Thus says the Lord:
    "Stand by the roads, and look,
    and ask for the ancient paths,
    where the good way is; and walk in it,
    and find rest for your souls."
    But they said, "We will not walk in it"
    (Jeremiah 6:16).

ANCIENT PATHS

UNTANGLING THE COMPLEXITY OF DISCIPILESHIP

SCOTT MICHAEL RINGO

OCEAN GRAND

To my wife, for embracing the adventure of life with me while allowing me the privilege of being your Husband. For having courage to make the simple choices as we learn to love more and raise a content and joyful family. You believed in me and made it possible for me to listen and follow Jesus into this. Thank you for your lunch hours, early mornings, and late nights to make my "farmer writing and grammar" look and read fantastic.

To my daughter and son, I've thought about you as I carefully wrote each word of this book to you. My hope is that it will become a well-worn instruction manual from which you gain a lifetime of learning that you do not need to discover for yourself. May it be like gems washed upon the beach of life from treasure ships, a priceless treasure that will preserve your life and give you hope, joy, peace, strength and the instructions to live a simple disciple-making life.

To those I've traveled beside, may you find the Ancient Paths and rest for your souls.

*Thank you to Debbie, a friend of the family for your excitement about this project.
Cover design and book formatting
by Scott Michael Ringo.*

ANCIENT PATHS

Published by Ocean Grand

Virginia Beach, Virginia

Copyright © 2014 by Scott Michael Ringo

All rights reserved.

Cover Design: Scott Michael Ringo

Photo: Shutterstock

First Edition 2016

Printed in the United States of America.

No part of this book may be reproduced in any form or by any electronic or mechanical means, including information storage and retrieval systems, without written permission from the author, except for the use of brief quotations in a book review.

Permissions

Scripture quotations are from the ESV® Bible (The Holy Bible, English Standard Version®), copyright © 2001 by Crossway, a publishing ministry of Good News Publishers. Used by permission. All rights reserved.

Scripture quotations marked MSG are taken from THE MESSAGE, copyright © 1993, 2002, 2018 by Eugene H. Peterson. Used by permission of NavPress. All rights reserved. Represented by Tyndale House Publishers, a Division of Tyndale House Ministries.

No portion of this document or design may be reproduced, stored in a retrieval system, or transmitted in any form outside of its intended use without written permission.

All emphasis in Scripture quotations has been added by the author.

ISBN 978-0-6927974-6-4

eISBN 978-1-7356637-6-0

CONTENTS

Journaling Through This Book	xi
Introduction	xiii
Preface	xv
1. God's Economy	1
2. God's Creation	30
3. God's Love	60
4. Jesus' Love	76
5. An Extraordinary Life	94
6. Significant Life	110
7. Complicated Life	125
8. The Simple Message	135
9. Becoming Sons and Daughters	151
10. Our Story	159
11. We Have To Embrace His Kingdom	176
12. Life on Purpose	194
13. Jesus' Joy	213
14. Enough is Enough	237
15. Interactive Relationship	267
Epilogue	280
Appendix	283
Chapter Questions	284
Accepting Jesus	295
What Will You Do?	299
Next Steps in Discipleship	301
Notes	307
About the Author	315
Titles by Scott Michael Ringo	317

JOURNALING THROUGH THIS BOOK

Journal

At the end of each chapter are some journal pages. Journaling is a great way to hear Jesus in what we learn. It is also a great way to keep a diary of notes, thoughts, and action steps from the lesson. There are questions for each chapter in the appendix which are good for journaling. Once the study is finished and the pages filled out, it is a great resource to return to time and time again to take action to transform our communities and make more disciples of Jesus.

I highly encourage you to take time and listen to Jesus and fill up the journal pages. If you are reading this in an electronic format, you can make digital notes right in the notes section of the application.

Each chapter has questions at the end that you can use individually to help you journal about what you read, or even with a group.

JOURNALING THROUGH THIS BOOK

Explanation of Spelling

Throughout this book I have purposely not capitalized the name of satan. I understand that it is a name and in the English language the rules say to capitalize all names. I do not consider satan to be worthy of capitalization and choose to break the grammar rule in order to not capitalize the enemy of which he is.

Explanation of Grammar

I am a husband, father, disciple of Jesus, and a writer. I am not an editor or a grammarian. I have written millions of words in my lifetime from college papers, blog posts, books, and letters. Rarely has my grammar been a factor in effective communication. Others along with family, friends, grammar and style checkers have been through this book many times. We have put a decent enough effort in making this book readable. In my opinion, people spend too much time and money on perfecting a piece of writing. Let us face that writing is never perfect. While I want to provide you with writing that is distraction-free of grammatical and style errors, it is doubtful I can afford that perfection. I write because I enjoy writing, and enjoy teaching. Perhaps you enjoy editing? If so, feel free to edit this work. Send us the errors, and we will make sure they get corrected. For the rest, please look past the massive imperfection.

Chapter Questions

In the appendix are questions for each chapter. These questions can be used for journaling or for discussion as a group study.

INTRODUCTION

To borrow a quote from James A. Baldwin:

I love America more than any other country in the world, and, exactly for this reason, I insist on the right to criticize her perpetually.[1]

In that same spirit, I love the Church. Not that I wish to criticize her, but encourage her through love, back to the true mission for which Jesus left for her. To encourage her to consider changing even her finest actions, or dismiss them altogether, so she can again find her true direction and commission, fulfilling it and bringing hope to a dying world. I have many responsibilities, but none greater than this: to last, to encourage the Church to finish her work. I want to be the Church's greatest encouragement and defender of the faith.

PREFACE

I will tell you right up front I did not write a book because I knew what to write. Instead, I wrote this book to know what to write. I wrote this book to see what God might say to me. It is not a crazy thought God speaks to people, and not any crazier than I could write what I hear God saying. I have always been able to hear God best when writing. I found years ago, when I needed to hear God about a major move in my life, God could write through me what He wanted to say. Much like the authors of the Bible did, except this was God speaking to me. This is not a typical book where the author plans out the chapter and the message of the book ahead of time. Instead, it is a journey with no particular destination other than to find greater intimacy with God by creating this book with Him. I am on a quest to hear what God will say to me, and maybe you, if you join the journey.

I imagine everyone has at least a small part of them that longs for interaction with a higher being who can give them purpose and fulfillment, not to mention the answers to all their questions. Think of it, a way to know you're doing the right

PREFACE

things, working in the right job, marrying the right person, and living the right life.

I know God wants to have direct interaction with us; He always has. You don't have to be a scientist to take a look at the eXtreme Deep Field photo[1] of 5,500 galaxies taken by the Hubble Space Telescope to know there is a creator.[2] Billions of galaxies for as far as the telescope can see do not happen by accident. Neither does it take a brilliant mind to see from the stories in the Bible that God yearns to interact with us. In fact, throughout the Old Testament, He audibly speaks to people. I have wished many times that God was that direct with me and would give me the blueprint for my life.

It is hard for many to imagine God's desire to interact with us because He is not as tangible as we think we need. At least that is our perception. I admit I have struggled throughout my life wishing that God was more audible or located where I could go to visit to get my questions answered. Most of my life, I have assumed He is silent and lets me drift on the currents of life wherever they take me. I don't believe that, but many times it feels that way. You may feel that way too? Yet, I have not been careful as I should have to listen for His voice.

I have not spent my entire life adrift on the currents of life without at least some bearing. Many times the direction I need to take has been so clear I could not have missed it if I had wanted. Yet, when I look back at those times to dissect them, they were a very intricate weave of smaller events and decisions that landed me in the right in the middle of doing the right thing. Looking back at all the events that got me to where I am today, I am amazed that I got here at all.

If we care to know a direction we are to go, God will show us, and speak to us, so we can understand. He encourages us, urges us on to the right conclusions. He can even reinforce the exact thing we are writing about memorably. Sometimes this direction is immediate and other times, as I will mention later, God chooses the right time. But you already know this, don't you?

Not even two pages into writing this book and of God's interaction with us, my two-year-old son has crawled into my lap with a tear rolling down his cheek, wanting interaction with me. He is now sitting in my lap, in front of the computer, facing me with my arms on either side of him as I type. My heart is yearning for God to interact with me now, and my son has shown me his wish for the same thing from me.

Eventually, my son pulled me to the floor to read through picture books where he dazzled me with correct identification of objects and letters. It should not amaze me he got most of them right as we have worked on them together. But it's challenging being a parent and wanting your child to learn at a quick pace. Yet each child is unique and learns from the day they are born to be unique.

But making the right choices in life is more challenging than the correct identification of a leaf, right? Given my son is two, he has a million words to choose from and only a year of experience to draw from since he first saw a leaf. I have 20 times the life experience to draw from, yet have a tough time remembering the right way to treat someone.

Many times I wonder if God is as amazed at me when I get a decision right. Even though I should know the answers, there are a myriad of possibilities to choose from when faced with a decision.

Here is a perfect example. Before starting this book, which I have been thinking about for years, I wondered if I should do something different with my time today. Not knowing how to start this chapter, I wrote the first thing I long for today, interaction with God. Not more than a minute later, my son is in my lap asking for the same thing I am longing for from God. Again,

PREFACE

a very intricate weave of smaller events and decisions that landed me in the right spot.

As most authors do, I did not plan this book out so it would be nice, neat, and ready for marketing. Nor did I plan to begin this book on hearing from God or that I am qualified to do that. I am most likely the last person who could give you a formula on this topic. Nor did I plan the chapters in this book or what I would write, but I started where every book should start, right at the beginning. This will allow me to explore the challenges I have and allow Jesus to speak to me through writing.

It is God's answering our deepest questions by beginning this book, reminding me that anyone can hear God. While many, including myself, say, "I can't hear Him," what we are saying is, "I don't hear Him the way I want to hear Him or when I want to hear Him." Instead, as my son reminded me, we rarely want God's answers and direction enough to seek Him out no matter what it takes. How many times have I jumped up into God's lap, tears rolling down my face to show Him I am longing for His attention? As we will see throughout this book, God created us to have a relationship with Him. He went to incredible lengths to create the space for us to find Him and interact with Him in our daily life.

How would I feel if each of my friends and family sought me out only when they needed something from me? Yet, many times that is how I have interacted with God. I have sought Him out and demanded answers to life's challenges. Rarely enough have I sought God out for a simple relationship with Him. I can come up with answers for my life on my own, but God's plan for my life is a better choice.

"Simple" and "gospel" are rarely two words that many see together. I will venture to say that many believe the gospel message is not simple, but complicated. Yet, the gospel of the Kingdom that Jesus proclaimed was easy for His followers to understand. The gospel of the Kingdom of God is that Jesus came to restore our relationship to God our creator. God not only wants to speak to us, but He will go to great lengths and is only a breath away when we need Him.

Through writing this book, I am reminded of how much God wants to speak to us. Countless times before, God has given me a fresh understanding of the words He spoke to other men, which they wrote in the Bible. God never stops speaking and I have to remember that God's words written many years ago are timeless and they apply to each of us. From time to time, I've gotten caught up in trying to find what I perceive as a fresh and exciting word from God. There are many times in the Bible where men seeking God went back to the ancient teachings which God already spoke. They looked again at the blueprint that God established through other Godly men and Jesus himself to navigate their way. That is what God has done with me; He has taken me back and given me a fresh understanding of the ancient paths He established thousands of years ago for me to live and be victorious.

We live in an age where disaster for our families, churches, country, and economy looms with no hope of recovery. The fact remains, one day it all fails and the end will come. During Jesus' ministry, He paints for the disciples a vivid picture of how the end of the days on earth will look:

> As he sat on the Mount of Olives, the disciples came to him privately, saying, "Tell us, when will these things be, and what will be the sign of your coming and of the end of the age?" And Jesus answered them, "See that no one leads you astray. For many will come in my name, saying, 'I am the Christ,' and they will lead many astray. And you will hear of wars and rumors of wars. See that you are not alarmed, for this must take place, but the end is not yet. For nation will

rise against nation, and kingdom against kingdom, and there will be famines and earthquakes in various places. All these are but the beginning of the birth pains."

"Then they will deliver you up to tribulation and put you to death, and you will be hated by all nations for my name's sake. And then many will fall away and betray one another and hate one another. And many false prophets will arise and lead many astray. And because lawlessness will be increased, the love of many will grow cold. But the one who endures to the end will be saved. And this gospel of the kingdom will be proclaimed throughout the whole world as a testimony to all nations, and then the end will come. (Matthew 24:3-14 ESV)[3]

I do not bring attention to this to be a doomsayer, but as someone who has the potential of half their life ahead of them and young children growing up, I have to keep in perspective that the challenges that my children and I face will only get worse. Considering that, I must look to Jesus for how to live our lives and continue to love others amid a world in turmoil, broken economy, and the challenge of our faith in Jesus at jeopardy.

Just days after God finished creation until now, lawlessness continues to increase in the world at a rapid pace. Just 2,349 years after creation, God destroyed everyone but Noah and his family with a flood because the world had become so wicked. Another 1,719 years after the flood, God's chosen people had once again disobeyed God so intensely that He sent a prophet Jeremiah to warn them that if they did not repent and turn back to God, He would allow their enemies to destroy them and overtake Jerusalem where they lived for giving up on Him, worshiping other gods, and the works of their own hands. The house of Israel and Judah refused to repent and God delivered the judgment He promised and allowed their enemies to take their people, city, and everything they owned.

God warned His chosen people through the words of Jeremiah over and over to turn back to Him and stop worshiping other gods and not give in to the surrounding lawlessness, but they refused to listen. God, the creator of the cosmos and everything in it, was patient with His warnings to Israel and Judah to no avail.

In Jeremiah 6, God pleads with Jerusalem to turn from her wicked ways and shares the disaster that looms on the horizon for their disobedience. Reading through the first 6 chapters of Jeremiah sounds like what God could say to us today. While God is full of grace, He detests sin, worshiping anything but Him, and Godlessness. God promised man after the flood He would never again send a flood to wipe out humankind. Yet, He loves His children enough that when they disobey, He will discipline them. God defines the boundaries of right living for those who worship Him through warnings and discipline.

Chapter after chapter in Jeremiah God asks His chosen people to repent but they refuse. God continues to repeat His warning of the pending disaster for their wrongdoing. But the people do not repent.

It is easy to see the parallels of words God wrote to His chosen people just 2,646 years ago and what He might say to us today.

> For from the least to the greatest of them, everyone is greedy for unjust gain; and from prophet to priest, everyone deals falsely.
>
> They have healed the wound of my people lightly, saying, "Peace, peace," when there is no peace (Jeremiah 6:13-14).

Wanting to learn how to live victorious today by God giving me a fresh understanding of the instruction He gave His chosen people through Jeremiah, one verse jumped out.

> Thus says the Lord:
> "Stand by the roads, and look,
> and ask for the ancient paths,
> where the good way is; and walk in it,
> and find rest for your souls."
> But they said, "We will not walk in it"
> (Jeremiah 6:16).

Is it possible in a world where lawlessness will continue to increase, and the love of many will grow cold that my soul can still find rest? Since the day God created man, He has given us the answers to live a successful life. God should know; He created us, the cosmos, and how our life is best lived within it. But like the people of Jerusalem, we refuse to listen.

I find a special interest in the imagery God uses in this verse. Roads by definition have covered or at least improved surfaces, so that travel is easier and more efficient. When I hear "road" the image I get is a smooth surface with gentle turns used by many types of transportation and traveled by many. Roads are the means of getting from point A to B in the quickest time and the most direct route. Contrast that image of a road with a path. A path is a trodden way, a footpath.[4] When I imagine a path I think of adventure, beauty, intrigue, mystery, and discovery. I associate paths with hiking trails that follow a winding course. Paths are not always easy nor walked by many, but the satisfaction is in the journey itself, not in the destination alone. There is a different way of life lived on paths, and they are typically narrow and the way less traveled. The word path is often used to describe a way of life.

In this verse, I hear God saying to stand by the roads you have widened, modernized, and made so easy to traverse that anyone can travel them. Instead of continuing in a way not designed by God, stop. Look and ask for the ancient paths that God established when He created the world, and He will show them to you. It is on those less traveled, adventurous ways of life you will find rest for your souls.

Even Jesus referenced that the path that leads to life is hard, narrow, and only found by a few.

> Enter by the narrow gate. For the gate is wide and the way is easy that leads to destruction, and those who enter by it are many. For the gate is narrow and the way is hard that leads to life, and those who find it are few (Matthew 7:13-14).

God promises that by looking and asking, it is possible to find the ancient paths where the good way is and walk in it, and can find rest for our souls. I've lost track of the times I have tried to figure out my life. It is stressful and the choices and possibilities are endless. Yet here, God promises that by looking and asking we can find the ancient paths, where the good way is and walk in it, finding rest for our souls. By following a clear path that God has for my life, I will find rest for my soul.

Not only will I find rest for my soul, the journey includes walking throughout my life with God and what He has planned for me. That was God's purpose for creation: for us to be in relationship with God in the garden.

One way to find God's ancient paths is to study the blueprint the disciples, including Jesus Himself, left for me through their examples and the written word of God to help me navigate my way. These are the ancient paths He established thousands of years ago for me to live and be victorious.

King David understood this well and relied on the written

PREFACE

word of God to help him find these ancient paths. "Through your precepts I get understanding; therefore I hate every false way. Your word is a lamp to my feet and a light to my path" (Psalms 119:104 & 105).

I've always loved to hike and camp. Before having small children, I spent many weekends during the spring, summer, and fall hiking and camping. Whether it was in the U.S. or Europe, solo or with friends, the trails were where I spent my time. A favorite quick trip of mine was a seven-mile hike along a bubbling stream and a series of waterfalls. I could hike in early on a Friday, spend the weekend, and hike out late on a Sunday. Much like the children in The Lion, the Witch, and The Wardrobe[5], each time I entered the trail I was at once transported to a mythical land. It would have not surprised me if fairies and animals that could talk had joined me during my hike. Perhaps they did. I wrote a good many of my early stories and blog posts sitting by the fire in that world that felt a thousand miles from reality. Most times I clambered out to civilization in the dark because I could not tear myself away from the serenity at the proper time to hike out in the light. Each time near the end of the hike there was a spot where a sound I had almost forgotten made me stop in my tracks. I would often have to remind myself that it was the sound of a road and the "door to the wardrobe ahead." Like Peter, Susan, Edmund, and Lucy, the time had stood still while I was in the forest. When I came out to the road after several days I could understand a bit of what Adam and Eve felt when banished from the Garden of Eden.

As God's ancient paths that give rest to the soul, it is those memories of hiking and others that our family is making that I draw on when life grieves us by various trials (1 Peter 1:3-6).

God promises we can find the path of the good way by being diligent to look and ask for them. Jesus reminded the disciples that if we ask the Father for the good things, He is faithful to give them to us. I know Jesus followed those ancient paths and through his example and teaching He encouraged the disciples to do the same.

> Ask, and it will be given to you; seek, and you will find; knock, and it will be opened to you. For everyone who asks receives, and the one who seeks finds, and to the one who knocks it will be opened. Or which one of you, if his son asks him for bread, will give him a stone? Or if he asks for a fish, will give him a serpent? If you then, who are evil, know how to give good gifts to your children, how much more will your Father who is in heaven give good things to those who ask him (Matthew 7:7-11)!

Just over 2,000 years ago, Jesus Christ, the Son of God, finished His work of complete restoration. Jesus came to bring restoration to every part of humanity including our souls while we are on this earth.

Through understanding and knowing Jesus, we can become the sons and daughters of God He made us to be. We can become His disciples and make disciples ourselves. Thus says the Lord:

> Let not the wise man boast in his wisdom, let not the mighty man boast in his might, let not the rich man boast in his riches, but let him who boasts boast in this, that he understands and knows me, that I am the Lord who practices steadfast love, justice, and righteousness in the earth. For in these things I delight, declares the Lord (Jeremiah 9:23 & 24).

ONE
GOD'S ECONOMY

God has provided me with what I need today.
Tomorrow is tomorrow.
-Scott Michael Ringo

I imagine that if most people who believe in Jesus could choose whether to guess at all the decisions in their lives or follow a custom-designed plan created by Jesus, most would pick the latter.

It is possible you are reading this book and do not believe that God created you. You may not believe God created you with a custom-designed purpose and direction for your life. I assume if you are, you would want to know if there was a divine plan for your existence. What if Jesus knows how to give you the most potential for your life and will guide you through it?

To discover such a plan from Jesus, we need to start by consulting Him to figure it out. That is where I had to start again several months ago. Life had piled up on me. It was nothing specific, and I couldn't put my finger on what was wrong, but I needed to simplify life. I needed a direction to follow. I needed to know the direction I went could have success, not failure. So I asked the only person I knew would know the answer; I asked Jesus. When I asked, I was hoping for a complete A-Z plan laid out in front of me; but I received something so much simpler.

When we need answers, most of us go to someone to ask for advice. I ask advice from Jesus, and yes, many times, Jesus talks back. It is not as weird as you might think. One of the simplest ways that Jesus speaks to me is through the Bible, the word of God, and that word is Jesus Himself.

> In the beginning was the Word, and the Word was with God, and the Word was God. He was in the beginning with God. All things were made through him, and without him was not anything made that was made. In him was life, and the life was the light of men. The light shines in the darkness, and the darkness has not overcome it (John 1:1-6).

Jesus is the word of God. Notice how the second sentence begins with "He." He was present with God in the beginning. So Jesus and God were together in the beginning when they made me. It makes perfect sense that going to the source is the best place when I need answers. When Jesus answers me, many times He speaks to me through the Bible.

HOW TO TALK TO GOD

When things get messed up, I've learned to start back at the beginning. That is where Jesus started with me. But before we jump to the beginning, my change in direction started with a monumental life lesson that changed my life and perspective forever. Perhaps you know The Lord's Prayer. The story is in Matthew and in Luke, where Jesus is praying one night. When

He finishes, the disciples ask Him to teach them how to pray. As believers, having a conversation with God is an activity we should want to know well. Talk to God, and He talks back to us. At the disciple's request, Jesus teaches them a simple prayer. Pray then like this:

> Our Father in heaven, hallowed be your name.
>
> Your kingdom come, your will be done, on earth as it is in heaven.
>
> Give us this day our daily bread, and forgive us our debts, as we also have forgiven our debtors.
>
> And lead us not into temptation, but deliver us from evil (Matthew 6:9-13).

Here is how it breaks down: Father, holy, and revered is your name. You are God; we are not, and we are humble in your presence. We submit to Your kingdom, and we want what You want. Give us enough food to feed us today and forgive our sins in the measure we forgive the sins of others who have wronged us. Now that you have forgiven us from our sins keep us from sinning again and protect us from evil and satan.

This differs from how most of us pray each day. I know in my own prayers I am needier and ask for more things. Let us be truthful, we need a lot of things, right? Not that it is wrong to ask for things we need, but do I need the things I ask for? You know, assess genuine needs from perceived ones. Could we not get all we ask for because we ask for what we want but not need? That is more the norm than the exception. Therein lies a truth that should change anyone's life and, should I continue to apply it, brings a great amount of freedom. As I will later share, I had let myself get to a dark place through false comparison.

After the prayer, both Matthew and Luke share some more teaching Jesus gives to the disciples, which I believe clarifies how much God wants to interact with us, and where our focus is best served. It is these teachings I want to focus on because they give us an incredible glimpse into God's economy.

FORGIVE OTHERS

Jesus' teaching continues:

> For if you forgive others their trespasses, your heavenly Father will also forgive you, but if you do not forgive others their trespasses, neither will your Father forgive your trespasses (Matthew 6:14-15).

I've never thought about forgiveness as a value in God's universal economy. In The Lord's Prayer, Jesus teaches us to pray for forgiveness and includes our forgiveness of others as a condition of our forgiveness. In case we missed it, He adds this clarification statement so we can't get the meaning wrong. It is not a choice to forgive others; it is a condition for our own forgiveness from God. It's easy to understand: God, the creator of the universe, went through the agony of dying on a cross for something I should have died for, not Him. He forgave everyone for all their sins and any sins they would commit. The first step to being a part of God's economy begins with forgiveness. God desires that, like Him, we forgive others of all their sins as though our own forgiveness is contingent upon it.

FASTING

Many people cringe when the word fasting comes up. It's true for me. The order it shows up in this teaching is key. In these verses, Jesus starts with a directive on living with less. First, I should assess my actual needs; then fast to put it into perspective. Fasting in its general term is doing without something, many times food, for a period. The reaction for many is to skip a meal, a day of meals or even something simple, like doing without our favorite pastime activity is uncomfortable. The practice of fasting is a whole other book, but it is worth looking into as the Bible has a lot to say about it. For the Pharisees, the religious leaders, fasting was a religious act they liked to get noticed for. They wanted everyone to notice how spiritual they were, so they would fast and make it a public spectacle. Intentional self-denial is not a practice I like to engage in. I want more: more stuff, more food, more everything. As we find out below, God's economy doesn't work like that. Jesus says:

> And when you fast, do not look gloomy like the hypocrites, for they disfigure their faces that their fasting may be seen by others. Truly, I say to you, they have received their reward. But when you fast, anoint your head and wash your face, that your fasting may not be seen by others but by your Father who is in secret. And your Father who sees in secret will reward you (Matthew 6:16-18).

When God asks us to do without, whether it is for a season or forever, He expects us to do it with joy and dignity. When God is asking us to do without something, He wants to do something within us, and He is not asking us to do it as a show to others. I am quick to see that God's provision and interaction for me are personal, intimate, and carries with it some conditions. It reminds me that throughout the Bible, there are examples of people who obey God's commands, and God is "with them," while others disobey and suffer the consequences of God not blessing them. Grace covers all my sins, but it does not give me a license to continue to sin with reckless abandon.

My own children give me a good perspective of how obedience brings them my blessing and disobedience brings them discipline. Not that I enjoy disciplining them, but as a parent, because I love them, I want to teach them correct behavior, so they can live life to its fullest.

TREASURE

Jesus adds:

> Do not lay up for yourselves treasures on earth, where moth and rust destroy and where thieves break in and steal, but lay up for yourselves treasures in heaven, where neither moth nor rust destroys and where thieves do not break in and steal. For where your treasure is, there your heart will be also (Matthew 6:19-21).

I admit that I am looking for God to interact with me and speak in monetary and direct answers to what I perceive is my immediate need. My prayers are less likely to include something that is a heavenly treasure. In developed countries, most of us do not need our next meal, a cup of water, clothes (because we have none), or shelter. No, my prayers and need for immediate interaction with God are many times future-focused and material. While future direction and items I want are valid concerns for me, I need to realize that God is more interested that store up heavenly treasures. It is also a great reminder of how He expects me to use the direction and provision He gives me. Next, He says:

> The eye is the lamp of the body. So, if your eye is healthy, your whole body will be full of light, but if your eye is bad, your whole body will be full of darkness. If then the light in

you is darkness, how great is the darkness (Matthew 6:22 & 23).

How many times is the interaction I want from God based on something I've seen? Like a kid in a toy store, I see something, and it is on my list of needs in an instant. However, it takes thinking to justify the item, and most of the time, I can. When I say it out loud, my justification sounds much like a spoiled child explaining why they need the latest toy. My personal economic system of needs revolves around money or success to get the stuff I think I need.

The word Jesus uses for healthy in the Greek is clear, or *haplous* translated to English as single or whole. The Greek word for full of light is *phōteinos*, which means composed of light; of a bright character. It means my eye is a lamp, like a candle illuminating everything that comes into me. If my eye is clear, my whole body will be full of light and of bright character.

Let me share that my family is simple in our accumulation of material goods. Much of our success in that area comes from living in a two-bedroom condo for the ten years my wife and I have been married. When the kids came, they took over the bedroom, that was my office from which I worked at home. I moved downstairs to a small desk in the family room. Without storage space, you can't hold on to a lot. A house with an office and a yard for the kids to play in has been on my prayer list for the last 6 years! Not having that house has been a source of personal defeat in my life. It's worn on me, torn me up, and made me feel ashamed.

Yet, considering the last few verses, I've been looking with my eyes for a treasure on earth, a house to store up inside it even more treasure. Until now, I had not realized I have been praying,

"Lord give me my daily bread" and believed a house should be part of that daily allowance. I am not saying that if you live in a house, it is wrong. For now, in our lives, God's plan for us is right where we are. We live in a condo with a beautiful water view out the back. There is a bed for each person, and ample living space, way more than many people I've visited in developing countries. You know what? We're just fine. Though I wish we had a bigger kitchen, a yard for the kids, an office, and a garage to putz around in, each member of our family has enough. As the stress and shame built up, my wife has been telling me for years that what we have is all we need. This is not the first time my wife has been the one who trusts God in His provision better than I do.

Stress is a killer. As you can see from the discovery above, we bring all kinds of misery on ourselves. For the last years, I've battled stress. Stress about our government, stress about the money we will need to retire one day, and stress about how we will afford to pay for our children's education. I have been stressed and beating myself up because I cannot provide a single-family house for us. You see where I am going with this. I have stressed about things like our government I cannot control and things that are so future-based I could never figure them out. We have a home, just not the one I think we need. Ha, our kids are 2 and 6 years old. Who knows what kinds of education, scholarships, or funds might be by the time they reach college? I am years from retirement, years from needing to pay for college, and sorting out our government will not happen overnight. I have allowed my eyes to wallow in the wrong life images, and like the verse says, the darkness was great. Our family is fine, yet I have worn myself out over what I want and think I need now. I have been lighting my body with a terrible light. You might imagine my world has been dark, and my character dim.

HEARING FROM JESUS

I want to add; I started this book not knowing what I should write and in a dark place. I knew I needed time to hear from Jesus. Maybe that is why you are reading this book. God has been changing my perspective of Him this year and helping me climb out of a dark hole. A hole I put myself in from worry, stress, and doubt. During this, my grandfather, who I loved like a father, passed away unexpectedly three months ago. It was a terrible loss. I've known him my entire life, and when he died, a huge pillar in my life crumbled. As Paul reminds us:

> Humble yourselves, therefore, under the mighty hand of God so that at the proper time he may exalt you, casting all your anxieties on him, because he cares for you. Be soberminded; be watchful. Your adversary the devil prowls around like a roaring lion, seeking someone to devour. Resist him, firm in your faith, knowing that the same kinds of suffering are being experienced by your brotherhood throughout the world. And after you have suffered a little while, the God of all grace, who has called you to his eternal glory in Christ, will himself restore, confirm, strengthen, and establish you (1 Peter 5:6-10).

In a very somber place over losing my grandfather, I was full of anxiety, and satan was on the prowl and had me, his prey, cornered. So I wrote, asking God for His wisdom:

> If you don't know what you're doing, pray to the Father. He loves to help. You'll get his help, and won't be condescended to when you ask for it. Ask boldly, believingly, without a second thought. People who "worry their prayers" are like wind-whipped waves. Don't think you're going to get

anything from the Master that way, adrift at sea, keeping all your options open (James 1:5-8 MSG).

I am already seeing I who was not interacting with God just a mere six thousand words into writing. I am learning along with you, and already the darkness is dissipating. Jesus goes on in Matthew 6:

No one can serve two masters, for either he will hate the one and love the other, or he will be devoted to the one and despise the other. You cannot serve God and money Matthew 6:24).

In our present-day, it is very hard for me to understand slavery. Throughout my life, I have seen movies and heard stories of the first 12 slaves who arrived in America in 1619, near to where I write this in Virginia. Slavery in the United States would not be illegal until 1865, and twelve million people had lived their lives as slaves in a free country. Eight million slaves would never taste freedom before they died. The last state to abolish slavery was Maryland in 1972 when the last slave was free. It is a terrible story of American tragedy.

Even though slavery is illegal in the United States, the US Justice Department estimates[1] there are still 17,500 people trafficked into slavery every year. They estimate twenty-seven million people around the world still live in slavery. I add this information to remind myself that while I struggle over not having the latest stuff, millions of people lack even the basic freedom.

GOD OR MONEY

I mention slavery because the word Jesus uses for serve in verse 24 above in the Greek, *douleuō*, means slave. The verse is clear that I must pick a master to be a slave, either God or money. The wording is plain; there is not a grey or safe area. Within this verse are the undertones of choice between life and death: physical, spiritual, and even moral. Physical in the sense that treasures on earth relate to stuff with which we surround ourselves. Physical stuff carries literal, mental, and emotional weight. When I get a house full of stuff, I sense that weight. It is easy to understand that there is nothing in a house full of stuff that has any heavenly treasure. Yet it costs time, money, even freedom to get and care for it. It doesn't take a lot of stuff to get trapped. For some, it's a car, boat, or even a hobby.

Each of Jesus' teachings above has a distinct choice to make: either treasures on earth or heavenly treasures, either good light or bad light, slavery to God, or slavery to money. It is plain that God's way brings life and the other way, death. The other thing I notice is how core these choices are to the human spirit. As I read through these choices, my mind fights to hold on to both while my soul longs for life. All kidding aside, this is the battle for my soul.

Another interesting facet to this choice between God and money is that the first choice is the creator of the universe while the other, money, is the world's form of barter. God created life and sustains life, while money is only the perceived means to sustain life.

It reminds me that God is an eternal being who has always existed. God created everything, including man and money. Throughout history, man has continued to fail by worshiping other gods. Chief among those gods are money and riches. Besides a choice between the two, there is a clear warning it is impossible to serve both God and money. If you serve money, you will hate and despise God. The word Jesus uses for "you cannot" is *dynamai*, which conveys the lack of power by one's own ability, resources, or favorable circumstances to be a slave to both.

It is a scary thought that by serving material goods and money; they have the power over me to withhold the choice to serve God. Serving money robs me of the free choice God has given me to serve Him. If I serve or am a slave to money, I cannot serve God.

In what a person puts their trust to sustain their life is a clear choice. They either trust God, the one who sustains all life, or money, the tool that God gives me to barter for goods.

So what does it mean to serve or be a slave to money? The Greek word used is *douleuō*. That word means to become a slave, submit to, yield, or give oneself up to.

In practical terms, when I determine my own wants or needs, I do so outside of God's plan. An example is for me to accumulate treasures on earth but is not God's will. That choice is simple when I allow my eyes to become clouded with desire and not His will. As in the earlier example of my desire for a house, I had determined to provide for that desire regardless of God's plan. To do so, I need to go beyond God's plan for sustaining my life and look to a smaller god and become a slave to money to provide that house for myself. I wanted the house enough; I counted on my ability to make money to provide for my need. Yes, making money is how you buy a house. But if that house is not God's plan, then it is a Godless process. I engaged the process, and in doing so, added great darkness to my life and became a slave to money. I invited stress and agreed to unbiblical, time-consuming work to gain it. My willingness to do this resulted in traveling a path to provide for myself what I perceived God was unwilling to do for me. If I had purchased the house, I would have agreed to the Godless chains of slavery for many years until I could sell the house or pay it off. It would have affected my family, my health, and my walk with God, while the entire time not understanding why God was making it so hard to afford the house. I would have agreed to be a slave to money and not to God.

We've heard people say, "My eyes were too big for my wallet." Unfortunately, for most, banks make this process much too easy by issuing credit cards. Credit cards are spending someone else's money that God has not provided you. With the quick swipe of a credit card, you can sign the line as a slave to the bank and money until you pay off the desire you purchased and buy back your freedom. Too many times, people take bank approval as their answer on whether to buy something. In reality, the bank approves loans to make a profit on a loan. They use the money they borrow to buy items they cannot otherwise afford. The practice of borrowing money to provide for ourselves is so common it is rare to find an individual who does not owe money to someone. People spending money they do not have, to satisfy their desires unapproved by God, fuels the world's economy.

NEEDS

One of the best ways to keep from serving the master of money is to live within our means and keep God involved in our buying decisions. God will provide for our needs as long as we do our part to work smart while keeping our eyes focused on our heavenly treasure. Jesus continues:

> Therefore I tell you, do not be anxious about your life, what you will eat or what you will drink, nor about your body,

what you will put on. Is not life more than food, and the body more than clothing (Matthew 6:25)?

Whoa! I am quick to admit I have wrapped myself up in what I perceive I need and want when I've not needed a thing in reality. In fact, so wrapped up, I missed God's interaction. As you will recall, God's interaction or lack thereof is how I started this book. God has been here the whole time I was piling on the stress, guilt, and shame. He has been interacting and integral in providing all I need. God was here the whole time saying, "Scott, I've got your back. I've supplied all that you need. You are focusing on getting yourself into the wrong stuff. Relax, don't be anxious. Instead, focus on storing your treasures in heaven and I will take care of your future."

I have food, clean water, and clothes. I have a lot more than that. Yes, I have everything I need for today, and that is all that matters. God has provided for me today, and I can rest in that.

Now back to the question: if there was a perfect plan for your life or day, and you wanted to know it, would God show it to you? Jesus says:

> Ask, and it will be given to you; seek, and you will find; knock, and it will be opened to you. For everyone who asks receives, and the one who seeks finds, and to the one who knocks it will be opened. Or which one of you, if his son asks him for bread, will give him a stone? Or if he asks for a fish, will give him a serpent? If you then, who are evil, know how to give good gifts to your children, how much more will your Father who is in heaven give good things to those who ask him (Matthew 7:7-11)!

As I reflect on my prayer life, it's rare when I've asked for my needs rather than my wants. For years, even my entire life,

God had already met my needs. I have never gone a meal without food or night without a roof unless I chose to. Even the nights I camped, I had the choice of a tent. Long international flights where airlines expect you to bring your own food were not the most comfortable. But even on the flights, there were peanuts and crackers. I have had it all and more every single day of my life.

How many people worldwide in developing countries would love to have the food, clean water, and shelter I have for one week? No doubt, most people in the world would take the basics of food, water, and clothing and feel they were living in luxury.

We live in a culture and a country that has programmed us to think we need more. We feed an insatiable appetite for stuff. Although this is no surprise to us, when I am forced to look at what I have and assess my needs, I'm sick. My life overflows with enough. I am not opposed to a minimalist view, but neither do I believe God requires that. At least for myself, I must acknowledge that God is providing what I need.

I doubt there are many reading this book who lack basic needs to live. Even if someone gave you a copy of this book because you could not afford it, I doubt you are on the verge of starvation. If you can afford to buy this book, I assume you do not need what this book costs to buy food, clean water, clothes, shelter, or necessities. Sure, it is possible you have overextended yourself and are in debt up to your eyeballs or put yourself in a position where you have a temporary need.

If you're overextended, it is most likely because, like me, you thought you needed something God wasn't providing and bought it yourself. Now it takes time and effort to pay that off. In fact, there are hundreds of thousands of people who have satisfied their own perceived needs in this exact way.

Matthew 7:7-11 promises, God has given me good things.

He has given me amazing things, and for all my life, He has taken care of me. I'm still alive, so I did not starve. I've never had a day I lacked clothes. Though I do not wear the latest fashion, people are not laughing at what I wear, nor should it matter. Maybe, like you, I thought I had a lot of needs. I was also wondering why God was so quiet about my needs. A quick evaluation under God's microscope, and I see how rich I am with the plenty He has provided me.

Years ago, a wise person encouraged me to be content in my circumstances. If I was not content, then I could not trust God that He was supplying and would continue supplying what I need. No doubt, I've forgotten that wise counsel time and time again in my life.

In context, Matthew 6:9-13 has a lot to say. Going back to the prayer, Jesus taught the disciples it might seem it lacks depth. It sounds like such a simple prayer that children learn. I think my needs are bigger than a children's prayer can address. Now when I read it, I see it asks for all the right things: nothing more, nothing less. I am discovering God's desires for my life are much simpler than the lofty goals and material wealth I've set for myself. Could a prayer this simple outline of how simple and basic God's economy is? Paraphrased the prayer says this:

- God, I acknowledge You are Lord, and your name is Holy.
- Bring Your kingdom of heaven of which is restoration, and I am a resident.
- I want Your will and Your plan for my life.
- Give me enough food and provision to sustain me today.
- Forgive my sins in the measure I forgive others.
- Keep me away from sin.
- Protect me from evil.

- I acknowledge your kingdom is the kingdom to which I belong, and it is your power and glory to which I pledge and give my life forever.

Even as I write this, my mind, programmed with all the years of wants and dreams, is trying to convince me I am too literal. God wants to bless me and wants me to have enough. He wants me to have everything this world offers that I need. He wants me to be happy and live a long, fulfilled life, right?

Yes, God wants to bless me, not by the world's standards but by His. By understanding these teachings of Jesus, I see that my perspective differs from what Jesus means by blessed. He is blessing me, and I have far more than most of the world and more than Jesus himself had in material possessions when He walked this earth. That I own more than Jesus had should be a clue I've got my wants and needs skewed. Yes, God wants to and is blessing me. Through a simple prayer, I see how God wants to bless me is not the way I imagined. The fact is, never in the Bible does God promise me a comfortable life, nor does he say He will give tremendous monetary or material wealth. As we will find in the next chapter, God's blessings look very different from the worldly blessings I have been striving for.

God is not asking us to abandon our dreams and desires. Instead, take a few minutes to reevaluate, refocus, redefine, and align them to His will for our lives. By aligning our dreams and desires to God's will, we will most likely find our pursuits less material-driven but more fulfilling. Most of us have set our dreams and desires too low by basing them on stuff, achievements we want, and the world's definition of success. Wealth in God's economy may appear very poor compared to the world's standards.

SIMPLE LIFE

I see an invitation in this simple prayer to a simpler life than the world has been persuading me to live. A life, less driven and more focused on others than on myself. I have known this because, at this invitation, my soul inside leaps with joy. It also makes me consider the stuff I have accumulated around me. To be certain, I have been anxious about more than food, drink, and clothes that Jesus warns not to be anxious about. Most can agree that the possessions from the most valuable to the least have not brought long-term happiness or contentment. So why do we listen to the message the world markets to us instead of that of Jesus?

In practical terms, is not a simple life — well — simpler? The less we buy, the less we own. The less we own, the less we must maintain and organize. Everything about possessions costs time, money, and emotional stress. What we have is weighty and does nothing but tie us down and complicate our lives. Most of the time, our stuff doesn't improve our quality of life or happiness. Instead, it is dramatic how that which we accumulate takes away from our life.

As my mind reels and questions the literal meanings, I will paraphrase a few truths I am learning:

- God desires for me to forgive others in the measure I want forgiveness.
- Do not make a spectacle out of what God asks you to do without, either temporary or permanent.
- Do not place your focus on treasures on earth but place your focus on treasures in heaven. If you focus on heaven, your heart will focus there too.
- The eye is the candle that illuminates everything

that goes into your body. If your eye is healthy[2], your whole body will be full of light.
- It is impossible to serve God and money; you must choose.
- Do not be anxious about even life necessities like food, drink, and clothes.
- Ask Jesus for your actual needs, and He will provide.

There is no need to get caught up in stuff or to focus our lives on it. If God has blessed you with extravagance, then God has put you in a unique position. God trusts people to distribute His wealth to those who need it. God does not give wealth to individuals, so they use it on themselves. Instead, God entrusts those to whom He gave wealth to be wise and distribute it to those who need it. Could it be the current wealth in the world could end all the needs in the world in an instant? It is an interesting thought everyone working together, each bringing their part, could abolish all needs in the world. Could it be God has already provided for everyone's needs, and we cannot see it because we focus on ourselves? Some have knowledge, others skills, the unemployed an abundance of time, the wealthy have money, and the list goes on. Could all the world's resources brought together, end hunger, thirst, and the needs around the world? Everyone would need to pitch in, some would need to downsize, and others would have to liquidate assets. Yet others might have to give up their vacation or free time.

The current global wealth is $241 trillion dollars[3] and there are about seven billion people alive. If that wealth was evenly distributed, every man, woman, and child would have around $34,000. So yes, temporarily there is enough wealth in the world to raise everyone well over the US poverty levels[4].

Oxfam estimates[5] that the richest 1% own close to half the world's wealth.

It would take serious economic restructuring to work. Yet, in monetary terms, God has supplied $34,000 dollars for every man, woman, and child in the world. There is an abundant amount of land in the world if redistributed for everyone to raise their own food. As I write this, there is over one acre of arable land or farmable land for every person in the world. An acre of land would give every person the ability to raise their own food.

We cannot look to others to begin the process. Instead, we must look at what God has entrusted to us and be faithful. That starts with the correct evaluation of what we need and redistribute the rest. By embracing a simpler lifestyle and trusting Jesus more for what we need, it frees us to redistribute more of what He has given us, whether that is time, resources, skills, or money.

Regardless of whether the rich or ourselves will redistribute the world's wealth, God will provide what we need. Money and resources do not fall out of the sky to those that need it. Instead, money and resources travel from one human's hand to another. Understanding that God takes care of my basic needs should entice me to give from my abundance to others in need. While it is easy to see that the richest 1% should do something with the abundance of their money, it is easy to forget that most of us reading this book have extravagant wealth when compared to most of the world's population and should do our part without regard to what others do.

I will be the first to admit that when I do not believe there is an endless source to take care of my need, I feel the need to hold on to what I can. By asking God for my daily needs, changes my perspective on retirement. It is not the earthly stuff I should want; it is the heavenly. I can serve God, or I can be a slave to money, a minor god. To be a slave to money, I will also supply for my own needs. Doing so, I will need to get and keep all the money I can get ahold of. Remember, the choice between being a slave to God or money is a choice between the creator of everything or money, which God created: the world's form of barter. It's always better to choose the source.

RETIREMENT

I mentioned not focusing on retirement, and, interestingly, nowhere in the Bible is retirement mentioned. Retirement is not a Biblical pursuit. Retirement is a term created as recently as 1883 by Chancellor Otto Von Bismarck of Germany. In, "The History of Retirement, From Early Man to A.A.R.P.," Mary-Lou Weisman writes:

> In the beginning, there was no retirement. There were no old people. In the Stone Age, everyone was fully employed until age 20, by which time nearly everyone was dead, usually of unnatural causes. Any early man who lived long enough to develop crow's-feet was either worshiped or eaten as a sign of respect. Even in Biblical times, when a fair number of people made it into old age, retirement still had not been invented and respect for old people remained high. In those days, it was customary to carry on until you dropped, regardless of your age group—no shuffleboard, no Airstream trailer. When a patriarch could no longer farm, herd cattle or pitch a tent, he opted for more specialized, less labor-intensive work, like prophesying and handing down commandments. Or he moved in with his kids.
>
> In 1883, Chancellor Otto Von Bismarck of Germany had a problem. Marxists were threatening to take control of Europe. To help his countrymen resist their blandishments,

Bismarck announced that he would pay a pension to any nonworking German over age 65.[6]

Only one hundred thirty-two years after establishing retirement, its pursuit has taken precedent in every working person's agenda the world over. Agreed, one verse in the Bible written by King Solomon states:

Precious treasure and oil are in a wise man's dwelling, but a foolish man devours it. (Proverbs 21:20 ESV)

Yet, Jesus Himself had much more to say about the subject. Jesus said, "Do not lay up for yourselves treasures on earth" and included in His teachings, "Do not be anxious about your life, what you will eat or what you will drink" (Matthew 6:19 & Matthew 6:25). Given those verses, it makes sense the Bible would be absent in addresses getting the most yield on your 401K or high yield investment strategies. God did not forget to include instructions on creating the fail-safe 401K for a comfortable retirement. Instead, God is clear about where we are to store up our treasures:

> But lay up for yourselves treasures in heaven, where neither moth nor rust destroys and where thieves do not break in and steal. For where your treasure is, there your heart will be also (Matthew 6:20-21).

I write this not as someone who has this figured out, but as someone who, I hope like you, wants to learn how God's economy works best. As a middle-aged husband and father of two, there is real tension as I read these verses. I have learned most of my life to save toward retirement. In fact, I have never had that thinking questioned before now. It takes genuine faith to help others with my extra rather than stashing it. Strange that I should say genuine faith as if I have been operating in areas where only fake faith will suffice. It is tough to have faith that God will supply for all our needs. The challenge is, what God might supply for and what we perceive He needs to supply are on two different lists. Right? Now we are talking about our future when we are older and supplying for our own needs will be even more difficult. That requires blind faith because when we are older, it is hard to supply for ourselves as effectively as we do now. Ouch! It is uncomfortable to think I have more faith in my ability to supply for my needs than to trust them to the creator of the universe. I am reminded of the simplicity of God's economy. Putting enough money aside and investing in the right ways for retirement has always been confusing. Yet, here God says to trust Him and don't worry about tomorrow. Jesus says, "Therefore do not be anxious about tomorrow, for tomorrow will be anxious for itself. Sufficient for the day is its own trouble" (Matthew 6:34).

Chapter 12, in the book of Luke, includes parallel verses of Jesus' same teachings on these subjects. In case I need a black and white example, Jesus includes one here:

> Someone in the crowd said to him, "Teacher, tell my brother to divide the inheritance with me." But he said to him, "Man, who made me a judge or arbitrator over you?" And he said to them, "Take care, and be on your guard against all covetousness, for one's life does not consist in the abundance of his possessions." And he told them a parable, saying, "The land of a rich man produced plentifully, and he thought to himself, 'What shall I do, for I have nowhere to store my crops?' And he said, 'I will do this: I will tear down my barns and build larger ones, and there I will store all my grain and my goods. And I will say to my soul, "Soul, you have ample goods laid up for many years; relax, eat, drink, be merry."' But God said to him, 'Fool! This night your soul is required

of you, and the things you have prepared, whose will they be?' So is the one who lays up treasure for himself and is not rich toward God (Luke 12:13-21).

God's economy is simple and not complicated. Trust God for everything, starting with my essential needs all the way through to my retirement.

God has provided me with what I need today. Tomorrow is tomorrow. -Scott Michael Ringo

It is also clear that God's economy centers on my obedience, my actions, and faith. How I respond to God and others is the currency used in God's economy. For example, in Matthew 7, Jesus says:

> Judge not, that you be not judged. For with the judgment you pronounce you will be judged, and with the measure you use it will be measured to you. Why do you see the speck that is in your brother's eye, but do not notice the log that is in your own eye? Or how can you say to your brother, 'Let me take the speck out of your eye,' when there is the log in your own eye? You hypocrite, first take the log out of your own eye, and then you will see clearly to take the speck out of your brother's eye. Do not give dogs what is holy, and do not throw your pearls before pigs, lest they trample them underfoot and turn to attack you (Matthew 7:1-6).

Whether it is judging others, forgiving others, or trusting God for my provision, my faith and actions determine how God rewards me. It is easier to look at someone else and deduce your course of action based on what they do. Jesus knows that it is an easy way to think. So He addresses it with clear teaching. We like to apply this verse to other areas of our lives, which might not be as sensitive.

It is no mistake that Jesus puts this teaching right in the middle of talking about these vital challenges for our heart. He wants us to look at these areas of our own lives and get them right. My relationship with God is one-on-one and what others do or don't do are not factors in my obedience to God. God's economy and governance is not a democracy. I, like everyone else, must make my decision about every teaching in the Bible. As a man, the issues covered in Matthew 6 and 7 are tough. Men can fight; we like toys; most are driven to work hard and store up stability for our families to be secure to the ends of their lives. Most of all, we want to provide well for our family, and we have been taught all our lives there is no one looking out for us but ourselves. We have also bought a lie that it is up to each of us to provide for ourselves. Jesus changes all that right here. He says we can choose: we can provide for ourselves or trust God to do it. In one fell swoop, He also changes our perspective on what that provision looks like: "our daily needs." That takes real trust and complete surrender to trust God daily for our needs and not to load up our storehouse for the winter.

> Look at the birds of the air: they neither sow nor reap nor gather into barns, and yet your heavenly Father feeds them. Are you not of more value than they? And which of you by being anxious can add a single hour to his span of life? And why are you anxious about clothing? Consider the lilies of the field, how they grow: they neither toil nor spin, yet I tell you, even Solomon in all his glory was not arrayed like one of these. But if God so clothes the grass of the field, which today is alive and tomorrow is thrown into the oven, will he not much more clothe you, O you of little faith (Matthew 6:26-30).

I love nature shows, especially the ones that explore

animals that I never knew existed. One theme that is very clear in nature shows is how each animal and plant has its own unique set of skills and ways to survive. This theme Jesus mentions in Chapter 6. The birds live day-by-day, never storing up quantities of food or making elaborate houses for themselves. Yet, God takes care of the birds that He never sent His son to die for. Jesus came to die for us, the humans.

We really want this; we want God to provide for us, but we are many times too busy providing for ourselves. I do not know about you, but I am tired of striving to provide. It is easy to look at how God provides for the birds or even others and forget this promise in the Bible that He will feed and provide for me. We also have to keep in mind that we need to be content with what He feeds us and how He clothes us. We might not be eating Filet Mignon every day or wearing the latest brand name fashion, but He will take care of us. God loves to give exceptional gifts; it says so in the Bible.

> Ask, and it will be given to you; seek, and you will find; knock, and it will be opened to you. For everyone who asks receives, and the one who seeks finds, and to the one who knocks it will be opened. Or which one of you, if his son asks him for bread, will give him a stone? Or if he asks for a fish, will give him a serpent? If you then, who are evil, know how to give good gifts to your children, how much more will your Father who is in heaven give good things to those who ask him (Matthew 7:7-11)!

Even though the Bible steers us away from living the rich and famous lifestyles, a simple life focused on the needs of others sprinkled with exceptional gifts from God is an amazing life.

Yes, God wants interaction with us, and I can see part of

that interaction is how He supplies for my needs. He also wants me to trust Him to supply for those needs as He determines. There is not a more intimate expression than to give life and then to sustain that life. God gave me life, and He wants to be the one to sustain it. He wants me to trust Him for my needs, whether that is food, clothes, shelter, or even my health. If I choose, I can strive to supply all that myself, which never works out.

Journal Pages

This is a great opportunity to journal what you are learning or the action steps you want to take based on this lesson. Doing so will keep all your notes and journaling in this book as future reference. Start by taking a few minutes to pray and ask Jesus to bring to light all you are learning and what transformational changes you can make in your life. If you are reading this in an electronic version, make a digital note and journal.

Journal Pages

TWO
GOD'S CREATION

Experts estimate half of the world has never heard the name of Jesus or the story of Him in the Bible. Growing up in the United States with a church on every corner, sometimes two, it is very hard to fathom that half the world does not know the story of Jesus. I am fortunate I have known about Jesus all my life. Yet, it did not hit me how fantastical the story of Jesus was until the first time I told it to someone who had never heard it. To my amazement, coming out of my mouth was a story that rivaled every fairy tale, adventure, and drama ever known to man. The listener's face was as one hearing the most imaginative, made-up story ever told. Yet, I could tell they felt sure they knew the story from somewhere. God stitched this ancient story inside the fabric of the soul of everyone. The Bible explains that God has revealed Himself to everyone through His creation, and no one is exempt from the punishment of death as the just payment for sin. Paul writes,

> For his invisible attributes, namely, his eternal power and divine nature, have been clearly perceived, ever since the

creation of the world, in the things that have been made. So they are without excuse (Romans 1:20).

Had I not researched how these sixty-six books got compiled into the book we know as the Bible, it is hard to believe. They compile the most extravagant and incomprehensible love story anyone could ever imagine. The Bible's story comprises the most breathtaking journey of God the Creator pursuing and loving His creation over the entire course of history. The dawn of this journey is ancient, the risk is deadly, and this lover's perseverance is unquenchable. Then to make the story incredulous, the aim of this love, adventure, and pursuit is you and me. It is staggering a story; this stupendous is more validated and proven than any other historical writing piece. A story that traces the creator of the cosmos in His quest to find and captivate humanity. You and I are the prime focus of creation and the ultimate motivation for everything that has happened since God created time until this very minute.

While sounding very egotistical and arrogant, it's unnerving that I think God began time and created everything that has ever happened since that time because of me. I understand that. The fact remains, as we will discover, that He did so that I would worship and glorify Him. An entity who has always existed in eternity, who made Himself known to us as God, created us and everything in the cosmos. He created everything we know to exist, including man, in six days.

> In the beginning God created the heaven and the earth. And the earth was without form, and void; and darkness was upon the face of the deep. And the Spirit of God moved upon the face of the waters (Genesis 1:1 & 2).

God has always existed in eternity and even created the

heavens during the first six days. God did not need earth, us, or even heaven. He had existed without them forever. He had a plan, and it was us. Everything God created He gave to us. He created a marvelous world: the animals, food, everything we needed, even companionship.

> So God created man in his own image, in the image of God he created him; male and female he created them.
>
> And God blessed them. And God said to them, "Be fruitful and multiply and fill the earth and subdue it, and have dominion over the fish of the sea and over the birds of the heavens and over every living thing that moves on the earth." And God said, "Behold, I have given you every plant yielding seed that is on the face of all the earth, and every tree with seed in its fruit. You shall have them for food. And to every beast of the earth and to every bird of the heavens and to everything that creeps on the earth, everything that has the breath of life, I have given every green plant for food." And it was so (Genesis 1:27-30).

Wow, what extravagance. He gave us life, the earth and everything on it. That was the plan; He gave it all to us and said to fill and conquer it. Adam and Eve, who God created, took care of the garden, and God took care of them. It sounds perfect, doesn't it? The plan was simple. God began time and created heaven and earth for us. Once God finished creating all creation and putting everything in place, He saw it was good. Hebrew, the original language of the Old Testament, says it was *pleasant* to Him. "And God saw everything that he had made, and behold, it was very good. And there was evening and there was morning, the sixth day" (Genesis 1:31).

Six days before, only God, Jesus, and the Holy Spirit existed: the Trinity, in perfect harmony forever in eternity. Six days later, there is heaven, earth, man in the garden, and planets hurling through space. Then this mystic creator, powerful enough to make us, says it is pleasant. He liked it. As we will see, He loved us, and He says we are pleasant. Of course, He did; it is majestic; it's amazing. Man existed in a perfect creation with dominion over everything for eternity.

On the seventh day, God rested. Not from exhaustion, but it says:

> Thus the heavens and the earth were finished, and all the host of them. And on the seventh day God finished his work that he had done, and he rested on the seventh day from all his work that he had done (Genesis 1:1 & 2).

No more creating, and no, evolution did not grow things from that point on, God finished the heavens and the earth (vs. 1).

My wife and I enjoy creating. Each year since we met, we handcraft the Christmas gifts we give to our family. Now that the children are old enough, they help us make the gifts. We start in October, and we finish just before Christmas arrives. It is fantastic to create a memorable gift and see the expression on a person's face that receives it. It is special to give and received knowing that real-time and thought went into its creation. With two small children, our gifts are less elaborate than initially, and we try to get them involved in the crafting. In the end, we need to rest. But the closer we get to Christmas Day brings the satisfaction and anticipation that comes from giving gifts we made. Each year we vow that is the last year of creating gifts until the kids are much older. But so far, when October rolls around, we once again find inspiration.

God exhausted? A perfect, eternal entity is no worse for the wear after creating the cosmos. Instead, He completed it, and it was perfect. He sat back and enjoyed it, loved it, and delighted with the pleasure He got from it. It must have been immensely gratifying to see animals and humans functioning perfectly and enthralled in the creation He created.

It is easy to forget God did not create a few two-dimensional props. He created a working, self-sustaining creation that continues to create even now. Imagine every discovery that continues to amaze us even today. He created it all in the beginning. Genetics, DNA, brains that learn, cells that reproduce, plants that sustain life, and galaxies as far as we can see. Everything God created works together perfectly. No doubt in man's haste and greed to get more than our daily needs met, we try our best to throw creation off balance, yet left alone, it rights itself.

In the garden that God made for man, besides every tree that produced food, He created two unique trees:

> And the Lord God planted a garden in Eden, in the east, and there he put the man whom he had formed. And out of the ground the Lord God made to spring up every tree that is pleasant to the sight and good for food. The tree of life was in the midst of the garden, and the tree of the knowledge of good and evil (Genesis 2:8 & 9).

It is mind-boggling how the garden must have looked. Imagine Willy Wonka's chocolate room, yet a billion times better. It had every tree that God ever created that produced food. Unlike the pictures you may be familiar with that have the man and woman next to a few fruit trees, this garden was jam-packed with every shape, color, and taste a person could ever want. The Garden of Eden was huge. Remember, every animal that ever existed on the earth was present in the garden, not to mention a perpetual ecosystem that, to this day, continues to sustain itself. Even today, scientists believe there may be up to fifty million types of animals alive. Then God added one warning:

> The Lord God took the man and put him in the garden of Eden to work it and keep it. And the Lord God commanded the man, saying, "You may surely eat of every tree of the garden, but of the tree of the knowledge of good and evil you shall not eat, for in the day that you eat of it you shall surely die" (Genesis 2:15-17).

"Yeah, sure God, with everything you've given us we don't need any stinking fruit from the tree of the knowledge of good and evil. We've got more than enough. We're good."

Rewind. God put us in the garden with peaceful bliss for eternity. So what happened to our peaceful bliss? Maybe you are not feeling you are living in a perfect garden, huh? There was one problem. We forgot a very important warning from God, the always existent being from eternity.

This warning from God means He gave man the free will to disobey that warning. What? No electric fence, front door with a deadbolt, or even a moat? He put the tree of the knowledge of good and evil out in the middle of the garden and said, "Don't touch or you will die?"

THE NAMING GAME

Life was going well, perfect to be exact, and God brought all the animals to the man and let him name them. It is crazy when you think of God interacting with us and giving us a role in His creation.

I love hanging out with my children. My daughter is six, and she names and renames her dolls, parts of the house, even me. My wife and I have different names each day as she casts into the incredible adventures she dreams up. There was a time when my daughter, like my son, who is two, would mix up the names for things. We loved it, and for longer than we should have, we let her get the names wrong because they were such cool words. One of our favorites was when she would say, "I'm fust-a-ated" for frustrated. It was amusing because she would put a pout on her face and act so discouraged. It did not hurt that her frustration had come from something very trivial to us, big to her, and she had tried to use such a big word for such a young child.

How cool would it be for God, who had created all these amazing animals, to bring them to you for names? How long would that take to name all the animals? According to The World Book Encyclopedia, "So far scientists have named and classified over 1 1/2 million animals." [1] That is only the number they have renamed, remember Adam named all the animals. He would have named up to fifty million kinds that experts believe to be alive today. That is over 600 twenty-four-hour days, more than a year and a half if he named one each second.

Amidst naming the animals, it was clear to God and Adam none was a good helper for Adam. The man was alone, and he needed a helper. So God made a helper for him. A woman, the last thing created by God, and the man called her woman. Creation was complete, the world was perfect, and everyone lived happily forever.

Well, not quite. Remember, God told them they could have everything except the tree of the knowledge of good and evil and warned them they would die if they ate from it? It would seem a warning that strong is enough never to set foot in that part of the garden.

It has been rare that I've seen a poisonous snake in the wild. In the United States, as long as you can get to a hospital, only a handful of snakes are poisonous enough to kill you. I, unlike others, would not mess with a snake that could kill me. Only days ago, I was fishing from the bank. As I was casting, my foot stepped into a slight dip between two rocks. My mind told me that my foot did not land on solid ground, but something softer and moving. When I looked at where I stepped, my foot was standing on a coiled up water moccasin who had been sunning itself between the rocks. Bracing for the bite, and before I could even think, my body had jerked back ten feet with a surge of adrenaline that had my heart pounding for five minutes afterward. Though the snake did not bite me and I continued to fish 30 yards from that spot, the encounter had me glancing for it and other snakes between each cast. Before long, the once peaceful day of fishing had lost its appeal, and I headed home.

There is no sign of how much time elapsed from perfect bliss to the woman's encounter with the snake in the garden. The Bible seems to show it was only days that man and woman enjoyed the perfect life together in the garden when it all ended.

> Now the serpent was more crafty than any other beast of the field that the Lord God had made.
>
> He said to the woman, "Did God actually say, 'You shall not eat of any tree in the garden'?" And the woman said to the serpent, "We may eat of the fruit of the trees in the garden, but God said, 'You shall not eat of the fruit of the tree that is in the midst of the garden, neither shall you touch it, lest you die.'" But the serpent said to the woman, "You will not surely die. For God knows that when you eat of it your eyes will be opened, and you will be like God, knowing good and evil." So when the woman saw that the tree was good for food, and that it was a delight to the eyes, and that the tree was to be desired to make one wise, she took of its fruit and

ate, and she also gave some to her husband who was with her, and he ate (Genesis 3:1-6).

The man and woman had a perfect life, without even neighbors. But, just days after creation, and before man created enticing television commercials, the salesman arrived. Like many commercials, it was selling something they did not need but appeared to make their life complete. The fatal mistake the woman made was to want something which God had not provided for her. The way verse 6 reads, it might even be the very first time she looked at the tree of the knowledge of good and evil. The serpent, a real serpent influenced by satan, convinced the woman that God kept something from her. She looked at the tree, and she desired it, what it might give her, and provided for herself from a source God made off-limits.

In chapter one, I mentioned that our eyes, the window to our bodies, can persuade us to override God's provision for us and persuade us to provide for ourselves. Here in the garden is where man decided for the first time to provide for himself regardless of the limitless bounty that surrounded him.

Again, remember the magnitude of that garden was the size of a small country. "And out of the ground the Lord God made to spring up every tree that is pleasant to the sight and good for food" (Genesis 2:9). The garden surrounded the man and woman with every kind of tree that has ever existed that was pleasant to the sight and good for food. If there ever was an endless buffet, when time began, man and woman lived in it. Yet, an all-you-can-eat-buffet was not enough. The serpent convinced the woman she needed more than her "daily bread," and convinced her it was worth dying. Rather than believe the Creator, she believed the serpent, part of creation. Believing the creation instead of the Creator is a lie, many scientists still believe today. "But the serpent said to the woman, 'You will not surely die. For God knows that when you eat of it your eyes will be opened, and you will be like God, knowing good and evil'" (Genesis 3:4 & 5).

This is a great lesson for us to learn. Even today, God surrounds us with His limitless provision. Everything is God's to grant us if He chooses. Many times it might not be as obvious as the literal garden the man and woman had right in front of them. But even that obvious, satan still convinced them they needed one more thing. The woman first looked and then desired the only thing God had not provided for her and got it for herself. Notice how chapter 3 starts, "Now the serpent was more crafty than any other beast of the field that the Lord God had made. He said to the woman, 'Did God actually say, "You shall not eat of any tree in the garden"?'" (Genesis 3:1)

Two things about that verse get my attention. First, the original Hebrew word for crafty is *àruwm*. That word means subtle, shrewd, crafty, sly, or sensible. How many times has God not provided me with something I am certain I should have, and I hear a subtle whisper to provide it myself? The first thoughts of getting something for myself outside of God's provision start very inconspicuous; I hardly notice I have had the thought. Maybe it's just an image of me with that item or gadget. It might be the thought of how it will make me feel, or with drugs, not feel. Sometimes what we want most that God is not providing is escape or numbness.

Coming up with a sensible reason I need something has been a good ploy to get me to provide for myself. Once I have the subtle thought, my mind can work out why I need what I want in practical terms. I can come up with all kinds of reasons I should have it: how it could save me time, money, or even improve my social status. Given enough time, we can usually justify a buy or consider it a sensible choice. For example, I could buy a house that costs me family time, exorbitant interest, keeps me from helping those in need, and causes stress. I can justify that buy because my family can have the room it needs to function, and at the end of 30 years, it will have appreciated in value. The long-game is my personal favorite way to make something practical or justify the wisdom of having it.

What about time? We are busy at breakneck speed with never enough hours in the day to do everything. If you raise children, then you sign up for at least 18 years of dedicated child-rearing. Small children grow into teenagers counting on a good family life to train them to be adults. First, they need a good place to learn the basics as children. Then as they continue to adulthood, you become their mentors, guiding them through adolescence. Many children suffer because of an over-commitment of their parents' time or their parents' commitments to supply for their wants outside of God's provision.

Children get stuck in daycares, with strangers raising them, with family, or with babysitters while their mom and dad are away doing what they must to pay the bills or enjoy free time. It is not practical or sensible to expect parents to be at home with their children every day and evening, is it?

The choice to have and raise children is a choice to sacrifice your time, freedom, and many times your peace. Children need their parents' time not only when convenient, but even when it is not. You had a baby knowing full well it takes many years before they are self-sufficient. You say you are not good with kids; if you have one, it is time to get good. I know many parents reading this disagree and their, "me-time" is a touchy subject. If your children could make a choice, would they want you at home raising them or be at the gym, the girl's night out, or maybe the golf course? Adults must make the right choice to empty their schedules for their children because children cannot make it for them, or can they? My wife and I stay amazed at how other parents with children carry on lust as they did before children. Once they are older, the children carry on in life as though they do not have parents. Maybe they did not.

of that which we can provide for ourselves for the obedience that God desires. Research in 2014 shows that working fathers spend 35 minutes a day with their children while mothers spend a whopping hour.[2] The list is endless of how we can trade the practical and sensible benefits Those statistics provide an example of parents being so busy providing outside their means that they ignore the children God has entrusted them to raise.

We must work, and through that, God supplies our "daily bread." Yet, if we are satisfied with God's daily provision, we have the time for both children and rest. A simple life with simple provision is all a family needs.

The second point that strikes me about the conversation between the woman and the serpent is how the serpent makes the woman second-guess what she heard God say. "He [satan] said to the woman, 'Did God actually say, "You shall not eat of any tree in the garden"'" (Genesis 3:1).

I've had times when I knew God's word and what I must do to be obedient, yet I second-guessed it. I am sure that has happened to you. Yet, in this verse, when the woman repeats the exact command God gave them not to eat or even touch the fruit, the serpent twists the truth with a flat out lie. This is important to learn that satan takes whatever means possible to kill, steal, and destroy (John 10:10). He has no qualms about lying or deceiving to win, nor does he play fair, for he is playing for your very soul.

But the serpent said to the woman, "You will not surely die. For God knows that when you eat of it your eyes will be opened, and you will be like God, knowing good and evil" (Genesis 3:4 & 5). When they ate the fruit, it opened their eyes, and for the first time and the rest of their life, they knew evil.

Until that time, all they knew was good, perfection, and total bliss. But by believing satan instead of God, it forever changed them. It forever changed the world.

The woman believed satan that God's perfect provision for them was not enough and that God was holding something back from her she should have. Remember the verse in Matthew Jesus shares about the eye is a lamp that either fills your body with light or darkness?

> The eye is the lamp of the body. So, if your eye is healthy, your whole body will be full of light, but if your eye is bad, your whole body will be full of darkness. If then the light in you is darkness, how great is the darkness (Matthew 6:22 & 23)!

Her eyes looked upon the only thing she did not have and, in an instant, immersed her whole body, her husband, and all humankind into darkness. Since that time, the darkness of sin has been great.

In a short time, days since creation, the woman had forgotten God's position as the creator and ultimate authority. He was the one who created her and everything on which she was standing. God even created the serpent and satan, who was influencing her instead of believing God. God can and will give us everything we need. Many times things that God created, such as people, satan, friends, and television, will try to persuade us we need something God is not providing us, and it will tempt us even if it means chancing death for it.

As with the first man and woman, death may not be immediate or even physical. Yet, when you determine to provide for yourself, it will cause the death of something: family, time, freedom, life, etc. How many times do we repeat that story in the Bible? Like the first woman not satisfied with her daily provision, throughout history, every man, woman, and child since that time has fallen victim to satan's lies.

Something I find interesting is the bait the serpent uses and why the woman even cares about this bait. "The woman saw that the tree was good for food" (vs.6). We have to remember there are thousands of different types of trees in the garden that were all good for food. God had created every tree that has ever known to man and good for food. With so many trees and creation only days old, I doubt the woman could have seen half the trees that bore fruit. Yes, the tree of the knowledge of good and evil was good for food, but so were thousands of more trees that God did not forbid her to eat or touch.

Second, the tree was "a delight to the eye" (Genesis 3:6). It could be this tree was more delightful looking than any other tree in the garden. But there is no sign that this tree was more delightful than any of the others. I've never seen a tree so delightful looking I will risk my life to try its fruit. Since God's creation was perfect, including the trees, they all looked amazing!

Third, the woman saw "that the tree was to be desired to make one wise." Ah, what is this? The Hebrew word used for the phrase, "to make one wise" is *sakal*. Sakal is to be prudent, to be circumspect, wise in understanding, to prosper, or to have success. Bingo! I want to examine this, so we understand what I believe the woman saw in this tree. It was not just a food tree and delightful to look at. It had the magical lure of something that promised to assure her future happiness.

The New Oxford American Dictionary[3] The New Oxford American Dictionary[4] defines "prudent" as acting with or showing care and thought for the future. It defines "circumspect" as wary and unwilling to take risks. It defines "prosper" to succeed in material terms; be financially successful. The woman in this amazing creation, with God supplying her with an endless, all-you-can-eat buffet, while having dominion over the entire earth for eternity, wants to take out an insurance policy. The verse with the Hebrew meanings reads this way:

> So when the woman saw that the tree was good for food, and that it was a delight [desirable] to the eyes, and that the tree was to be desired to make one wise [acting with or showing care and thought for the future and wary and unwilling to take risks, saw that it promised to help her succeed in material terms; be financially successful], she took of its fruit and ate, and she also gave some to her husband who was with her, and he ate (Genesis 3:6, emphasis mine).

Concerned for the future and wary of taking risks, one look at the tree, and she was quick to eat the fruit that promised material and financial success. As the saying goes, "The apple does not fall far from the tree." Isn't that just like the things that tempt us? Six-thousand years ago, the first woman was most likely not concerned with financial success, but she was for her future. Only days after God created her, and with everything she could ever want, she was shopping for insurance policies. Dictionary definitions change throughout the ages to apply to culture. Read with today's definitions of those ancient Hebrew terms; they are dead on to what we today will risk our lives for. Concerned with the future and wary of taking risks, given a tree that bears fruit that promises material and financial success, most of the world would eat heartily even at the risk of death.

What in the world, or garden, had the woman concerned over prudence, circumspect, being prosperous, or ultimately successful? Women and men are different. Maybe she had concern over her ability to bear children? God told them, "Be fruitful and multiply" (Genesis 1:28). Today, it's a valid concern, with millions spent on fertility drugs, artificial insemination, and egg donation. Perhaps she was concerned about being a good wife or mother. Whatever had her looking out for herself, even though six-thousand years is between us, we do not differ all that much from the first humans. Whatever the reason, she rolled the dice and gave the fruit to her husband for the success he might gain from it as well.

Interestingly, the same success they were attempting to get for themselves by eating from the forbidden tree is one of the same desires today. Second, trying to provide for their future outside of God's provision was their undoing. It took the universe's creator six days to create the cosmos, animals, and even man. Now, look at how fast and sorrowful that celebration of life and perfect creation unraveled because Man looked outside of God's provision.

> Then the eyes of both were opened, and they knew that they were naked. And they sewed fig leaves together and made themselves loincloths. And they heard the sound of the Lord God walking in the garden in the cool of the day, and the man and his wife hid from the presence of the Lord God among the trees of the garden. But the Lord God called to the man and said to him, "Where are you?" And he said, "I heard the sound of you in the garden, and I was afraid, because I was naked, and I hid myself." He said, "Who told you that you were naked? Have you eaten of the tree of which I commanded you not to eat?" The man said, "The woman whom you gave to be with me, she gave me fruit of the tree, and I ate." Then the Lord God said to the woman, "What is this that you have done?" The woman said, "The serpent deceived me, and I ate" (Genesis 3:7-13).

At once, the man and woman are frantic, and they try to

cover up their disobedience. In too familiar fashion, they hide from God. Even after the instantaneous knowledge upgrade of good and evil, they misunderstood who God was. I cannot imagine the chaos that ensued just after eating the fruit. Now deceived, they knew they had disobeyed God; and they knew they needed clothes. For the first time, they needed to figure out how to create something for themselves: clothes. Up to this point, God created and provided everything for them. Once they decide to provide for themselves, they are going to need to keep creating, fast! They had to fashion fig leaves together to conceal their nakedness. They did that out of fig leaves? Surely fig leaves were not the largest leaves they could have found. Today fig leaves are about ten inches long and still a term used to convey something inadequate or embarrassing. The snowball was rolling downhill, and it was only gaining speed.

I can imagine the man and woman hearing God's footsteps in the garden. There was something different in His stride. Instead of a brisk, expectant gait of one wanting to see His created beings, was it a slower, more solemn one? God called out to man, "Where are you?" because, for the first time, the man and woman were hiding from Him. Up to now, did they run to meet Him when they heard their creator coming? Not that He did not already know where they were or what they had just done—He knew! This time, they hid in fear and embarrassment.

Then the excuses flew. The man blamed the woman, and the woman blamed the serpent. Just a newborn, humanity had crashed, and the sin that introduced death had entered a perfect creation. I hear the heartbroken tone of God as He asks the woman, "What is this that you have done" (Genesis 3:13)? He knows that in one swift blow, they have separated themselves from Him, the garden, and eternity for a long time. He is now separated from His creation, which He delighted in. For a few days, creation was perfect as it had been for all eternity, but the man broke it. God seeing down through history understands, more than anyone, the magnitude and depth of what had occurred. Disobedience causes sin, and sin carries a consequence.

The party was over.

A DEADLY DISEASE

This is a picture of what happens each time we provide for ourselves instead of relying on God's provision. How many stories do you know of a father who has provided for his family's needs through his own efforts and destroyed a family, his children, and his own life? Though he might not have dismantled mankind with him, to his family, he destroyed their perfect bliss. Our landscape is littered with children, teenagers, single mothers with babies, homeless, and veterans that are hurt, estranged, and void of a bright future because the man leading them decided his provision was better than God's.

Dads, husbands, and even our government hinder the lives of those who followed them into "eating the fruit" to secure their future, material, and financial success. They now abandon those that followed and trusted them, as they are on to their next conquest, chasing the moving target of success. Meanwhile, they leave in their wake the temporary passengers who were prisoners on their last voyage. A tragedy that leaves them handicapped, depressed, and challenged to trust again.

The few times I flew on an airline in the last years, I am saddened as the boarding task begins. Exuberant, the gate attendant announces the airline is proud to welcome their frequent flyers class. As we later board, the first-class section is full to the brim with those that fly so frequently they get first-class or business class upgrades. While sitting in those cushy seats looks inviting, my heart breaks for their occupants and their families because of the exorbitant price of success they pay to sit just in front of a cloth curtain inches from my seat. I can hardly allow my eyes to meet theirs because, though they look important, I know the hours I get to sit on my comfortable couch with my family or on my floor playing with my kids while theirs is vacant. Free vacations, hotel rooms, and front row seats in a plane cannot be worth the time it costs to be away from family and friends.

In a data brief released by the Centers for Disease Control and Prevention,[5] they reported that drug use was on the rise in the last decade and the most prescribed drug for 20 to 59-year-olds was antidepressants.

In a data brief released by the Centers for Disease Control and Prevention [6], they reported that drug use was on the rise in the last decade and the most prescribed drug for 20 to 59-year-olds was antidepressants.

It is not just fathers lured into the trap of eating the forbidden fruit from the garden. Teenagers, mothers, and even church pastors have destroyed their lives and the lives of others while dining on its allure. The taste of that outlaw fruit from the garden has become so addictive our culture serves it up day after day as the main course in schools, colleges, and even churches. Like flies around a rotting corpse, millions attend week-long feasts disguised as business seminars and webinars to sample the fruit prepared different ways as though they were attending a wine tasting. Even bookstores devote entire sections to cookbook-like manuals that teach different methods of preparing the fruit for daily indulgence. Those who engorge themselves at these feasts and devour the pages of these manuals are the norm, not the exception.

It should be easy for us to understand the woman's enticement at the tree's enchanting attraction because, like her, we are a culture immersed in concern for the future and wildly driven to material and financial success. All the while, this pandemic disease carries with it today the same strain of deadly DNA to separate us from God that it did in the garden. Just as the first woman, God gives us the free will to contract this deadly virus and, it's worth mentioning, to spread it. Since that day, the taste of that fruit has never left the human palate. Bigger, better, more, and quicker is the prognosis of the human condition. Add to this; no one cares we have this condition that steals our joy, life, time, families and destroys our lives. It seems normal, so normal that parents encourage their children to contract the disease as quickly as possible by lavishing them with toys and the latest fads as soon as they can crawl.

It's not the success that is the problem. Remember surrounding the man and the woman is the abundance created and supplied by God. If anyone ever lived with prosperity, affluence, wealth, riches, and opulence, it was the man and woman in the garden. What trips us up is why and how we gain success. Moreover, how we define success can be the bigger deception. I believe it is important to note; it was not the serpent's deception that caused the woman to sin. Desire causes sin, and the woman desired something she perceived as success instead of being content with what God had provided for her.

If you are not content in your circumstances, then in essence, you are telling God His provision for you is not enough. When God's provision for you is not enough, then you will look for more provision or a provider you believe will give you what you need. When you look for that provision or provider, you will need to look for it outside God's provision. If you look outside God's provision, you will get deceived. Don't get deceived. Why? Because nothing is as good as God's perfect provision. Nothing. Therein is God's definition of success: to be happy and content with what God provides while keeping in check the responsibilities He has entrusted to you.

Let us get back to the story. Surrounded by the abundance of everything created, the woman and the man ate the fruit of the tree of the knowledge of good and evil, which was the only thing forbidden to them by God. They went into a panic attack, blamed everybody and everything but themselves, and are standing in front of God, half-clothed in fig leaves they threw together. It is a scene too familiar when I have gone outside of God's provision and tried to "make it happen" for myself. I look and sound as though I have tried to take care of myself. I decide I need something that God is not providing for me. When my solution comes apart, I create a fix. My patch looks terrible. When God shows up, I am frantic and create a cover-up and hide. When God asks me to come clean, I give Him my rehearsed excuses and blame everything and everyone but myself. Not much has changed since the garden; I act as though I was the first man myself.

ETERNITY ENDS

> To the woman he said, "I will surely multiply your pain in childbearing; in pain you shall bring forth children. Your desire shall be for your husband, and he shall rule over you."
>
> And to Adam he said, "Because you have listened to the voice of your wife and have eaten of the tree of which I commanded you, 'You shall not eat of it,' cursed is the ground because of you; in pain you shall eat of it all the days of your life; thorns and thistles it shall bring forth for you; and you shall eat the plants of the field.
>
> By the sweat of your face you shall eat bread, till you

return to the ground, for out of it you were taken; for you are dust, and to dust you shall return."

The man called his wife's name Eve, because she was the mother of all living. And the Lord God made for Adam and for his wife garments of skins and clothed them. Then the Lord God said, "Behold, the man has become like one of us in knowing good and evil. Now, lest he reach out his hand and take also of the tree of life and eat, and live forever—" therefore the Lord God sent him out from the garden of Eden to work the ground from which he was taken (Genesis 3:16–23).

Life is about to get very hard for the first inhabitants of the earth. What is God's tone here as He hands out this judgment? Is it searing, apathetic, gentle, or heartbroken? How we read God's tone as He hands out the punishment and bans man from the garden can make a distinction in how we view God.

After everything God did to create the world, the animals, and man, God's tone is grace and love even in humanity's darkest hour. It is here in this desperate minute of man's existence we see God's love. Grace is unmerited favor. He could have decided the experiment of creation did not work, destroy everything: heaven, earth, and man; and go back to peaceful bliss and eternity.

The man and woman stand before their creator, naked and without a defense. Their fate hinges on the next words that come from God's mouth. God spoke them into existence, and with the very next word, they could cease to exist. Poof.

Instead, God banishes them from the garden, and He does so with grace. This is the part of the story I forget. One word, one breath from God, and creation, man and history will end. God made it with His spoken word, and He could have as easily spoken it out of existence. He owed them nothing; He set the rules, and they broke them. From the beginning, God's plan was to create heaven, earth, the animals, man, and for them to live in eternity in perfect bliss. It was not God who made a mistake; it was man. Do not forget, God is all-knowing, so He had no problem seeing down through history to even you and me. So, for Him to continue the story, He knew even then what it would cost. It will cost Him His Son, Jesus. How many of us would show grace to someone who spilled coffee on us? What would it take to have grace and love for someone that would cost me my only son?

> In the beginning was the Word [Jesus], and the Word was with God, and the Word was God. He was in the beginning with God. All things were made through him, and without him was not anything made that was made. In him was life, and the life was the light of men. The light shines in the darkness, and the darkness has not overcome it (John 1:1-5, emphasis mine).

The eternal Trinity: God, Jesus, and the Holy Spirit faced a decision that will cost them one of their own. John says it best in verse 16:

> The true light, which gives light to everyone, was coming into the world. He was in the world, and the world was made through him, yet the world did not know him. He came to his own, and his own people did not receive him. But to all who did receive him, who believed in his name, he gave the right to become children of God, who were born, not of blood nor of the will of the flesh nor of the will of man, but of God. And the Word became flesh and dwelt among us, and we have seen his glory, glory as of the only Son from the Father, full of grace and truth. (John bore

witness about him, and cried out, "This was he of whom I said, 'He who comes after me ranks before me, because he was before me.'") For from his fullness we have all received, grace upon grace (John 1:9-16).

On that day, standing before God, the man, the woman, and each of us received, "grace upon grace." Jesus, the true light, present at that moment in the garden of Eden, who made all things, will die for us. God set the price. Man made the purchase, but Jesus will pay for it with His life.

This is not only the story of how history began, but how history would play out. From the time God spoke creation into existence until the end, God will never leave. He will always see things through to the end. Ten times throughout the Bible, God promises us with these exact words, "I will never leave you nor forsake you" (Hebrews 13:5).[7] It is God's promise.

I say, "how history would play out" because, regardless of what man did in the garden, God's plan will go forward. Let me explain. When God sets out to do something, He always completes it. It is His nature to be perfect. Because man made a fatal error does not change who God is or what He set out to do. God made the heavens, the earth, us, and all creation. He put in motion a directive that man, woman, and the animals would live forever in eternity, right? Does it seem possible that man, a created being, could thwart God's plans? No. The man did not change God's plans through disobedience in the garden. God gave the man and woman the free will to be a part of His plan if they so chose. When the man and woman looked outside of God's provision for themselves by disobeying His rules, sinning, they chose not to be a part of God's plan. Instead of destroying them, He set them outside the garden to live out their lives in His grace. When one generation fails, God sets them aside, then starts with the next generation and continues his plan.

> And Adam knew his wife again, and she bore a son and called his name Seth, for she said, "God has appointed for me another offspring instead of Abel, for Cain killed him." To Seth also a son was born, and he called his name Enosh. At that time people began to call upon the name of the Lord (Genesis 4:25-26).

I believe that God is all-knowing and realized we would make the wrong choice at a time in history. Since the day God created man, he has always had a choice whether to be a part of God's plan and eternity with Him. Only now we will need to choose God rather than satan, taking steps to accept His plan for our lives.

Let me give you a simple example of this complex scenario. Our family eats dinner together every evening, and rarely has either my wife or I missed a meal with our children. We cook at home and infrequently eat out. We want our evenings to be family-oriented and quality family time. Our children are fantastic eaters and prefer vegetables and fruit to any other food. There have been times each of them has been less than excited about something we fix. We set dinner on the table, and they have the choice, free will, to eat dinner or not. We do not fix alternatives. It is their choice if they decide not to eat what we fix. Missing one meal will not harm them. At any point during dinner, food is available, and they can eat. Once we finish dinner, dinnertime is over, and food will be available again at breakfast.

If our children decide not to eat the food we fix or at the time for dinner, they have that choice. Their decision has no bearing on the food being served, the time we eat, or anyone else who wants to eat. Our plan for dinner stays its course. Each child has the choice to be a part of dinner or exclude themselves. We make provision that, if a child wants to opt back in during dinner, they can with no consequence. Once dinner is over, we wash the dishes and close the kitchen until breakfast.

Grant me the liberty to compare this to God's plan for eternity. He set it in motion, and man opted out. God provides, through Jesus' death, burial, and resurrection, that we can opt back into His eternal plan up to where Jesus comes back. After that, the "kitchen's closed." Let me add; neither of our children has ever missed an entire meal.

God, in His all-seeing and infinite wisdom, gave us provision for us to get back to the garden. But before we get to that, let me briefly revisit the Lord's prayer and show you something I discovered.

I often ask myself how I can avoid the same mistake the first woman and man made in the garden. Remember, God's warning to not touch or eat from the tree of the knowledge of good and evil or you will die? It is the same gentle nudge to get it right He gives us today.

We must remember, it was not the fruit of the tree that caused death. God did not say do not touch or eat the tree because it is poisonous and will cause death. It was the act of disobeying God's command, sinning against God, that removed them from eternity in the garden and set them on the path of death. Through obedience, God continued to make a way for His chosen people to follow, have a relationship, and spend eternity with Him.

Four thousand years later, God sent Jesus into the world to complete God's plan for a way for all people to get into God's plan of eternity. In one simple prayer, Jesus teaches us how to avoid, in our own lives, the tragedy that happened in the garden.

> Our Father in heaven, hallowed be your name.
> Your kingdom come, your will be done, on earth as it is in heaven.
> Give us this day our daily bread,
> and forgive us our debts, as we also have forgiven our debtors.
> And lead us not into temptation, but deliver us from evil (Matthew 6:9-13).

From chapter one, readers will remember it breaks down like this: Father I glorify your name; You are God, and we are not. We submit to your kingdom, and we want what you want. Give us enough food to feed us today and forgive our sins in the measure we forgive the sins of others who have wronged us. Keep us from temptations and protect us from evil and satan.

Think about this prayer considering what the woman faced in the garden. This prayer would have reminded her of her place as a created being not equal to the eternal God who created her. She needed to focus on the abundance she had that surrounded her, rather than the only thing, the tree of the knowledge of good and evil, she did not. Whatever the enchanting seduction that tree had on the woman, being content with what God was supplying could have made all the difference in resisting the temptation. Obedience to God was the knowledge of good and evil she needed to concern herself with. She did not need to be like God, which was the temptation that satan offered. No doubt, she needed God's protection from temptations and evil.

That simple prayer is powerful. The things that were a threat in the garden are the same things we face today. Jesus knew exactly how to tell the disciples and us how to pray. He knew how I need to pray to avoid my own garden tragedy. He was there in the garden and has been present at every human debacle since. I find it intriguing that Jesus' arrest was from a garden, then tried, and condemned to death, to take my place for the sins committed in the first garden. It is crazy how simple this prayer seems on the surface, yet it is what I need to pray every day.

Here again, God shows me what I thought was a complex task of praying is simple. The story of creation is even simple. God made everything.

Man sinned by disobeying God. That is where we are today, outside the garden. Like the first man and woman, we are living out our lives, outside the garden and outside eternity. Through a simple prayer, God gives us the formula for living out our lives in a broken world with the hope of eternity until His plan is complete:

- Glorify the Creator, God
- Submit to God's kingdom
- Be content with how God supplies your daily needs
- Repent for your sins and forgive others
- Resist temptations and
- Guard against evil

But as I mentioned before, when God put His plan in motion, the mistake in the garden did not thwart His plan. The story continues, and man, woman, and the animals will again live in the garden with the Trinity forever. How?

As the lyrics from the song "Woodstock" by Crosby, Stills, Nash & Young say, we are "Caught in the devil's bargain, and we got to get ourselves back to the garden."[8]

Journal Pages

This is a great opportunity to journal what you are learning or the action steps you want to take based on this lesson. Doing so will keep all your notes and journaling in this book as future reference. Start by taking a few minutes to pray and ask Jesus to bring to light all you are learning and what transformational changes you can make in your life. If you are reading this in an electronic version, make a digital note and journal.

Journal Pages

THREE
GOD'S LOVE

Fortunate for us, the lyrics, "And we got to get ourselves back to the garden," from the song "Woodstock" are wrong. God has a plan to bring us back to the garden and eternity.[1] But it will not be through our efforts, but through His son Jesus.

But before the story gets better, it gets worse. This morning is a noble example. While writing, my two-year-old son woke up in a terrible mood. He was unhappy through breakfast, and his mood continued to degrade until the morning was a complete mess. If you have children, you recognize the disposition where nothing changes their state of mind. No matter what you do or give them, they continue on a destructive path.

To make matters worse, he got into one thing after the next with objects off-limits. First, the refrigerator, then my desk drawer, and onto something else, and I felt I was chasing a live pinball around on his highest-scoring game yet. Each time I bounced him back into play, the level of his dissatisfaction and crying increased.

That destructive path is much how the first 1,656 years

outside the garden went between man and God. Man multiplied on the earth and along with that murder and mayhem. Complete wickedness, and God was sorry He had made creation.

> The Lord saw that the wickedness of man was great in the earth, and that every intention of the thoughts of his heart was only evil continually. And the Lord regretted that he had made man on the earth, and it grieved him to his heart. So the Lord said, "I will blot out man whom I have created from the face of the land, man and animals and creeping things and birds of the heavens, for I am sorry that I have made them" (Genesis 6:5-7).

It does not take much to imagine what it must have been like; look at the world today. We have not changed one bit, except to get even more deplorable. Still, there was a man named Noah, who the Bible says, "... found favor in the Lord" (Genesis 6:8). Whew, Noah saved our skin, because the Bible says, "Noah was a righteous man, blameless in his generation" (Genesis 6:9). Once again, this time through Noah, God showed us grace and spared the world. You can't say God doesn't give second chances. God has Noah build an ark and put in it his family, two of every unclean animal, and seven pairs of every clean animal. Then God wipes out the rest of creation with a flood. One hundred fifty days after the rain starts and water covers the globe, eight people and the animals walk out of the ark with a fresh start, and God starts again.

It is at this point in the story, just 1,656 years from when God created us, that I grasp the depth of His love. Besides having grace for the second time, the word which comes to mind is patience. What in all creation could give this majestic being any interest in watching us bumble through it yet again?

GOD'S HEART

To understand, we need to go back to the sixth day of creation. By the end of the fifth day of creation, God had created the light, heavens, earth, seas, plants, trees, sun, moon, stars, sea life, and birds. On the sixth day, God created all the land animals and insects. As God's last task of creation, He makes man and woman in His own image.

Then God said, "Let us make man in our image, after our likeness. And let them have dominion over the fish of the sea and over the birds of the heavens and over the livestock and over all the earth and over every creeping thing that creeps on the earth."

> So God created man in his own image, in the image of God he created him; male and female he created them.
>
> And God blessed them. And God said to them, "Be fruitful and multiply and fill the earth and subdue it, and have dominion over the fish of the sea and over the birds of the heavens and over every living thing that moves on the earth." (Genesis 1:26-28).

Here lies the reason God has the grace, patience, and willingness to let man start over again and again. God said, "Let us make man in our image, after our likeness" (Genesis 1:26). God made us in our entirety, just like Him. The word used in the Hebrew for likeness is *děmuwth*. At this point is where it gets good, and we can understand to what extent of His image He made us. The author uses "likeness" translated *děmuwth* two more times in Genesis 5:

"This is the book of the generations of Adam. When God created man, he made him in the likeness of God" (Genesis 5:1).

"When Adam had lived 130 years, he fathered a son in his own likeness, after his image, and named him Seth" (Genesis 5:3).

These two verses, written a verse apart, give us an exact meaning of the word "likeness" or *děmuwth*. "When God created man, he made him in the likeness of God" (v.1), and "When Adam had lived 130 years, he fathered a son in his own likeness, after his image, and named him Seth" (v.3). It is easy for us to understand how alike Adam and his son Seth were, right? But it is hard for us to accept that God made man very much, or even just like Him. Our sin changes a lot, including how we view ourselves. We act, feel, and think opposite to God with sin operating in our lives. For those that want to burn me at the stake for heresy, notice I did not infer God made us equal to Him but in His image. Let's think through this.

You might remember, God made man perfect without sin. "And God saw everything that he had made, and behold, it was very good" (Genesis 1:31). In reality, how could God, who is perfect, make anything less than perfect?

God made us as eternal creatures, just as God is eternal. Jesus references we are eternal several times in his ministry. The first time is in John 5, after Jesus heals a paralyzed man lying beside the pool at Bethesda on the Sabbath. Next, He teaches those watching. Amidst that teaching, Jesus says, "Truly, truly, I say to you, whoever hears my word and believes him who sent me has eternal life. He does not come into judgment, but has passed from death to life" (John 5:24). Realizing that God made me much like Himself helps me understand why He gave us many chances to get it right.

Several years after I married my wife, I remember the exact moment she showed me the home pregnancy test with the pink stripe on it. A flood of emotions washes over every soon-to-be parent when that moment arrives. If you are a parent or soon-to-be, you know what I'm describing. I felt amazed, confounded, joyful, and inadequate all at the same time. I believe the nine months of pregnancy are as much for the developing mother and father as for the developing baby. It gives you time to get your brain around the changes that are taking place. Just when you think the nine months are going by too slow and you have it all figured out, you are sitting with a little bundle in your arms and wondering if you could have a couple more months to prepare. I was awestruck looking at my daughter in my arms; there was an incredible love for her, for which I had not prepared myself. Sure, during the nine months, my love for her had been growing. When I held her in my arms, my love bubbled over. I had made another human from myself. Through creation, God gave me the physical ability to create another human that I would father for the rest of my life. My creation was only possible because gave the command to multiply; even so, it was my limited creation.

It is crazy how the pregnancy and birth of a child changes so many things about a person in a positive way. I stayed with my wife the couple of nights required in the hospital after the birth, basking in surreal joy. I will never forget that first night in the hospital and even have a self-portrait to prove it. Our daughter stayed in the room with us, and they provided a see-through bassinet for her to sleep in. My wife was asleep; she had accomplished an incredible nine months of endurance that rivaled any triathlon competition a hundred times over. The clear bassinet was there for the baby, but it seemed so institutional and foreign for a newborn baby to sleep in. Besides, I couldn't bring myself to put her down. It had been a 15 ½ hour trek for all three of us that day, and we had reached exhaustion. There I sat with a newborn baby in my arms, my daughter! The dim light of the room illuminated her face, and I couldn't stop watching her. Every movement of her lips, her hands, her nose were captivating. She was perfect; the world was perfect; our family was perfect. I remember my heart was so full of thanks to God for bringing this little girl into my life, for bringing my wife into my life. I thought my heart would explode just looking at her. Then I realized the love I had for her. Wow, the love I had for her was immense, rich, and deep. For the first time, I realized just a fraction of how deep God's love for me must be. I would do anything for this little bundle; I knew it. I would protect her with my life, just as I had promised her mother I would for her.

Life was perfect, just the three of us, perfect blissful family. As the weeks and months passed, she tried to talk, to crawl, and then it happened. One day my beautiful and innocent daughter became much less innocent and disobeyed me. As she continued to grow, she made more mistakes, and because of my love for her, I gave her chance after chance.

Even after experiencing the jarring reality that children will disobey, a few years later, the pregnancy test was again positive, and this time we had a son. This time we thought we had prepared and knew what we were in for — not a chance. Nine months of waiting, nine months of preparation, and our hearts changed again forever. It was miraculous. Again, nights awake watching his every movement, marveling at this baby I had a part of creating. Then one day, as if he had taken his cue from his sister, he too disobeyed. Even though they continue to disobey from time to time, I still love them, care for them, and want to spend every one of my waking hours with them.

Still, at night as I am headed to bed, I sit in their room and watch them sleep. Other nights I wake up in the middle of the night and go to their room to watch them, marveling. We have thousands of videos taken on our phones of them doing whatever amused us. Our children enthrall us. Yes, I would die for each one of them.

Understanding how much my children mean, it is easier to understand the depth God loves me. Along with raising children comes great times of frustration. It confounds parents all over the world what children are capable of. To the degree they amaze, is the same degree to which they can frighten. My wife and I cringe at the thought of what they might do once they are teenagers.

The life of a parent is never dull. One hour you're thrilled, and at another, you can't believe what you're looking at. At one moment, they have never been cuter, and another, they terrify you. The last six years of my life, blessed with children, have been the best and the most challenging years I've experienced. Their capacity for food, care, love, entertainment, and baths is endless. Yet, even with the challenges, I would never trade a second of my life with them for the most tranquil beach in the world. Not even if it had a waiter serving endless Mudslides. Life with children is rich, unpredictable, selfless, and yes, pure joy. You know you're a parent when one of your most proud moments in life is when your child went to the bathroom for the first time on the potty. I cannot explain the exuberance which goes through your mind. The thrill that a child could learn to use the potty is liberating.

And in case you have never experienced the magnitude of a catastrophic world disaster, let me explain. My daughter was almost four, and she was playing in our family room as I was working from home. Mind you; I was in the same room and on the phone. It started with a sneeze, and then I coughed as I realized something was amiss. As I looked to see what was causing me to cough, I saw my daughter dancing like a princess, emerging from a thick fog. You know the kind they use in plays and concerts. There was light streaming into the room from the glass sliding door behind her. It was surreal like I was looking at a scene from a fairy tale. Then my mind caught up to what I was looking at. She was emptying the last of a 22-ounce bottle of baby powder, the economy size, over the top of her head. By now, half the powder was like a dusting of new-fallen snow and the other half suspended in the air like fog. If you have never experienced this stage effect in your own home, then I should tell you that the initial wow factor is only half of how cool it is. Baby powder is special. Because it is so fine, it takes hours to settle and floats through the entire house. In the meantime, you cough your head off while trying to clear the air. Hours later, the whole house has a thin layer of white powder. As you dust and vacuum, it reanimates the powder allowing you to dust again and again. I am sure that if you analyzed the dust in our house now over one and a half years later, there are trace amounts of baby powder still present. The experts warn you to keep poisons locked away in a cabinet, but they do not warn you of the dangers of baby powder.

Regardless of the challenges or near-death experiences, I love my kids, and I would never walk away from them. Never.

GOD'S IMAGE

That love I have for my children is part of God's image; He embedded it in my DNA. No matter what they do, I'm their dad, and I am cheering for them. The love that God has, for me is God's DNA. Our Father, God, made us in His image. I understand that no matter what I do, He is still my Father, and He is rooting for me. "For God so loved the world, that he gave his only Son, that whoever believes in him should not perish but have eternal life" (John 3:16).

Remember those three chances God gave us? The first chance He gave was when He created us. Yet we messed that up and, instead of destroying us and all of His creation, He had mercy. God gave us a second chance and set us outside the garden, the perfect eternity He made for us. One thousand six hundred fifty-six years later, humankind was so evil that God was sorry He made it, and only because of Noah, He gave us a third chance. But God loved us so much that having us live, yet be apart from Him for eternity, was not His plan. God loved you and me so much that He gave His only Son that, through His death, we again would have eternal life with Him. Though it cost Him His Son, He is bringing us back to the perfect garden for eternity with Him.

Yes, God had a plan when He created us. God included a fantastic plan that included giving us a free will. A plan that even encompassed us disobeying Him in the garden and a plan that will bring us back to living with Him in eternity. Since the day He created us, God has been relentless to pursue us throughout history as a lovesick Father and creator. He knew what history would look like, and He knew what it would cost Him. Now can you hear the tone in God's voice in the garden when He asks the first woman, "What is this that you have done?" (Genesis 3:13). Just days into a perfect creation, to make it right again, it would not only cost God six days of creating. He knew it would cost Him His Son. Can you see how crazy it was that the woman was looking outside God's provision for her success? How insane it is that we look outside God's provision for our own wants, desires, and success? This eternal being, God, needing nothing, desired to create us and give us a perfect life. Besides everything He had already done, our thanks for that was to cost Him His Son. God has watched us bumble through history, pursuing success, riches, fame, power, and even lesser desires. The free will God gave us has allowed us to reject Him, yet go on living right in front of Him. That cost Him His Son, not that He had to, but because we were worth it to Him.

I cannot imagine what it would be like to watch my children love everyone but me, want to be with anyone but me, or even ignore me. We have a custom in our home at bedtime. We get the kids' pajamas on, brush teeth, and give them their last sips of water. Then we sit as a family and sing "Twinkle, Twinkle Little Star," and "Jesus Loves Me." Then we say a prayer together. Since writing this book, we say "The Lord's Prayer." Then my wife and I each put a kid on our backs and haul them to bed. Once in bed, we give them kisses and hugs. Our son, at two, gives great slobbery kisses. He is at the age where he thinks it's amusing to refuse to give kisses and hugs every once in a while. It's hard not to let those refusals become personal. Sometimes he will kiss one of us and refuse to kiss the other. If he refuses, we resort to begging for those juicy slobbers. Sometimes we don't win him over and have to close the door without them. It is heartbreaking, and my mind wonders what I did that he doesn't want to give me kisses. He is laughing and thinks it's a game; he means nothing by it. Each time I have to remind myself that he is two and does not understand how deep a missed kiss goes to a parent. I cannot explain it any simpler than God does in His own handwriting:

> Beloved, let us love one another, for love is from God, and whoever loves has been born of God and knows God. Anyone who does not love does not know God, because God is love. In this the love of God was made manifest among us, that God sent his only Son into the world, so we might live through him. In this is love, not that we have loved God but that he loved us and sent his Son to be the propitiation for our sins. Beloved, if God so loved us, we also ought to love

one another. No one has ever seen God; if we love one another, God abides in us and his love is perfected in us. By this we know that we abide in him and he in us, because he has given us of his Spirit. And we have seen and testify that the Father has sent his Son to be the Savior of the world (1 John 4:7-14).

God is love. That elusive elixir called love we have been searching for all our lives as humans is God. Not only is love from God, but that same love is also God Himself. You may be like me; I have gone through my entire life thinking love was something that God did. Instead, I need to view God in a whole another way. Love and God are the same. That is what it says, "... because God is love" (vs. 8). Love is what every human is after, right? Through that lens, God becomes more than just some religion or a belief; He becomes life itself.

God, literally being love, showed us that love by sending His Son Jesus, so we could live and have life. Not only a life here, but by bringing us full circle back into the garden for eternity. Yes, life here is better because we have hope in our souls of eternal life with God that is coming. Everything is better when there is something good at the end. Remember that verse at the beginning of the book about how the end of life on this earth ends?

> Then they will deliver you up to tribulation and put you to death, and you will be hated by all nations for my name's sake. And then many will fall away and betray one another and hate one another. And many false prophets will arise and lead many astray. And because lawlessness will be increased, the love of many will grow cold. But the one who endures to the end will be saved. And this gospel of the kingdom will be proclaimed throughout the whole world as

a testimony to all nations, and then the end will come (Matthew 24:9-14).

Together, these two verses are a great insight into whether we know love or are just going through the motions. It is both a comfort and a warning for all humanity. The comfort is if we know God, we know genuine love because God is love. For it says, "Beloved, let us love one another, for love is from God, and whoever loves has been born of God and knows God" (1 John 4:7). In addition, if we know God and love one another, God abides in us, and He perfects our love. That is our assurance that God abides in us. "No one has ever seen God; if we love one another, God abides in us and his love is perfected in us. By this we know that we abide in him and he in us, because he has given us of his Spirit" (1 John 4:12-13). To know the emotion of love, you have to be born of God and know God. The opposite is the impossibility to know genuine love unless you know God. "Anyone who does not love does not know God, because God is love" (1 John 4:12-13).

We find the warning in Jesus' explanation of the end of the world. As lawlessness increases, the ability to love will also be challenging. If we allow our love to grow cold, coupled with the verse above, we will no longer know God. The word know in the Greek is *ginōskō* which means no longer perceive or feel God. I know from multiple experiences, it is tough to keep loving someone who violates the law or is unethical and therefore harms us. But we must remember that Jesus, who was fully man, died on a cross, taking our lawlessness, saving us. That is the picture of love He also expects us to live.

Through my kids, I understand the joy God gets as He interacts with us. Playing with my children is one of life's greatest successes. I also know to the extent God loves to be with me because there is nothing I would rather do than play and interact with my kids. My son and daughter soak up my attention, and it is never easy to resist them wanting to play with me. They are the center of my wife's and my attention, thoughts, and dreams. First, my wife and I had a fantastic life together; we needed nothing more to enjoy life or each other. Together we enhanced our lives with children. We knew our lives would never be the same and would be an exploration of epic proportions. Our children would be born with free will. It would require us to live out the rest of our lives as a sacrifice to teach, train, and help them grow into adults who could do the same for their children. We are helpers and teachers to show them the way through life. When our children came, they enhanced our life, and our romance for each other melded into a family. Now our children are as big a part of our lives as anything else. Because of that, our lives and our relationship with each other is family, not just a couple.

It's very much like the story that started our life. God, Jesus, and the Holy Spirit, three separate identities in one person—the Trinity lived in eternity together in perfect harmony. They needed nothing more, and forever they have always had a fantastic existence together. Not explained why in the Bible, together they embarked on an adventure. They created a cosmos with eternal inhabitants, set in a perfect world, and given free will. They knew this venture had risks. Once created we have been the center of their attention, thoughts, and dreams. Though we cost them the life of one of their own, Jesus, they made the sacrifice because they loved us so much. When we used our free will to disobey them, Jesus sacrificed His life to adopt us back into their eternal family. When we choose His sacrifice for our sin, our relationship with them is a close family, the family which we have longed for since the garden. As we will learn, our adoption is not as a distant relative but as sons and daughters.

It is not a coincidence that those two stories are similar, as the Trinity made us like them in every way. God, Jesus, and the Holy Spirit, the triune Trinity, created us as a family, just as my children are born into my family. Though it is rare, children can walk out on their parents. When minors in the United States do, they become wards of the state they live in. Either their parents did not take care of them well or believed their parents were not taking care of them. They grow up in orphanages or foster homes, and the state takes care of them until they are of legal age. When we listened to satan in the garden, we made a choice to go outside God's care and live outside His kingdom. We walked away from God and into satan's care, choosing satan rather than God for our future. We became a ward of satan and if we want to leave that care we need someone to save us, to adopt us.

There would come a man, a God-man, to save us, and His name would be Jesus.

"She [Mary] will bear a son, and you shall call his name Jesus, for he will save his people from their sins" (Matthew 1:21).

Journal Pages

This is a great opportunity to journal what you are learning or the action steps you want to take based on this lesson. Doing so will keep all your notes and journaling in this book as future reference. Start by taking a few minutes to pray and ask Jesus to bring to light all you are learning and what transformational changes you can make in your life. If you are reading this in an electronic version, make a digital note and journal.

Journal Pages

FOUR
JESUS' LOVE

> *If you took the love of all the best mothers and fathers who have lived in the course of human history, all their goodness, kindness, patience, fidelity, wisdom, tenderness, strength, and love and united all those qualities in a single person, that person's love would only be a faint shadow of the furious love and mercy in the heart of God the Father addressed to you and me at this moment.* [1]

My son and daughter are distinctly male and female. Since my daughter's birth, I have enjoyed and become skilled at engaging the princess theme for the last six years. It is incredible how a small girl can take her daddy into a delicate and feminine world where everything is soft and beautiful. It is a pink world where everything is innocent, gentle, and full of hope. She has taken me on long walks just to look at flowers and marvel at leaves. I've attended the opening night of her dance recital performed right in front of the couch in our living room. Mind you, no three-minute preview, but a full-blown ticketed event that lasts half an hour! At her request, she and I have gotten married 100 times, and my role is both the father of the bride, giving her away, and the groom. After our wedding ceremony, we go back to our home, which she has prepared, and she cooks a meal for us to enjoy in the candlelight. I have enjoyed hundreds of homemade meals she has spent hours preparing with plastic food. Sometimes she makes the food from Play-Doh, and the designs are more intricate than a French chef's. She dresses up and puts on play makeup and asks me how she looks. Of course, she is asking me if she looks as beautiful as any princess could ever look. No matter if it is the dead of winter, her go-to clothes is a dress and nice shoes; it is a struggle to get her to wear pants. She talks to boys on play phones and has me play sick, so as a doctor, she can fix me up and then mothers me back to health as I lay on the couch. As my teacher, she has taught me my alphabet, numbers, and everything else she has current knowledge. And yes, we've had the grandest adventures. She travels the world right in front of me. Sometimes, she takes me with her, and other times, she waves goodbye and leaves me behind, reminding me that she will want to be more independent one day. We've built forts in Africa from blankets thrown over chairs; we've sailed the oceans together in boxes. I've served many lunches to her from cantinas in Mexico to beach shacks in Jamaica. You never know from minute to minute when you will need to snap into character to live out the next adventure with her. Like her mother, she is captivating in every way. Both she and her mother have ground off many of my sharp and rigid edges. My favorite of all the inherent values my little girl has is the thousands of times she spontaneously tells me, "Daddy, I love you," followed by kisses and hugs. If you don't know by reading, she melts my heart. She has what every little girl has deep inside her: a princess, a mother, and a homemaker that wants to love, to be loved, to help, to nurture, and to make the world around her the Garden of Eden. "Do you see me? Asks the heart of every girl. And are you captivated by what you see?"[2] John Eldredge writes, "Every woman has three desires that are essential to her heart. Every woman yearns to be fought for, wants an adventure to share, and wants to have a beauty to unveil."[3]

Every one of those three desires of a woman's heart, John mentions, is played out every day right in front of me by my daughter. It is my question to answer, or else she will look to another boy or man to answer it. Whether the answer is right or wrong, empowering, or hurtful, every girl finds an answer to that question. She will find the answer one way or the other, and it is best if that answer comes from me, her father.

Yes, my daughter is a woman in every way, and it's easy to see who she will grow up to be. She will be beautiful, captivating, nurturing, and an adventure junkie. Whenever she meets that special man who will take my leadership place in her life as a husband, he will need to fight with his life for her. The extra terrible news for him is I fought with diligence and without reservation for my daughter's heart. She knows what a warrior for a woman's heart looks and smells like.

On the male side of our roost is my two-year-old son. He encompasses everything God created in a man. Once he progressed to crawling, the household shifted from being weighted more on the feminine track to a level playing field. Even at two, he makes his presence known as a man. He is not timid one bit to insert his masculine leadership role even when standing up to his six-year-old sister.

It's been refreshing because he rescued me as a father from everything being soft, pink, and cute in his hero nature. Blue is his favorite color, not by any influence of ours but by his own choice. He is rough, tough, and self-sufficient to where he might be okay if he walked out of the house today and made his own way.

From the first time, he could scoot his way to his own interests, cars, boats, trucks, tractors, trains, and planes came to life under his puppetry. My daughter enjoys those objects to a degree, but my son stays engrossed in them throughout the day. His favorite, and mine also, is when he insists I get on the floor, and he runs the cars and trucks around my limbs as a racetrack and off-road racing venue. It is the best stuff in the world when your son includes you in the focus of his play. He is fascinated with how things move and fit together. He marvels at how car wheels move, trucks roll over obstacles, and cities get built using Legos. As he ponders these discoveries, you can see the builder, engineer, warrior, and survivalist jotting mental notes he will use later in life. Even at two years old, he builds his masculine skills to take him on adventures, fight battles, win the princess by rescuing her from the castle, and then romance and take care of her all of her life.

As a father, he has rekindled a part of my life I had forgotten as my son invites me back into the world I had spent my days in when I was a child. While writing this, I realized that somewhere between junior high and high school, I walked out of a special place that I have deeply missed since then. A place where I could do anything, be anyone, and dreams always come true. Every day was a new adventure, villains lost, good guys won, the open landscapes were beautiful. I was always the hero when there were princesses to be rescued. Thinking back, it is as if I forgot that magical world overnight. Much like when God set the first man and the first woman outside the garden, the world's message became predominant.

When I first saw my son open the door to that world I had forgotten, there was a sentimental longing to be there again myself. I remember my father being with me every chance I gave him in that magical world where everything my mind imagined would happen. I do not remember when my dad was not leading the charge, fighting the dragon, or sailing the high seas with me in that world. I remember my father enjoyed it as much as I did. So as my son found the door into that world, there was not a second of hesitation as he looked back, inviting me to join him. Once again, dawn broke for a father and son in that world of endless possibilities. Come to think of it; it is about as close to the garden of Eden as we will ever experience on this side of death. As I remember, there was never a moment's hesitation for either my father or grandfather to jump headlong into that world with me. They were like anxious children that couldn't wait to storm into the next adventure with me. There was always a toy or something they built in the garage that pulled us as a father and son or grandfather and grandson into the next marvelous expedition. One of my favorite memories is my father inviting me to build a hovercraft alongside him from miscellaneous things found around the garage. It was magical to be a part of transforming a bunch of spare parts into a working toy. It must have taken an entire day to build and paint, but it seems like in my memories an hour after we started it purring in a nearby mud puddle. After being a part of that, I felt my father could build anything. It was hundreds of times like that with my father showing me he enjoyed and delighted in doing things with me, which added the most value and love into my childhood.

It has been refreshing to be back in that world I had so long forgotten as a man. I'm confident it is part of God's design that when a male in each new generation is born, they invite the older generations back into a world where anything can happen, where they can find their hero side again. I have a special affection for that world and never want to forget it again.

My wife and I are careful about the information, TV, and movies our children take in, chief amongst that programming with violence and witchcraft. It surprised me that my son began crafting everything into guns at about one and a half years old. Puzzle pieces, sticks, forks, you name it; they were all guns. "Pow pow." What? Where did that come from? Yes, with no instruction from me, my son realized deep down inside him, he was born into a battle to fight. It is inherent to his nature as a man that he learns to fight the battle for his soul, country, princess, and kingdom. He is already preparing himself for battle at two years old. To men, John Eldredge writes, "They may be misplaced, forgotten, or misdirected, but in the heart of every man is a desperate desire for a battle to fight, an adventure to live, and a beauty to rescue."[4]

Like my daughter with her feminine qualities, each of the masculine attributes that John mentions are present in my son. As John explains, he must also answer the question, "Am I a man? Have I got what it takes...when it counts?"[5]

Though my son's and I's adventures are just beginning, I can already see that together; we will conquer the deepest caves, the highest mountains, win back countless princesses, explore the galaxies, and discover innumerable universes all before he is fourteen.

My son has a few years of training to go, but his natural manhood and strength already show. Even at two, it is easy to see he will grow up to be a powerful man, and whatever his battles, he will defeat every foe that stands in his way.

As far as his question, "Am I a man and do I have what it takes ... when it counts?"[6]

Starting today and the rest of his life, my thrill, and privilege as a father, is to stay involved in his life and reinforce his journey to manhood. Through battles, adventures, and preparing him to romance his princess, I will help him develop his God-given masculine skills and verve. My son already has what it takes to be a courageous man in every sense of the word. That manhood is given to him by God when He made him in His image. He is a dangerous, adventurous knight in shining armor. He is the answer to humanity of what it is to be a man, and soon enough, He will realize that. Together my son and I will stay the course for which God created Him. As father and son, we will change the world together and restore a broken world. What will my son become? I know he will be twice or even three times the man I am and live out everything God meant him to be.

Deep down inside, isn't that the dream of every father? To train up his children to be a force to be reckoned with, vibrant, alive, and full of worth? No, there is no greater calling in life nor as grand an adventure as a father than to help his children through their first years of life to hone their individual gender skills to be a tribute to humanity and their creator God. There is no greater compliment given a father than to be given children and serve them to reach their dreams.

> Don't you see that children are God's best gift? the fruit of the womb his generous legacy? Like a warrior's fistful of arrows are the children of a vigorous youth. Oh, how blessed are you parents, with your quivers full of children! Your enemies don't stand a chance against you; you'll sweep them right off your doorstep (Psalms 127:3-5 MSG).

As far as the world I left behind as a teenager; I will do everything within my power to make sure my son and I never close the door to that magical world ever again. I know these things about my children not by wishful thinking but because God made them in His image.

In contrast to my beautiful princess daughter, my son is a warrior: fierce, wild, and a prince who will grow into a king. Nothing will stand in his way to win or fight for his princess. Jesus came to us as a gallant knight in shining armor: a king, dangerous, adventurous, free, and focused on his mission that nothing, not even death, would deter. The fact is, He came to die for each of us. Jesus came to earth with the greatest of battles to fight, the most heroic adventure to live: to rescue and win His princess, His creation, us.

On a quiet night like any other, in a little town called Bethlehem, God staged His final victory over the mistake man made in the garden. Since the dawning of creation and man's terrible mistake, the world, the universe had been waiting for this night. Jesus showed up on our doorstep as a baby to rescue us.

THE RESCUE

It seemed like almost any other day in the bustling city of Bethlehem, Israel. The town was crowded past capacity for weeks by weary travelers from all over the country. By decree from the Roman Emperor, Caesar Augustus, they had converged on Bethlehem to be counted in a census.

Later than expected, a teenage couple engaged to be married entered the edge of town, exhausted from a 90-mile journey that took more than a week on foot from their hometown of Nazareth. To add to their weariness, Mary— the female, had made the trip pregnant. For Joseph, the father, it had been an adventure: up and down mountains, through a river, and the wilderness of Judea all with an expectant wife. They arrived after such a grueling trip only to find no comfortable place to stay and rest. The city was full. Yet God had a plan for them, an extraordinary plan.

Though they had come to Bethlehem for a census, God had another much more significant purpose. God had brought Mary and Joseph to Bethlehem for a night, unlike any other. Through this couple, God was staging His rescue of us. Not since God had walked in the garden with the first woman and first man, would God ever be as close to humanity as He would come this night. At the center of the cosmos was this teenage couple with the baby inside her. As the labor pains began, few others but the humble couple noticed or cared, as they too were away from home and distracted by their own circumstances. In uncomfortable surroundings, far away from home with much less than adequate care, the young mother strained through the pain of childbirth. Likely, Joseph had never assisted the birth of a child. Whether a sympathizing woman jumped in to help or not, Joseph mustered the courage and did what little he could do to comfort and help his wife through the unbearable pain and suffering. They understood that there was never a more precious gift given to the world than the child born that night.

Oh, but while few men understood what this night meant, all heaven and hell knew that God was staging the most significant rescue ever known— the recovery of all humanity. Though it might have seemed to the young couple they were alone, the hosts of heaven, the demons of hell, satan, and God Himself had their full attention. For the baby who Mary carried inside her was Jesus. For the first time since God formed the first woman from the man's ribs, Jesus would again touch the hands of a human. Once born, as all new-born babies do, Jesus would curl his fingers around the finger of Mary, around each of our fingers. Through that grasp, He would pull us out of our sin, once and forever. For the first time since creation in the garden, man would reach out and have physical contact with a member of the Trinity. The circle was again complete. From that night on, anyone who believed He was the savior would touch the heart of God. For those throughout the ages who wondered about God, oh, from this night forward, He would be very real.

God, through His infinite love, had sent His Son, Jesus, to rescue us. Through Jesus, God would bring the ultimate and complete restoration for our mistake in the garden.

> For God so loved the world, that he gave his only Son, that whoever believes in him should not perish but have eternal life. For God did not send his Son into the world to condemn the world, but in order that the world might be saved through him (John 3:16-17).

God had not forgotten us when He placed the first man and woman outside the garden for their sin of disobedience four-thousand years earlier. Instead, He planned the most incredible rescue mission the world would ever witness. It was long, dangerous, and the last act hinged on a young teenage couple, not yet married, being obedient to follow His plan. Less than nine months earlier, before the labor pains started, Mary and Joseph pledged to be married to each other. It was an exciting time and Mary, just like any other teenage girl of that time, felt her life coming together with the promise of marriage to an upstanding boy of the village. That was just the first step of a very unusual start for the young couple.

I can imagine Mary humming as she was going about her daily activity. She was happy; why shouldn't she be? She had caught the eye of Joseph, a righteous Jewish boy whose family had descended from King David. While carrying on daily life, she and her family were planning her wedding. She saw the life ahead of her that God had set in motion. She and Joseph would get married, settle down, and have a wonderful life. Joseph was a carpenter and skilled craftsman and would provide a good life for them. It is everything a young Jewish girl dreamt of, right? It would be perfect, and they would have a happy life together watching their children grow old.

Mary had a perfect life planned out, but God had something better. Remember, "Every woman has three desires essential to her heart. Every woman yearns to be fought for, wants an adventure to share, and wants to have a beauty to unveil."[7] The life Mary had planned was missing the adventure, and God was about to change that. At this time in the Bible when God wanted to get someone's attention, and He sent an angel to speak to them. Mary is going through her day, and an angel named Gabriel shows up.

> And he [Gabriel] came to her and said, "Greetings, O favored one, the Lord is with you!" But she was greatly troubled at the saying and tried to discern what sort of greeting this might be. And the angel said to her, "Do not be afraid, Mary, for you have found favor with God. And behold, you will conceive in your womb and bear a son, and you shall call his name Jesus. He will be great and will be called the Son of the Most High. And the Lord God will give to him the throne of his father David, and he will reign over the house of Jacob forever, and of his kingdom there will be no end."
>
> And Mary said to the angel, "How will this be, since I am a virgin?"
>
> And the angel answered her, "The Holy Spirit will come upon you, and the power of the Most High will overshadow you; therefore the child to be born will be called holy—the Son of God. And behold, your relative Elizabeth in her old age has also conceived a son, and this is the sixth month with her who was called barren. For nothing will be impossible

with God." And Mary said, "Behold, I am the servant of the Lord; let it be to me according to your word." And the angel departed from her (Luke 1:26-38).

Mary has her adventure now! Angels appearing have a way of helping people do the right thing. But what is most incredible about this encounter is that she can lose everything else she had been dreaming in one fell swoop. Mary is a good Jewish girl from an upstanding Jewish family, or else a righteous man like Joseph would not agree to marry her. Now she is pregnant, and she has to tell Joseph. Never had anyone become pregnant without trying, so most likely, he won't believe her. Besides that, she will tell Joseph that she will have the Son of God, Jesus? Every Israelite girl had grown up looking forward to the Messiah, Jesus. Now, it's Mary who will give birth to Him. In all reality, this will be a tough sell. Especially when she tells him, "But Joseph, I had an angel standing in front of me telling me these things." Either she will have a rough life ahead of her as a single mom, looked down on by society, or God would do a miracle.

When we take on God's adventures and trust Him, he always comes through. You guessed it. God does another miracle to get Joseph onboard.

> Now the birth of Jesus Christ took place in this way. When his mother Mary had been betrothed to Joseph before they came together she was found to be with child from the Holy Spirit. And her husband Joseph, being a just man and unwilling to put her to shame, resolved to divorce her quietly. But as he considered these things, behold, an angel of the Lord appeared to him in a dream, saying, "Joseph, son of David, do not fear to take Mary as your wife, for that which is conceived in her is from the Holy Spirit. She will

bear a son, and you shall call his name Jesus, for he will save his people from their sins." All this took place to fulfill what the Lord had spoken by the prophet:

Behold, the virgin shall conceive and bear a son, and they shall call his name Immanuel" (which means, God with us).

When Joseph woke from sleep, he did as the angel of the Lord commanded him: he took his wife, but knew her not until she had given birth to a son. And he called his name Jesus (Matthew 1:18-25).

Admittedly it's an extraordinary way to bring the most important of any human into the world. Find two upstanding teenagers in the community pledged to be married. Visit each of them by an angel so they will sign on to the plan. Then raise the eyebrows of everyone they know because the girl is pregnant outside of marriage. Now nine months later, they have a baby in less than desirable circumstances in a city far away from their family. Remember the words of the angel to Mary?

He will be great and will be called the Son of the Most High. And the Lord God will give to him the throne of his father David, and he will reign over the house of Jacob forever, and of his kingdom there will be no end (Luke 1:32 & 33).

Mary, exhausted, gives birth to her baby, Jesus, then wraps him up and lays him in an animal feeding trough. What?! The Bible says, "And she [Mary] gave birth to her firstborn son and wrapped him in swaddling cloths and laid him in a manger" (Matthew 2:7).

It's a picture most of us have seen at Christmas, where the baby Jesus, happy as any baby could be, is swaddled and laying on a bed of straw in a feeding trough. Most likely, it was a trough hewn out of stone, but a trough no less. Incredulous, the King of kings, the Son of the Most High, is born amongst the animals and laid to sleep in a filthy feeding trough? You must admit, there is no more humble way to come into the world. And if you know Him, there is no more humble King than Jesus.

Jesus, a member of the Trinity, creator of the cosmos, arrived on earth to not even a crib, but a manger. It would seem any person of importance, wealth, or a king, let alone Jesus Himself, would roll out the red carpets, demand the finest lodging, and the best care. Jesus is a member of the Trinity who created the galaxies, man, the earth, and everything, including its wealth. With four-thousand years to plan, He could have arranged for a better place for His mother to give birth? Perhaps a last-minute cancellation could have opened providing lodging somewhere in town? Anyone in Bethlehem who knew this baby was Jesus would be quick to give up their bed for Him. Through the ages, every Jewish person grew up hearing the prophecies and expected the Messiah. The Messiah's birth had been foretold throughout the Old Testament writings, which they held dear to their everyday life. This night, the city of Bethlehem was bursting at the seams, not for the expected birth of a savior, but instead for a census. A census that would ensure that Caesar, the Emperor, would get all the taxes he had coming to him. While all the known world was waiting for this night, only a handful of people would know it had come and gone.

From this night on, moderate and restrained presence would be a theme which Jesus would subscribe to while He walked amongst His creation. But why? He was the Messiah, the Son of God, coming to rescue all humanity. He had the ultimate authority and power that spoke planets into existence.

Never again since would a man or woman with the slightest bit of power or authority be so discreet. Most of us only need authority the size of a grain of sand to act as though we rule the world. So why was this birth so quiet and humble, so unnoticeable?

It is a fact: for the last three years of His life, time in actual ministry, Jesus would live a hunted life. It would be important that Jesus bring His gospel forward before his death on a cross. After all, if God orchestrated His birth through a virgin, might He arrange anything, including Jesus avoiding death, until He delivered His message? Even while Jesus was young, Herod, King of Jerusalem, had all the boys two years old and under in Bethlehem killed, in an attempt to murder Him. King Herod had heard from wise men that the King of the Jews had been born, which troubled him since he was the Jewish people's King. What king wants to give up his throne to another? Even amidst that massacre, God made an escape for Jesus. While there would be countless plots on Jesus' life, God had sent Him to die on a cross for you and me. For that reason alone, Jesus would never bask in the limelight of the public stage. Instead, He would live His life on earth in obscurity known only to a few followers to whom He would share the mysteries of life and those of eternal life.

No, the birth and life of Jesus was not quiet because God could not protect Jesus until the appointed time for His death. So why? The ultimate reason was love. Love is the reason the Trinity created history, from creation through to the end of the world. Love is why this quiet birth was happening in the first place, and love would be the reason this baby would grow up and face death on a cross just thirty-three years later. Do you see it? Jesus, part of the Trinity, is love.

From the first second of our creation, until the second you read this, God desires that we love Him. Love can only be given, never forced, and certainly not demanded by the person who receives it. When God created us, He created us with the free will to love or reject Him. God has orchestrated everything throughout history, even a quiet birth so that He would always be available to us, but never force Himself upon us.

God is love; it's His very essence. If you have ever experienced or given love, that love is God. Then God showed us the love He is by sending His Son, Jesus, so we can fix our relationship with Him we destroyed in the garden.

> My beloved friends, let us continue to love each other since love comes from God. Everyone who loves is born of God and experiences a relationship with God. The person who refuses to love doesn't know the first thing about God because God is love—so you can't know him if you don't love. This is how God showed his love for us: God sent his only Son into the world so we might live through him. This is the kind of love we are talking about—not that we once upon a time loved God, but that he loved us and sent his Son as a sacrifice to clear away our sins and the damage they've done to our relationship with God (1 John 4:7-10 MSG).

Journal Pages

This is a great opportunity to journal what you are learning or the action steps you want to take based on this lesson. Doing so will keep all your notes and journaling in this book as future reference. Start by taking a few minutes to pray and ask Jesus to bring to light all you are learning and what transformational changes you can make in your life. If you are reading this in an electronic version, make a digital note and journal.

Journal Pages

FIVE
AN EXTRAORDINARY LIFE

The best love is when it captures you unexpectedly. Come to think of it; maybe that is how all love comes when you least expect it. That way, you know it's not made up, and you can trust it. When I met my wife, there were instant sparks. Like in the movies, when the edges of the screen get fuzzy, and only the couple is in focus. Neither she nor I were looking for a romantic relationship. I had just returned from Europe from working with refugees and had moved to Virginia to finish a degree. She was busy with her own things. But in one instant, the paths our lives converged and melted into one. We were standing two feet from each other on a stage; she turned around and said, "Hi." We were at music practice. When the practice was over, we talked a few minutes before going home. During those few minutes of meeting her, heaven opened, and both our lives changed. I asked her to marry me 181 days after I met her, and our wedding was four months later on the same stage where we met. Her love captured me unexpectedly, and it was amazing. It was grace. The love my wife has given me is by far the greatest earthly gift in life I have ever received. Once I met her, you better believe I pursued and romanced her. As much as I tried, her love was only hers to give. I could not demand it, earn it, or force her to give it. I could only beg, which I did without shame. As you can guess, our love grew as we each gave each other first our interest, then our time, our trust, and then our devotion. It only took thirty-seven days to know we couldn't live our lives without each other. But we gave the love and trust we had for each other. Had I told my wife the first night we met that I loved her and she was the one I would marry, I doubt she would have ever talked to me again. Receiving love and giving love is a delicate undertaking. I live by a formula to give love 110% and expect nothing in return. In a marriage, showing someone you love them looks much like work; in fact, it is. Whether you are the male or female, just put your head down, do the housework, the cooking, the yard work, pay the bills, change the diapers and whatever needs done. Gender-related tasks in a marriage shouldn't exist; instead, you work together as a team to do life. My wife is the master of serving her family. The best way to explain my devoted wife is to include a message I wrote her on our tenth Anniversary just a few days ago.

> A Song to My Beloved Wife
> *God has blessed me with an excellent wife.*
> *She is more precious than all the world's riches.*
> *My very soul trusts her, and because of her, I*
>   *own the world, and everything life can*
>   *give me.*
> *My wife always looks out for my best interests*
>   *and never does harm to me.*
> *She takes care of our home and children with*
>   *excellence. Her meals are wholesome, rich,*

and delicious. Her food warms our family's hearts.

She wakes up every morning early to make sure our household starts right, and our family is ready for the day. Whether that is packing lunch, juicing vegetables, or prepping for the evening meal, she is diligent that our home is in order for the day.

She is always thinking of her family and others and is generous to everyone.

She is wise and frugal with our finances and makes good decisions so that our family is always taken care of.

She has great determination and verve so that she can overcome any challenge. She is mindful to keep her body, soul, spirit, heart, mind, and will in great shape. She always looks her best.

She is excellent with everything she puts her hands and mind to. She produces the best of everything she does so that she receives praises for all she does.

She is always careful with everything she allows into her and our family's mind, soul, and spirit so that our lives are full of light and not darkness.

She is never afraid of work or what it takes to care for her husband or our family. She is a skilled and crafty homemaker.

She loves those in need and is always ready and willing to help and care for those in need.

She is a woman at peace because she knows her

*home and family have no need or lack; they
are ready for life.*

*Through her diligence, her children and I are
always prepared for each day.*

*Through everything she does, she brings respect
to me. She gives me wise, thoughtful, and
discreet counsel that protects my
relationships with others.*

*She is powerful and honorable in everything she
does, and nothing challenges who she is or
her resolve. She knows who she is and
knows tomorrow will be just fine.*

*She is restrains in her words but when she does
speak it is always eloquent with kind and
wise knowledge.*

*She is meticulous concerning her household and
keeps our family well taken care of.*

*My two children and I can never thank her
enough for being such a woman among
women. We sing her praises every day
because she is the most outstanding woman
in the human race. She is our heroine, our
princess, queen, and rock star.*

*My wife is the most beautiful of all women ever
made by God, and no woman has ever done
womanhood as good as she.*

*Best of all, her characteristics is her love for
Jesus, who she embodies to our family. Our
family knows Jesus intimately because, in
her, He literally lives with us.*

*My prayer is that God will bless her immensely
because of her excellent character and
qualities that rival any other human.*

> *Bless and praise you, my wife, my lover, and excellent mother to our children. You have no challenger or equal among women. Let all mankind take notice; you are the most excellent wife.*
>
> Scott Michael Ringo to his wife.
> Adapted from Proverbs 31

There is no campaigning or fluff in that proverb; every word is true. There has ever been such an amazing woman, and I am honored to be her husband. That is how you love a man and a family. In return, our family stumbles over ourselves, trying to serve her. Mind you, we don't come as close as we want, but we give it our best.

With my wife by my side, I have experienced the best a man can in this life. She gives the deepest human love a man can ever wish for. She has been with me through the life adventures of giving birth to two amazing children, family trips, romantic getaways, and crafting our yearly Christmas gifts. I've been cared for, romanced, and nurtured by the most beautiful and captivating of women. Most of all, I have an amazing woman to fight for. I love how she loves me and tells me through word and deed every single day. She is my soul mate, friend, and lover. I can never go through life without her, nor would I want to. We are perfectly grafted together for the rest of our lives. Through the unexpected love of my wife, God has taught me how deep His love is for me.

God shows us His love in amazing ways if we open our eyes and emotions and look. It is impossible to miss Him showing us Himself all around us every day. When you look at the beautiful colors of fall, something inside tells you it's a glimpse of His beauty. When someone cares, deep inside, we know it is

His care we are feeling. A beautiful sunrise, majestic sunset, red and yellow leaves in the fall, the crash of waves on the beach, snow-covered mountains– it's all Him. All those experiences stir a yearning inside that pulls us toward something more than this life. While many reject this invitation of God's love, others embrace it with abandonment. It's the latter that find true meaning in life because, after all, God made life.

As I mentioned, when I met my wife, I had just returned from Europe, where I had been working with refugees. Imagine: you need a new life, so you take a risk, a very dangerous risk. The only way you can make a better life for yourself is by risking death. So you take all the money you and your family members have and pay it to some people who say they can get you to a better country. One refugee, I met arrived in Europe by stowing away in a shipping container that had a false floor just tall enough for him to lay on his back. He and the others scooted in until they were lying side by side, and the bottom of the container was full. He had brought food and water, but getting it to his mouth was tough because the container floor was right on top of him. They fill the container on top of the false floor on top of them with items they are shipping. The dark silence began. They did not know how long their journey would take or where it would end. It was over a month before they would arrive in Germany and the container opened. During that month, he was in total darkness. As people needed to use the bathroom, they did so right where they laid. The person lying next to him did not live through the trip, many did not, and He lay next to a corpse the rest of the trip wondering if he was next. Can you imagine the depth of the darkness with defecation and death permeating the air all around you? For many, the risk of their life didn't pay off; for others, it did. For those that made it through that dark, treacherous journey, there was an unexpected love that met them on the other side. Our team was there working with refugees of all kinds to give them hope, clothes, food, and friendship. We were there to show them, love, to show them acceptance. It was a good start to a new life for them. Someone cared and met them on the other side of a long-shot gamble to help them toward a new life. We gave those refugees the gift of love was not something they expected, or something we could have forced on them. Nor could they have demanded it from us. It was our expression of love to give, and for them to either receive it or reject it. We offered that love because we cared about their circumstances and wanted them to have a better life.

It is hard to understand the desperation for a better life to the extent I would risk my life. I've never been in that dilemma. Yet, I understand needing a change badly enough I would take drastic measures for it. I've been there several times; you might be there now. Just as we were there in Europe to give those refugees an unexpected gift of love, the night of Jesus' birth in Bethlehem He had come into the world for a similar purpose. Those alive then might not have realized it, nor do many of us now, but all of us were in a much worse place than those refugees were in for a month. No matter what we would have been willing to pay or gamble on a long shot, death was the only price that would pay for our sin and disobedience to God. Jesus came because God loves us, and because of that love, He would give His own life and die to fix our separation from Him that happened in Eden. He will never force Himself upon us, or make us choose Him. Thus, His birth was a quiet and humble one. Jesus was a gift for the world, but like today only those who realize their desperate separation from God and want Him in their life for eternity know the significance. Not much has changed in the last 2,000 years. Then, like now, few noticed the gift that God gave the world that night in Bethlehem. For those then and now who noticed Jesus' birth, no night since nor ever will compare. Two-thousand years ago was the birth of Jesus, the very son of God He sent because He loved us. God sent Jesus so we might have life through Him because of His sacrifice of death on a cross to once and forever fix the mistake that separated us from God.

THE FANFARE

Oh, but make no mistake, there was a fanfare on the night of Jesus' birth for those who looked. In fact, miracles happened of unprecedented magnitude. Then, like today, most were too busy with life to notice.

If you were a religious leader, it would have been the hottest ticket in town. This birth was no joke but the single most expected event in the religious world. In normal life, to be on the guest list you would have had to be someone important. Yet no religious leaders received an invitation– shocker! The list of invitees must have included the who's who of government officials and dignitaries? Nope. By invitation only, the guest list was a group of ordinary shepherds on duty that night watching their sheep. Shepherds? Yep, plain 'ole, hadn't washed for days, poor shepherds. The last-minute, hand-delivered invitation by the angels would have made Cirque du Soleil look like a flea circus.

> And in the same region there were shepherds out in the field, keeping watch over their flock by night. And an angel of the Lord appeared to them, and the glory of the Lord shone around them, and they were filled with great fear. And the angel said to them, "Fear not, for behold, I bring you good news of great joy that will be for all the people. For unto you is born this day in the city of David a Savior, who is Christ the Lord. And this will be a sign for you: you will find

a baby wrapped in swaddling cloths and lying in a manger." And suddenly there was with the angel a multitude of the heavenly host praising God and saying,

"Glory to God in the highest, and on earth peace among those with whom he is pleased!"

When the angels went away from them into heaven, the shepherds said to one another, "Let us go over to Bethlehem and see this thing that has happened, which the Lord has made known to us." And they went with haste and found Mary and Joseph, and the baby lying in a manger (Luke 2:8-16).

Here are ordinary shepherds out on the meaningless task of watching sheep. Something they have done hundreds of times before, a mindless job. Except for the occasional predator attacking the sheep, there was not much excitement. Every time I think about the shepherds and how insignificant their life was, it reminds me of the homeless. I believe God chose shepherds because, like the homeless, they were only ones that would appreciate this message of hope. I can see them lying on their backs looking up at the sky deep with more stars than they can count. Then blam, an angel appears with its customary greeting, "Fear not." It's amazing how the shepherds kept their hearts beating. It must be a hair-raising experience to meet an angel, and I love how they assure those they meet with "Fear not." The shepherds were fortunate that only a single angel appeared at first with the warning. Had the whole multitude showed up at once in the night sky, they might have been singing to lifeless shepherd bodies. The angels deliver their "golden ticket" invitation to the shepherds and put on the first live Christmas holiday spectacular for the shepherds. It must have been amazing; the sky lit up with angels, and "multitudes" sounds like a sky full. It's the words the angels sing that give me goosebumps. "Glory to God in the highest, and on earth peace among those with whom he is pleased!" (Luke 2:14)!

Jesus is God's peace offering. It was a glorious night for mankind, and a very stoic night for the Trinity. Having never been separate for eternity, the Trinity sent one of their own to straighten out our mess.

All my life, I have seen this song from the angels a little different than I do at this moment. Until now, I saw this Christmas scene through my eyes as a human. It is a glorious night; the angels are singing, and Jesus, the long-awaited Messiah, is born to save mankind.

Silent Night and the little town of Bethlehem, how still we see thee lie, right? But from the perspective of the Trinity, Jesus is absent from heaven to live thirty-three years as a man and then die a horrible death. This is the one and only Jesus, a member of the Trinity, who spoke the cosmos into being, who created us, now coming as a humble baby to change our diapers. When you see it from that perspective, the song of the angels is a magnificent overture performed, reminding us "Glory to God in the highest," because tonight He is sending Jesus to live and die for those that believe in Him so that there can be peace between God and man once more. Once again, like in the garden, God has spared man from destruction. Now it's up to us.

After all man has done, out of all the people in the world, God announced the birth of Jesus to everyday, ordinary shepherds. Most likely, the shepherds were simple hired hands who watched the sheep, nobodies. Can you sense their frustration in how their life was turning out? But God picked these ordinary men to be among the handful of people to witness this extraordinary event. Common as they were, out of everybody alive, they had the VIP invitation to the King of Kings' birth. If they had the time. I love the shepherd's response; it says, "And they went with haste" (Luke 2:16). As I write this, I wonder what that says about God that He would choose the ordinary in which to announce the extraordinary. This reminds me of another occasion where God finds ordinary people, frustrated with life, and gives them the front-row seat.

> On one occasion, while the crowd was pressing in on him to hear the word of God, he was standing by the lake of Gennesaret, and he saw two boats by the lake, but the fishermen had gone out of them and were washing their nets. Getting into one of the boats, which was Simon's, he asked him to put out a little from the land. And he sat down and taught the people from the boat. And when he had finished speaking, he said to Simon, "Put out into the deep and let down your nets for a catch." And Simon answered, "Master, we toiled all night and took nothing! But at your word I will let down the nets." And when they had done this, they enclosed a large number of fish, and their nets were breaking. They signaled to their partners in the other boat to come and help them. And they came and filled both the boats, so that they began to sink. But when Simon Peter saw it, he fell down at Jesus' knees, saying, "Depart from me, for I am a sinful man, O Lord." For he and all who were with him were astonished at the catch of fish that they had taken, and so also were James and John, sons of Zebedee, who were partners with Simon. And Jesus said to Simon, "Do not be afraid; from now on you will be catching men." And when they had brought their boats to land, they left everything and followed him (Luke 5:1-11).

It is an ordinary day for three ordinary, frustrated fishermen who had caught nothing the night before. In a matter of minutes, Jesus puts them in the front-row seat to fill a vital role in God's rescue mission to man. Once ordinary, now three of the disciples will spend three extraordinary years with Jesus, the Son of God. Throughout the Bible, God takes ordinary people and invites them to have a front-row seat in history. In fact, most of the Bible's legends were ordinary when God called them to do great things. One of my favorites is a boy named David.

About 1,040 years before the birth of Jesus, God, through a prophet Samuel, would choose a King to replace the first King of Israel. Saul was the first King of Israel. God chose Saul because God's people, the Israelites, demanded from God a physical king to reign over them. Samuel's role was to hear from God who He chose as King. Before that, God had appointed Judges, men who were not rulers but instead were a type of military leader and presided over legal hearings to make rulings concerning disputes. Saul fell from God's favor because he disobeyed Him. In choosing a new King, God told Samuel, "... Fill your horn with oil, and go. I will send you to Jesse the Bethlehemite, for I have provided for myself a king among his sons" (1 Samuel 16:1). During the selection process, Samuel listens to God concerning the seven sons present, and God rejects all seven. Samuel then asks Jesse if all his sons are present, to which Jesse explains that there is only the youngest, David, but he is watching the sheep. They send for David, and God instructs Samuel that he is to anoint him as the next king of Israel. I love this story because, again, God takes an ordinary, unlikely candidate and makes him King of Israel. In the family's eyes, David was the youngest son, drew the short straw by default to tend the sheep. From his writings in the Bible, you can tell he spent a lot of time in the pastures watching sheep. So it is an ordinary morning for an ordinary boy waking up on Bethlehem's hills after a night of watching the sheep. Perhaps the exact hills where just 1,000 years later the shepherds we discovered would be invited by a host of angels to see the baby, Jesus. David sees one of his brothers running out to meet him to send him home to meet Samuel. Minutes later, Sammuel anoints him King over all Israel! David is not perfect, and he makes big mistakes, but in a split second, God calls David, rather than a more obvious choice, to the extraordinary.

The Bible is full of stories like these where God chooses the ordinary to change history. Like I wrote before, the best kind of love is when it captures you unexpectedly. Jesus, with His love, unexpectedly captures these like countless others' lives throughout history.

Now it's up to us. The question is, like the shepherds, will we too go with haste to meet Jesus and worship Him? For the shepherds, their invitation was rather simple. Drop what they were doing, trust God that the sheep wouldn't take off, and be only a handful of the first people to see Jesus. It would have been worth losing the sheep and a job to see God in the flesh on earth! Or, as with the fishermen, will we too drop our nets of what we have known all our lives for our livelihood and follow Jesus into a new adventure? For the fishermen, it was a more gutsy move than the shepherds, but they knew Jesus was calling them to the real purpose for their lives. Their lives had led up to this moment and a choice that would forever determine the rest of it. How about David? In an instant, he accepts an invitation into a life-changing path that would encompass leading a nation, both as a military leader and judge. Samuel could have added, "There is no formal training since you are only the second king of Israel." Wow. Quite an epic life role to step into that changed his life and the lives of everyone in the world forever.

In each of these situations and the hundreds of others throughout history, God gently asks those He finds in obscurity to trust Him and respond to His love and role in life in varying degrees. Sometimes the task is simple, like with the shepherds, to believe in and worship Jesus. Did it change their lives? You bet. For the fishermen and David, the task was monumental; their obedience and sacrifice gave them both the front seat in what God was doing in the world and an epic role in history that took them the rest of their lives to complete. Ordinary people used by God to change history forever. For the majority reading this book, that is us. Is it hard to believe? If you are like me, you may feel, well, ordinary. Right?

Journal Pages

This is a great opportunity to journal what you are learning or the action steps you want to take based on this lesson. Doing so will keep all your notes and journaling in this book as future reference. Start by taking a few minutes to pray and ask Jesus to bring to light all you are learning and what transformational changes you can make in your life. If you are reading this in an electronic version, make a digital note and journal.

Journal Pages

SIX
SIGNIFICANT LIFE

I feel that most of my life has gone unnoticed by the world. You might feel that way too. Sometimes that makes me feel alone, and other times, very fortunate that my life is not on continual display. I believe most people think their life has little value as it whizzes past in a blur. Like the shepherds, fishermen, or David, for many, our lives are one day after another of a mundane, sometimes very frustrating life.

No matter how ordinary our life may be, something inside us compels us to strive to find significance. Every person wants their life to count. Have you ever looked up for no particular reason and noticed someone looked at you, and as you do, they smile? It is great when someone notices you. People do many things to get noticed and believe they are somebody, some good and some bad. Spending extra time at the office away from our families to get noticed for a promotion, buying sporty cars that get from point A to B just like the rest. How about seeking the fame that comes with being a musician, worship leader, or public figure? Sure, while the reasons for those pursuits may be well-intentioned, there is an element of notoriety and acceptance in all those. Even those who will go to great lengths to commit horrible atrocities such as assassinations, bombings, or overthrowing governments because they are so desperate for their life to matter. Try as we may, most of us will not experience the extent of love or awareness we want, though we might try everything to get it.

Some imagine that married life is the ultimate achievement for providing and receiving lifelong acceptance. Most find that statement to be false, but it all depends on the people's realistic expectations.

The movie, "Shall We Dance" illustrates this point well. It is a story of a married, successful executive in a big city who rides the train home each day from work. While riding on the train, he notices a beautiful woman through a dance studio's glass window. One night after again seeing the woman through the window, he jumps off the train on an impulse and signs up for dance lessons, hoping to meet her. Not immediately meeting the woman and continuing his dance lessons, he falls in love with dancing. He keeps his newfound passion for dancing from his wife, who gets suspicious about the extra time he spends away from home. Throughout the movie, the executive and his wife learn what is important to them. As it dawns on each of them what is important in their lives and marriage, the wife, Beverly Clark, answers the question about why people get married like this:

> We need a witness to our lives. There's a billion people on the planet... I mean, what does anyone's life really mean? But in a marriage, you're promising to care about everything. The good things, the bad things, the terrible things, the mundane things... all of it, all of the time, every day. You're saying "Your life will not go unnoticed because I will notice

it. Your life will not go unwitnessed because I will be your witness."[1]

Even in marriage, there are times of loneliness and times when pieces of our life go unnoticed. But if this story of Jesus is true, He created us because He wants a relationship far deeper and meaningful than any human relationship, even marriage. If you remember, in the beginning, Jesus not only created us but also created a paradise for us to live in. In the garden, He provided for all of our needs. As much as I love my wife and family and want to give the best to them, I can't give them anything close to what Jesus can provide. Jesus created each of us to have a relationship with Him. Whether we believe it or not, Jesus is present through every second of our lives, literally standing right in front of us. Why do we ignore this person, not to mention the creator of the universe, who dedicates His breath to every second of our life? With an insatiable wish to count in this life, why do we spend so much of our life focused on trivial endeavors? Like the first woman and man in the garden, we seek everything but Jesus to bring significance to our life. As Dallas Willard points out in The Divine Conspiracy, to be ordinary, "is a deadening agony for us."[2]

> This is why everyone, from the smallest child to the older adult, naturally wants in some way to be extraordinary, outstanding, making a unique contribution or, if all else fails, wants to be thought so – if only for a brief time.[3]

Dallas continues:

> Unlike egotism, the drive to significance is a simple extension of the creative impulse of God that gave us being. We were built to count, as water is made to run downhill.

We are placed in a specific context to count in ways that no one else does. That is our destiny.

Our hunger for significance is a signal of who we are and why we are here, and it also is the basis of humanity's enduring response to Jesus. For he always takes individual human beings as seriously as their shredded dignity demands, and he has the resources to carry through with his high estimate of them.[4]

Though it may seem your life exists in a meaningless vacuum, each of us lives for a specific time to complete a life's work that no one but you can do. Our "hunger for significance" can be the fuel to propel us to make the difference only we can make. Instead of by chance, Jesus mandates our existence, considering our lives necessary. Wherein, He equips us with His inexhaustible resources to succeed with a divine purpose that no other thrill on earth could match. Your life will count unlike anyone else's that has ever or will ever live. The question each of us answered is, for what will it count? But alas, if it were only so easy to grasp this truth, we would be too busy to read this book.

For most, it is not until the end of our life where hindsight helps us see how much more our life might have counted if we had all of our accumulated knowledge and wisdom from the start. The knowledge and wisdom of those who lived full lives and even those cut short give us a glimpse into our own futures. For at the inevitable end of many people's lives, there arises a profound knowledge they can share as they summarize the worth of their life as they experienced it. The simple truths are made holy as someone collects their life experiences and condenses them into a few sentences of parting wisdom.

It was my privilege to hear such a conversation from John Moorhead. John, diagnosed nine months before with terminal lung cancer, nearing the end of his life on earth, shared his parting thoughts on a podcast. The entire conversation left me lost for words because of the simple yet astounding truths He shared. But one statement he made more than any other made me shudder, "We never know what life has to offer until we manage to let go of what we believe it should offer." [5]

John, a physician, who is a picture of success for many, found that when given a diagnosis that his time was short, he changed his definition of what he thought life should offer. Letting go of his assumptions, he discovered a richer and more fulfilling life in his remaining years. Much of that was making people glad they had met him while engaging in a pursuit of taking God at His word of who He says He is in the Bible. Is not that the picture we get of the life of Jesus? Jesus did not come to earth to accomplish His own agenda; instead, He stayed focused on God and His Father's agenda. At any point during His time on earth, Jesus could have taken His eyes off the reason God sent Him. He had the same opportunities for distraction from His mission as we do today. Had Jesus looked at the temporary He could have made a nice life for Himself by giving into the opportunities to make money, gain fame, even overthrow the government and become king Himself. We must not forget the Trinity allows satan to rule this domain and can take it back at any time, which at an appointed time They will do. God made us in His image to reign for eternity over the cosmos, not only a minuscule planet called Earth with a temporary lifespan. Jesus stayed focused on the big picture. Like Jesus, we must stay focused that our time on this planet is temporary and finish the mission for which He purposed us.

At the start of Jesus' ministry, the devil himself offered Jesus the ultimate position of power on earth if He would abandon God's plan. The devil took him to a high mountain and showed him all the kingdoms of the world and their glory.

And he said to him, "All these I will give you, if you will fall down and worship me" (Matthew 1:8 & 9).

However, Jesus did not look at what He might gain for Himself from life. Instead, he kept His eyes focused on God, on ransoming our lives, and He had a richer, more fulfilling life than any man has ever had. Like John Moorhead, much of Jesus' life was making people glad they had met Him while revealing to them He was the Messiah come to give them life.

A lifetime of knowledge and wisdom is no small thing. Instead, it is the most valuable wealth one human being can accumulate and invest in others. That wealth is like gems washed up on the beach of life from treasure ships, now lost, which deposited their bounty. Though beautiful to the eye for all who gaze upon that beach from their lofty mansions, they are a priceless treasure for the beachcomber who rises early to walk its shores each morning. It is worth every ounce of strength it takes to carry the laden bags of treasure to his shack because it is worth more than money and will preserve his life. With it, he has gained a lifetime of learning, which he does not need to discover for himself with each gem he gathers.

No doubt, King David, mentioned in this chapter, passed on his wisdom and knowledge to his son Solomon. That provided insight, well beyond his years, to know what to ask for when asked by God. Early in his reign as King, God appeared to him in a dream and said, "Ask what I shall give you" (1 Kings 3:6-14). Instead of paraphrasing this conversation, I will let God and Solomon speak for themselves:

> And Solomon said, "You have shown great and steadfast love to your servant David my father, because he walked before you in faithfulness, in righteousness, and in uprightness of heart toward you. And you have kept for him this great and steadfast love and have given him a son to sit on his throne

this day. And now, O Lord my God, you have made your servant king in place of David my father, although I am but a little child. I do not know how to go out or come in. And your servant is in the midst of your people whom you have chosen, a great people, too many to be numbered or counted for multitude. Give your servant therefore an understanding mind to govern your people, that I may discern between good and evil, for who is able to govern this your great people?"

It pleased the Lord that Solomon had asked this. And God said to him, "Because you have asked this, and have not asked for yourself long life or riches or the life of your enemies, but have asked for yourself understanding to discern what is right, behold, I now do according to your word. Behold, I give you a wise and discerning mind, so that none like you has been before you and none like you shall arise after you. I give you also what you have not asked, both riches and honor, so that no other king shall compare with you, all your days. And if you will walk in my ways, keeping my statutes and my commandments, as your father David walked, then I will lengthen your days" (1 Kings 3:6-14).

Today many of us still need to learn, like the beachcomber and Solomon, that the greatest treasures in life are wisdom and knowledge. We need to learn from God's own words that wisdom, discernment, riches, honor, and long life come from Him. Those are His to give, and all the college degrees, endless hours of work, and time spent in the gym will not add one bit to our pursuit of them if God does not first grant them to us. It is pure arrogance for anyone to believe they can accomplish any success God does not grant.

King Solomon is the wisest and richest man who lived, even in today's standards. His estimated worth in today's money was upwards of one hundred billion. He experienced firsthand the degree to which wisdom and knowledge compare in value to wealth. God had granted Him all three. With that wisdom, King Solomon put this emphasis on the three, "For the protection of wisdom is like the protection of money, and the advantage of knowledge is that wisdom preserves the life of him who has it" (Ecclesiastes 7:12).

Charles Spurgeon, a prolific author, helps us to understand the relationship between the two:

> Wisdom is the right use of knowledge. To know is not to be wise. Many men know a great deal, and are all the greater fools for it. There is no fool so great a fool as a knowing fool. But to know how to use knowledge is to have wisdom.[6]

> In this present age, and certainly in our nation, more emphasis is placed on formal education each year. In 2011, more than 30 percent of U.S. adults 25 and older has at least a bachelor's degree, the U.S. Census Bureau reported.[7]

Many of those continue to get even more education. Many people are gaining book knowledge, but it is glaringly clear that most things in the world are getting worse and not better? Both King Solomon and Charles Spurgeon shed light on this. It is not the knowledge that preserves life; it is the wisdom of using the knowledge that protects the life of him who has both. If any man should know, King Solomon got the largest portion of wisdom of anyone. Instead, with all the knowledge the world has and is getting, we lack the wisdom to use the knowledge. For example, look at all the knowledge in the Bible, but only a small percentage of people boast the wisdom to use it even today. It is not that the Bible is hard to understand. Common men wrote the Bible to be read by common men. Perhaps knowledge without wisdom is nothing at all? Let us say you earned a college Professional Nanny Career Diploma. Yes, there is an actual diploma one can earn to be a Nanny. If you hated children and never used what you learned, there would be little benefit to the knowledge you gained.

God grants us wisdom as he did to Solomon. Wisdom begins with the fear of the Lord, and most likely, Solomon learned this from his own Father David's words, "The fear of the Lord is the beginning of wisdom; all those who practice it have a good understanding. His praise endures forever (Psalms 111:10)!

Solomon, who gained the most wisdom God ever granted an individual, repeats that and adds to it knowledge in his own writings in Proverbs:

> The fear of the Lord is the beginning of knowledge; fools despise wisdom and instruction (Proverbs 1:7).
>
> The fear of the Lord is the beginning of wisdom, and the knowledge of the Holy One is insight (Proverbs 9:10).

We would be "wise" to take heed and apply three gems included in those verses. For with them, wisdom and knowledge are promised to us.

- The fear of the Lord is the beginning of wisdom.
- Everyone who practices the fear of the Lord has good understanding.
- The fear of the Lord is the beginning of knowledge.

There is not anything inherently destructive about any of the instructions in the Bible. If a person used the Bible's knowledge strictly as a self-help manual following all its instruction, they would only become a better person. There is nothing in the Bible that doesn't strengthen a person to be a much better and well-rounded person. The gift of eternal life it offers is a gift, a nice bonus, for following through on its instruction. But take or leave eternal life after death, a person still becomes a better person for following its knowledge. Therein lies the key — without the wisdom to use its instruction to become a better person, it is just a book of knowledge. Let me add, as much as we value the gems of wisdom and knowledge left to us by great men and women that fill our libraries; we neglect the Bible's collection of knowledge indexed since the beginning of time. How much wisdom is there in that? If all humans living today read the sixty-six books of the Bible and use wisdom to apply their knowledge to their lives, every political, economic, national, and justice system could improve a one-hundred fold. If only.

If any man in history had it all, tried it all, indulged in every pleasure, and spoke from experience, it was King Solomon. In Ecclesiastes, King Solomon lists all matter of activities, pursuits, and endeavors he tried to find meaning. He concludes that everything was meaningless. Even great wealth, power, and the pursuit of work afforded no significance to his life. Then, as if to take away every hope of a life fulfilled, King Solomon concludes that even wisdom is vanity and meaningless. However, he leaves us with a perfectly cut diamond, uncovered from the heat and pressure of his vast wisdom, wealth, and pursuit of everything he did to find meaning. The gold miner's nugget, the gem of priceless worth that his life yielded was this:

> The end of the matter; all has been heard. Fear God and keep his commandments, for this is the whole duty of man. For God will bring every deed into judgment, with every secret thing, whether good or evil (Ecclesiastes 12:13-14).

This from a man, not perfect by any means, who had more opportunity than most to explore each of life's darkest valleys and cavernous joys.

The obstacles are endless, complicating the path that each of us travels to our unique purpose in life. Most of us believe our life will have significance if . Fill in the words that best fit in the blank. Most follow the well-worn wagon trails of those pioneers that went before seeking to find significance for their life. Yet when the trails converge, the weary travelers find, as King Solomon did, that most everything they journeyed for is meaningless. It is an endless cycle etched in time and stone, but disregarded by most.

A haunting example of this is the Estate Sale. I saw these while growing up as a young boy in a small farm town, known to me then as an auction. Yet it has taken me until my adult years to grasp the gravity of the plight. So imagine this, a person lived a large part of their life working hard each day, year after year, to surround themselves with their picture of success. This includes their house, car(s), furniture, and all they find valuable or believe they need. Then because of deteriorating health, death, they took on too much debt or failed to pay their taxes, everything dear to them is up for sale to the highest bidder. I might add that it is often a forced sale, and everything sold for pennies compared to the items' actual worth. Several years ago, walking through one of the few estate sales I've been to, it was difficult to ignore what I was witnessing. The estate sale reduced everything that was once the priceless treasures of a lady to a few thousand dollars. She had worked her entire life, eight hours a day, for the house and everything in it. The problem remained that tragedy caught up to her before she paid for everything. The lady spent her life doing what most people do, working, and accumulating stuff, searching for her life's significance. Not only did her pursuits and stuff turn out to be meaningless, but everything she had worked for was sold to others, scavenging her treasure in hopes of finding meaning and significance with it in their lives.

Estimates state from 2006 to 2014, more than five million homes were lost to foreclosure. Estimates predict foreclosure will strike another three million homeowners in the next three to four years.[8] The economy has been rough, and there is no sign it will get better soon. In their search for meaning, those in developing countries cannot get enough or big enough stuff. Even if it means borrowing up to one's credit limit at the risk of losing everything, the search for one's significance through what they own or perceive they need is an epidemic.

As I mentioned, our family has lived in a small condo for the last eleven years. It was not a conscious, long-term choice but one we grew to appreciate. When my wife and I first got married, like most married couples, we were looking for a place to rent and call our own. Several years later, when we thought we wanted to find a place to buy, home prices were high and more than we wanted to pay. The bank pre-approved us for a mortgage far above what we should borrow.

Sixteen families have moved in and moved out of the three closest condos to us in the last eleven years. In the last three years, the new owners did massive renovations on each of the condos. Not just updated, but from the ground up renovated. The condos are thirty years old, and repairs need to be done. The newest family purchased the condo beside us because they lost their big house in a foreclosure. Yet, six months the family dumped in more money as crew after crew did a complete top-to-bottom condo renovation. The common wall between us is the wall that I face while writing this book. They changed the wood floors twice in one year. It is challenging concentrating while writing this book with constant construction noise next door. Two and one-half months is enough to demolish and reconstruct the entire condo. The cost to renovate a condo on top of purchasing it is expensive. I understand buildings need to be updated and repaired, so I do not suggest people live in an unsafe place. Will the renovations be enough for the family to be content with life? Likely not. [I add a note to this as I do the final edit that family lived in the condo only months after completing renovations that took more than a year, to buy another house and move.] My point is as a nation, and many times as a human race, we search for our significance through bigger, better, and newer stuff. Yet even if we accumulate enough to rival King Solomon's assets and wisdom, we too will most likely find it all meaningless.

Like King Solomon, we spend our lives getting the stuff we need for our life to be meaningful and significant. For most, accumulating stuff, they believe they need a lifelong mission. At the end of their life, there is little, if any, time to enjoy what they collected. History shows, as with King Solomon and millions upon millions who lived after him, most will find that everything is a vapor and meaningless. As with the lady above, the estate sale will come, the vultures will grab up your stuff for pennies on the dollar, and it all was for naught.

Journal Pages

This is a great opportunity to journal what you are learning or the action steps you want to take based on this lesson. Doing so will keep all your notes and journaling in this book as future reference. Start by taking a few minutes to pray and ask Jesus to bring to light all you are learning and what transformational changes you can make in your life. If you are reading this in an electronic version, make a digital note and journal.

Journal Pages

SEVEN
COMPLICATED LIFE

Our story and ability to complete our mission has gotten complicated. God did not create us to live the way we do now. God created man to live in the garden, and He provided for Him. He did not intend for us to spend our lives accumulating stuff and remodeling condominiums in our search for significance and meaning. Our only job or occupation was to work and keep the Garden of Eden. God created us to live forever and placed us in a garden that He planted, which provided an abundance of food. Man had no need or concern about tomorrow. Each day brought the same love and generosity from God. To be frank, in the garden man had no need for clothes. We did not struggle with a lack of significance. Man counted because God made us and gave us the role in the only two jobs there were. Adam named the animals, and the man and woman worked and kept the garden. What else was there? It was a perfect world.

But that was not enough, was it? The serpent tricked the woman into believing she needed more than God provided. It's the same lie we are tricked into believing today. We are just as blind today to the lie as the woman was in the garden. We spend our entire life searching for a larger significance and meaning in our life. In doing so, we create a vacuum where there is never enough and spend our entire life trying to fill a limitless void. To be correct, satan keeps telling us the lie that we need the things that God has not provided for us. By believing the lie and waste our entire lives attempting to get what we do not need for others to sell at our estate sale.

Everything within us tells us if we don't take care of ourselves, no one will. It is even hard for us to believe King Solomon, the wisest man in the world. Yet for those of us who are still doubtful, Jesus, the one who knows our real need, restates again:

> Therefore I tell you, do not be anxious about your life, what you will eat or what you will drink, nor about your body, what you will put on. Is not life more than food, and the body more than clothing? Look at the birds of the air: they neither sow nor reap nor gather into barns, and yet your heavenly Father feeds them. Are you not of more value than they? And which of you by being anxious can add a single hour to his span of life? And why are you anxious about clothing? Consider the lilies of the field, how they grow: they neither toil nor spin, yet I tell you, even Solomon in all his glory was not arrayed like one of these. But if God so clothes the grass of the field, which today is alive and tomorrow is thrown into the oven, will he not much more clothe you, O you of little faith? Therefore do not be anxious, saying, 'What shall we eat?' or 'What shall we drink?' or 'What shall we wear?' For the Gentiles seek after all these things, and your heavenly Father knows that you need them all. But

seek first the kingdom of God and his righteousness, and all these things will be added to you. Therefore do not be anxious about tomorrow, for tomorrow will be anxious for itself. Sufficient for the day is its own trouble (Matthew 6:25-34).

The problem is the lie that surrounds us, which continues to persuade us to waste our life on that which will never satisfy. Instead, we must use the wisdom to apply the knowledge of God's instruction and stop feeding the estate sales. Even the slightest possibility that the story of Jesus is true should compel us to seek His wisdom and knowledge for our lives. The story of Jesus is the only story of hope which makes sense out of our life. Is the story of the Bible too good to be true that it dissuades us to believe? Can life be so brutal that we cannot believe a story of such hope and love? Is the Bible's answer to creation, life, and our purpose too simple to believe? Can the knowledge of science and incomplete theories be more believable than sixty-six books of history written by the eyewitnesses themselves? Did the forty authors of the Bible, speaking different languages, have nothing else to do with their lives than write sixty-six separate books comprising over 807,000 words, written over a time span of 1,500 years that melded together in perfect unity?

It can't be that this life is so wonderful that we don't need the story to be true. Even those like King Solomon and countless others who had everything admit that life itself lacks the ability to bring true meaning and fulfillment to life.

There comes a time in everyone's life, or at least there should when we stop listening to everyone else's opinions and decide for ourselves what to believe. Are you reading this book because you are on such a quest? If so, there is no more valiant pursuit. Even growing up in a Christian home, there was a point where I had to decide once and for always what knowledge I would base my life. I could not ignore the Bible, with its expansive knowledge and universal influence on the world. If you too, have determined or can consider the Bible to be true, then there comes the point where you must stop reading the cliff's notes or simply spending an hour on Sunday mornings listening to someone spoon-feed it to you. Instead, it would be best to decide what you will base your life on and take it as truth.

I can take the most influential book in history, its knowledge and wisdom, and apply it to my life and never look back. Or I can ignore the Bible and continue my life, never knowing what its decades of knowledge might afford my life. My faith in which I choose will decide whether I use God's knowledge to live my life or worship creation, which He made.

THERE ARE NO COINCIDENCES

Those who wrote the Bible books did so in the common language of the day that anyone could understand. Many of the authors of the New Testament, as you might remember, were common people. When we think of the Bible heroes and authors, we often forget they were very ordinary. Even as their stories developed, many of them were simple people being obedient to God. They wrote the books of the New Testament from their actual experiences with Jesus, written in every day, ordinary language. That common and ordinary men wrote so many books is proof in itself that these experiences were real. It is strange for eight men to write at least a book each and include each other as characters following a mythical God come to earth. It is more incredulous that at least eight men of varying occupations: a tax collector, a missionary, a physician, two fishermen, two carpenters, and a Pharisee who persecuted Christians, would write a book that supported and validated each other. Not to mention the books these eight men wrote identified them as followers of Jesus, who was crucified for sacrilege of their religion.

It's a simple yet incredible story. Whether you accept the incredible story of the God of the Bible or not, doesn't it make you want to find someone willing to go to this length for you? OK, try to forget everything negative you have experienced in a church or from religious people and think of what it means if this story of God were true. Whether you are like me and trust in Jesus or are hearing of Him for the first time, everyone wants their life to count. Regardless of your belief level, when you first consider having a relationship with Jesus, a mystical and sovereign being, it might not seem like something you need or want in your life. That is understandable given the weird spin many churches put on the life of those that follow Jesus. Throughout history, strange and inaccurate teachings have emerged from religious leaders. Even in the days of Jesus, religious leaders had turned following God into the task of keeping six hundred and thirteen laws. Let me add, Jesus rejected these laws. Then, as today, many religious leaders interpreted the Bible based on their personal preference. Consequently, people who did not know the Bible well blindly followed the personal preferences these men made into laws. Likewise, religious teaching passed through generations of religious leaders, and new interpretations were even created for new circumstances. This has often recreated Jesus and His message into an entirely different person and message than is in the Bible. Most times, the recreated Jesus is a mere wisp of who He is. In other instances, the Bible teachings created with an interpretative twist serve the men's agendas with misdirected authority. I understand those that find it difficult to follow this mere remnant of Jesus of the Bible. Nor do I encourage anyone to follow this created remnant of Jesus or those who have reduced Him to anything less than our loving Father. Let me add, I get it— much of the Jesus thing happening today and in many of the churches is strange. The whole religious thing is just wacky, and I don't enjoy being around it either. If you feel the same, you're not alone.

Yes, the "religious movement" and those that lead it often cause more hurt than the help they offer. Their message should show that Jesus accepts us as we are and is full of love, grace, and mercy. Jesus knows us. He knows our good, and even what we may assume is too bad for Him to forgive. He even knows whether we are a skeptic of Him. Yet He wants each of us just as we are; He gave His life for you. Let's say that if the story of Jesus is true, wouldn't you want to know the person who created you and then died for you?

Maybe the best way to illustrate this point is to go to the first pages in my children's storybook Bible. When things are difficult to understand or explain, I look at them from a child's perspective. The Jesus Storybook Bible begins like this:

> God wrote, "I love you"— he wrote it in the sky, and on the earth, and under the sea. He wrote his message everywhere! Because God created everything in his world to reflect him like a mirror— to show us what he is like, to help us know him, to make our hearts sing. The way a kitten chases her tail. The way red poppies grow wild. The way a dolphin swims. And God put it into words, too, and wrote it in a book called "the Bible." Now, some people think the Bible is a book of rules, telling you what you should and shouldn't do. The Bible does have some rules in it. They show you how life works best. But the Bible isn't mainly about you and

what you should be doing. It's about God and what he has done.[1]

Let me clear all the clutter. You don't need to go through any man, religious belief process, or any prerequisite to know Jesus. Jesus already knows you; He made you. He accepts you with all your weirdness, flaws, and skepticism. No matter how strange, far-fetched, or weird, you imagine Jesus maybe, at the very least, consider the possibility that the story of the Bible could be true.

What man can understand the Trinity, who created the cosmos, and set the stars in place? What mere human can explain a love so deep it moved Jesus to die a horrible death on a cross to be with you for eternity? A relationship with the creator is such an extravagant gift and the value so incomprehensible that men cannot resist appraising it according to the world's standards. It is as if God forgot to levy a price tag to get this gift and so men have set their own. From the day Adam and Eve set foot outside the garden, everything in life has carried a cost. So a promise of life after death, living with the creator for eternity, should carry a weighty price. Right?

Good or bad, we all have beliefs of what it means for Jesus to love us. Many cringe when reading those words; others feel dread, exhaustion, guilt, failure, and the list goes on. Does it bring up thoughts directed toward being a good person, going to church each week, or giving money to the poor? It might remind you of the things you have heard that you need to do to get your life straightened out to please Jesus. I am guessing a large majority associate negative emotion when you read those words. If so, those negative emotions result from false teachings men create. There are no prerequisites for Jesus to love and accept us.

If you're reading this book and never met Jesus other than

what you read here, then I hope you never resort to negative performance-based feelings when it relates to Jesus. Maybe you are one of the fortunate few who have no negative feelings about Jesus. But it hasn't always been like that, has it? No, most of us believe Jesus accepts and loves us based on our performance and that a hefty reordering of your life is required to be loved and accepted by Him.

Journal Pages

This is a great opportunity to journal what you are learning or the action steps you want to take based on this lesson. Doing so will keep all your notes and journaling in this book as future reference. Start by taking a few minutes to pray and ask Jesus to bring to light all you are learning and what transformational changes you can make in your life. If you are reading this in an electronic version, make a digital note and journal.

Journal Pages

EIGHT
THE SIMPLE MESSAGE

The message of Jesus is simple, but it has gotten very complicated in this day and age. So complicated and distorted that millions reject Jesus and the Bible like a bad disease before even considering it. It is not the message of Jesus that is the problem; it is what we believers have made the message of Jesus to be.

For many reading this book, it was in our darkest hour when we first met Jesus. The stories are endless of those who ignored their need for Him until the moment comes, and they have reached their impossible moment. All hope is gone, and in a last-ditch effort, they cry out, "God save me!" Guess what? He comes through even then. Even though they rejected Him all their life, He is only a breath away. He is there when you need him, and when you realize you need Him, His love, captures you. Jesus requires no prerequisite and no church attendance. He is there waiting for you. The first time you want Jesus in your life, He won't deny you access. That, my friend, is how it is regardless of your circumstance. Jesus has no hoops for you to jump through to get to Him. Jesus is patient to wait for you to ask Him into your life. Finding Jesus is never any weirder than that. Never.

The story of the Bible and Jesus' life is not a story to prove, it is a story to have faith to believe in. It's a story to fall into, much like love. When you love someone, you want to build a relationship with them, hang out with them, get to know them. Once you meet, or maybe you have already met Jesus, it's a relationship that you want to engage in. That is as straightforward as it gets; it's a personal relationship with the one who put you and everything in place.

The word "father" is difficult for some. Those who associate negative feelings with the word father struggle with yet another father figure who might or might not act as a true father should. For where I lacked, I apologize to my two children. Let me add that try as hard as I may; it is impossible to be a perfect father, as it is equally impossible to be a perfect person. I in no way condone those fathers who do not put forth a valiant effort. Fatherhood should be— forever— doing what is best for your children and your family. Fortunate for us, God is perfect, and as George MacDonald says, "Father—of the maker of fatherhood, the Father of all the fathers of the earth."[1] This is assurance He is a father that will never let you down. George says it like this:

> There may be among my readers—alas for such!—to whom the word Father brings no cheer, no dawn, in whose heart it rouses no tremble of even a vanished emotion. It is hardly likely to be their fault. For though as children we seldom love up to the mark of reason; though we often offend; and although the conduct of some children is inexplicable to the parent who loves them; yet, if the parent has been but ordinarily kind, even the son who has grown up a worthless man, will now and then feel, in his better moments, some

dim reflex of childship, some faintly pleasant, some slightly sorrowful remembrance of the father around whose neck his arms had sometimes clung. In my own childhood, my father was the refuge from all the ills of life, even sharp pain itself. Therefore I say to son or daughter who has no pleasure in the name Father, 'You must interpret the word by all that you have missed in life. Every time a man might have been to you a refuge from the wind, a covert from the tempest, the shadow of a great rock in a weary land, that was a time when a father might have been a father indeed. Happy you are yet, if you have found man or woman such a refuge; so far have you known a shadow of the perfect, seen the back of the only man, the perfect Son of the perfect Father. All that human tenderness can give or desire in the nearness and readiness of love, all and infinitely more must be true of the perfect Father—of the maker of fatherhood, the Father of all the fathers of the earth, specially the Father of those who have specially shown a father-heart.[2]

It is terrible for those that must interpret the word father by the things they have missed from a father. Even those of us who have great fathers, as George explains, only see a shadow of what the perfect father, God, can be to us. The thing I miss most about my own father is the separation I sense as I get older. From the time I left the house to go to college, the space between us seems to get farther and farther. I don't believe it is that he has any less interest in me, but the intentions are overcome with current tasks. I miss his interest in my life and time hanging out. For many fathers, pursuing what they believe they need to give their families take all the hours in their day. The few remaining hours of each day demand decompression and relief, so they can engage the next day. Too many children have suffered an absent father because that relief included chemical addiction that overtook even that father's good intentions of providing well for his family. No father who wanted to have children began the quest not to be a good father. Many fathers' lives get taken over by life itself, not that they intended for that to happen; instead, they were not intentional enough to keep life from draining their very being from them.

Let me offer this comfort for those who struggle with the word "father" about God. God created us because He wanted to be our Father. God was not forced into fatherhood, nor has there been anything else to distract His focus. Where fathers on earth get pulled by life's concerns and challenges, God does not. Owning and having created the universe, He has never needed to work a day in His life to provide for us. Nor does He go away on business trips, or pursue hobbies that steal His time from us. Instead, He is present every minute of every day. His love is perfect because God is love. He does not merely love us, but He is love itself. Love originates from God. The only thing to impede God being the perfect Father we long for is us, or to be more specific, our lack of interest in the relationship. Most of us aren't sure how to start a relationship with God. Many still hurt from relationships, are hesitant to dive into another, especially with someone invisible. But the only way to know if God is the perfect father is to give Him a shot. You have to experience God to understand what it means for Him to father you.

I am not a big fan of sweets or desserts unless they are over the top incredible. There is not much that makes that list. In 1999, I moved to Atlanta and, shortly after, stumbled upon a Krispy Kreme Doughnut store that was open twenty-four hours a day. Ok, I sought it out. If you know about Krispy Kreme Doughnuts, then you know about the "Hot Now" sign. Many Krispy Kreme stores are not only a doughnut store; they also make the doughnuts distributed to local grocery stores. When they cook those doughnuts, they display a big, red neon sign that says, "Hot Now." Go into the store during those times, and you can get hot glazed doughnuts as they come straight out of the oil and right after they run through a sugar waterfall. I am not exaggerating. If you have never had one, believe me when I say they melt in your mouth. This Krispy Kreme store in Atlanta ran the "Hot Now" sign twenty-four hours a day, seven days a week. Hot, glazed Krispy Kreme doughnuts are the perfect food. They are one of the few sweets other than my daughter's oatmeal cookies that make my list. When friends and family would visit me in Atlanta, the tour of Atlanta always included a stop at this Krispy Kreme Doughnut store. If they had never experienced fresh hot Krispy Kreme, I felt it was my obligation to introduce them. I led them through reciting the Krispy Kreme Doughnut promise printed on each box and then indulged. When my wife and I got married, I suggested a pyramid of Krispy Kreme glazed doughnuts for my groom's cake. If you are a Krispy Kreme fan, you understand the intense emotion that you are experiencing even as you read this. A few of my friends and family had never experienced the hot, fresh Krispy Kreme Doughnut. I guess it is possible you have not either. It's hard for me to believe there is a human alive that does not at least like these doughnuts, not to mention revere them. I can try to explain the experience, taste, perfection, and wow of a hot, glazed Krispy Kreme Doughnut. I can tell you how much they mean to me, my friends, and many people. I can try to persuade you to drive the time you must to grab one of these delectable sugar bombs. But until you experience one of these doughnuts for yourself, you can't fathom what the frenzy is about. Agreed?

Like Krispy Kreme Doughnuts, there are many experiences in life which you must engage in before you know its worth or benefit. You can assume you like or dislike something, but you can only have an assumption until you try it. You can form a theory of whether a relationship or friendship will be meaningful, but you cannot have firsthand knowledge at a distance. Look, touch, even read about a Krispy Kreme doughnut all you want, but until you put it in your mouth and taste it, you will never experience a Krispy Kreme doughnut.

It's the same with God— you can listen to others talk of Him, read of Him, but until you engage in a relationship with Him, you will never experience God.

Imagine the perfect father, and that's God. I know because, like the Krispy Kreme doughnut, I needed to know. It was too fantastic of a story, and everything in the world pointed to Him. I had tried many kinds of things to find meaning in my life. If He was the perfect father, I needed that in my life.

TWO PATHS

Because God loves us, he gives us free will to accept or reject Him. True love is not forced or demanded. Since God created us and the universe, it should be easy to trust that God is real and that He is our perfect Father. Yet, many of us have grown to physical adulthood before ever considering that God could be a valid theory for our existence or as our true Father. In part, that is a byproduct of growing up and blindly trusting our parents or whoever raised us. That blind trust could contribute largely to our belief, or lack of belief, in God as our Father. If our parents did not subscribe to God being true and our true Father, then safe among our childhood toys, we did not know of God. If parents proved to be trustworthy, then there was no reason to question or even think to question God's absence in our childhood academics. We did not need anything greater than our parents to give our lives meaning. God's love story was inconveniently left out of our childhood learning and a void left in its place, which one day we would wrestle with. But for many, science patched that void with a highly improbable, complicated theory of how the cosmos, earth, and man began. Science offers a substitute, absent of God, to explain how the cosmos and man began. A theory that is so complicated that even those who want to believe it say its probability is impossible.

Sir Fred Hoyle, one of Britain's best-known mathematicians and astronomers, in his 1981 book Evolution from Space (co-authored with Chandra Wickramasinghe):

> Calculated that the chance of obtaining the required set of enzymes for even the simplest living cell was one in 10^{40000} (one followed by 40,000 zeroes). Since the number of atoms in the known universe is infinitesimally tiny by comparison (10^{80}), even a whole universe full of primordial soup wouldn't have a chance.[3]

Arriving at adulthood without considering God as a valid theory puts people on two paths. One, they are comfortable with an impossible long-shot, 10^{40000} chance that God is not part of the equation. Well, that is until a circumstance puts them at the end of their rope, and they need a miracle. Evolutionist Sir Fred Hoyle mentioned above, was the person who coined the phrase "big bang" theory. He explained the long-shot theory like this:

> The chance that higher life forms might have emerged in this way is comparable with the chance that a tornado sweeping through a junk-yard might assemble a Boeing 747 from the materials therein... I am at a loss to understand biologists' widespread compulsion to deny what seems to me to be obvious.[4]

The second path is to realize that while the information about God may be different from what you once knew, it is wise to look into its validity. It is what intelligent beings do when confronted with new information: they check it out.

Think of it this way: it is likely if a person grows up with parents who subscribe to God being real and our true Father, then even the possibility of God's validity is easier for that person to accept. But just because a person did not have the advantage of knowing God at an early age does not discount God's validity, nor is it a wise decision to disregard the possibility.

Everyone grows up with limited knowledge of how the world works and the laws of physics. Just because we do not know about gravity does not mean it does not apply to us. Right? So a limited knowledge of laws or even God is not proof of their factual soundness.

God fathered us all and gave us life, whether we accept that or not. By not accepting it, we rob ourselves of the benefits of Him being our father and the benefits of knowing Him.

THE NOT SO SIMPLE MESSAGE

The next challenge arises when many attend a church, they step into one of 30,000 to 40,000 denominations with forty major divisions, each of whom might believe something different. I can be the poster child for those who have spent their life searching for a church to attend, and I am not alone. Finding a church to be a part of is a daunting task.

Therein might be the problem: instead of looking for a church to attend, should we instead be looking for like-minded people who believe in God to build relationships? My personal challenges arise from what I believe a group of people who believe in Jesus should do when they get together. The majority of churches I have attended, either by design or necessity, focus the main attention of their time on Sunday morning activities. Those activities range from sermons, Sunday school classes, and children-focused spaces. Depending on the church's size, that can also range from one centralized service, multiple services, or many environments all meeting and adjourning at different times during the morning. From my observation, the emphasis is on getting people in and out of the parking spaces and seats, yet giving them an experience for which they will sacrifice their Sunday mornings each week. Throughout the week, staff members usually paid, spend forty-plus hours in administrative tasks, music practice, message and lesson preparation, all focused on a Sunday morning performance. Depending on the church, there may or may not be other opportunities to get together in small groups to practice music, study the Bible, or even take part in self-help programs. From my inquiries of those that prescribe to these expressions, the reason for a once-a-week Sunday morning meetings stems from this verse in Hebrews:

> And let us consider how to stir up one another to love and good works, not neglecting to meet together, as is the habit of some, but encouraging one another, and all the more as you see the Day drawing near (Hebrews 10:24-25).

A once-a-week meeting requires a place to meet, and many churches have adopted a once-a-week expression that requires multi-million-dollar church buildings and a staff numbering more than the teachers of most public schools. I often wonder if this verse, rather than small group gatherings, justify the billions spent collectively to accomplish it each year, not to mention the billions of hours of preparation and volunteer hours consumed. Despite all they do, it is rare I leave church on

Sunday morning "stirred up to love and good works, while encouraged" by the people there. On the other hand, those involved in the service, from the pastor to the worship team, have lathered themselves into loving what they do on a Sunday morning with good reason because it is what they get paid to do. There is little time before or after the teaching time to get into any real conversation with another person. People hurry in at the last minute, drop off the kids at the children's program, then into the auditorium. After the large group teaching time, those with kids must promptly pick the children up so the second or third service attendees can whisk in and out. It's been rare to remember halfway through the week the teaching I heard just days before without consulting my notes.

This is my opinion and experience, and not meant to offend those who receive love, good works, and encouragement from Sunday morning and evening services. Yet I am not convinced these Sunday morning pit stops are the best expression of those who love Jesus getting together and encouraging each other. Are they even enough to recharge the batteries of those who attend them for the effort it takes?

THE SUNDAY MORNING SPORTS TEAM

Sunday Church gatherings remind me of the few professional sporting events I've attended. The doors open, and everyone files in and sits facing the center of the building where the professional players provide entertainment. A stop by the concessions can get you a coffee or tea to enjoy while you attend. Some churches are so big nowadays they use sports arenas to meet in. The game starts with a prayer and an anthem. Then players execute the plays they have practiced all week and the spectators cheer at each play's end. The game ends, everyone files out, very few indicating they know a single person in the building. A few stragglers hang back, giving pats on the back and high-fives, showing their approval of their team's win.

Growing up attending church services all my life, I've never understood them. The bigger the church, the less personal, and you can attend week after week, year after year, and never get to know anyone. At least not more than the obligatory greetings and acknowledgments customary for someone you see once a week for a few minutes. Conversely, the smaller the church, the more personal, yet it is tougher to break into the click. The challenge is daunting for a believer, nonetheless, a new believer in Jesus to find an enjoyable, meaningful, and personal experience among the millions of churches open for business little more than an hour a week.

Perhaps a church building to attend on Sunday mornings is not an ideal representation of the "Church." Instead, a small group of people (the Church) meet and have two-way conversations that build deep and meaningful relationships. Instead of supporting salaries, paying a church mortgage, and light bills, those that meet use their money to meet the needs of those around them.

In fact, the Bible highlights such a group, the disciples, who walked with Jesus and His followers:

> And they devoted themselves to the apostles' teaching and the fellowship, to the breaking of bread and the prayers. And awe came upon every soul, and many wonders and signs were being done through the apostles. And all who believed were together and had all things in common. And they were selling their possessions and belongings and distributing the proceeds to all, as any had need. And day by day, attending the temple together and breaking bread in their homes, they received their food with glad and generous hearts, praising

God and having favor with all the people. And the Lord added to their number day by day those who were being saved (Acts 2:42-47).

This is the simple message and life of the believer of Jesus, just days after Jesus had died a brutal death on a cross, rose again and ascended into heaven. This is the model and expression that gave those early believers the ability to "stir up one another to love and good works" while "encouraging one another."

Read it again; isn't this the group you want to be a part of? Please take a moment and absorb this picture compared to what most of us know of churches or small groups.

They devoted themselves to teaching, fellowship, eating together, and prayers. "Devoted" sounds very different from the way I've observed most Christians going through the week. It is tough for our family to get another family to come to dinner at our home once a month. But in this verse, they are hanging out, eating, and praying together daily. A group so active and close that, "... awe came upon every soul?" What needs to happen in a group of believers to evoke awe? Yeah, I am thinking something incredible. To add to the shock factor, the apostles had taken Jesus at His word and were doing signs and wonders. Just every day, ordinary people believing in and using the power Jesus had left them. Then the most intriguing part of the statement, "And all who believed were together and had all things in common" (Acts 2:44).

Really?! "All things in common" is hard to comprehend. Most Bible translations agree, the believers shared everything they had with each other. When anyone had need, they sold possessions and gave the proceeds to that person. The Message translation says, "And all the believers lived in a wonderful harmony, holding everything in common. They sold whatever they owned and pooled their resources so that each person's need was met" (Acts 2:44-45 MSG).

If that was not astonishing enough:

> They followed a daily discipline of worship in the Temple followed by meals at home, every meal a celebration, exuberant and joyful, as they praised God. People in general liked what they saw. Every day their number grew as God added those who were saved (Acts 2:46-47 MSG).

As I write, I am blown away at the emotions that well up inside me. This is the picture you expect of a group of people who have experienced Christ. It is no wonder "the Lord added to their number day by day those who were being saved" (Acts 2:47). Who wouldn't want to be a part of that? A group of glad and generous people living out life together, sharing everything they had. There is no better picture of the Church. No Sunday morning gathering or church building function could emulate what these new disciples in Acts lived. If this is what Jesus taught the disciples, why would we do anything differently? This sounds perfect, it is simple, and it works.

Not too many years ago, larger churches began encouraging their members to get into small groups. That emphasis allowed the church to grow larger while still being able to meet its administration's needs. Many churches realized that their members needed more in-depth study than they could get on a Sunday morning sermon. Besides, there were needs such as counseling, prayer, and daily interaction that staff could not provide, no matter its size.

Large churches are more like colleges because their design and emphasis is more suited to college-style Bible teaching. They pay administrative staff, teachers, buildings, and music programs from donations, and grants they receive. The Sunday morning message is more a once-a-week college lecture.

My point is not against those that establish and run churches. It is not against those who attend those churches. It is not against anyone. Instead, I wonder why we settle for less than what we read in Acts 2:42-47? How could we be content with anything less engaging? If you knew of a group of believers like this, would you want to be a part? If so, then why not begin living like this?

As believers, we are to be a family who learns together, eats together, and takes care of each other. A once-a-week gathering of any sort, be it teaching, eating, or encouraging one another, should never be normal. It should never be enough to settle for anything less than daily, two-way interaction and involvement in each other's lives. It will never be satisfactory to take care of ourselves and let those who have need suffer. The body of believers is to be no less a family than a family. This truth shared in Acts is no secret, and I suspect, just like me, when you read of people caring for and loving each other like this, your soul yearns for something this real, so genuine. It is time we stop buying into the "build it, and they will come" Sunday morning gathering and seek real and genuine family relationships. We need to return to the simple message and life of the believer of Jesus. It is this message, this love, and glad generous hearts that will show the world Jesus.

Just like our relationship with each other should be no less than family, neither should our relationship with God.

Journal Pages

This is a great opportunity to journal what you are learning or the action steps you want to take based on this lesson. Doing so will keep all your notes and journaling in this book as future reference. Start by taking a few minutes to pray and ask Jesus to bring to light all you are learning and what transformational changes you can make in your life. If you are reading this in an electronic version, make a digital note and journal.

Journal Pages

NINE

BECOMING SONS AND DAUGHTERS

The framework of our relationship with God should not differ from the relationship that exists on earth between children and their fathers. First we are children and then progress into His sons and daughters. Many forget these relationship roles only to walk away frustrated, hurt or confused. The role of a father and a child are different. God is always our Father, never are we His equal. In my life, I too ignored the correct role of son both with my father on earth and with my Father, God. By ignoring the correct relationship between a father and son, I too walked away frustrated, hurt, and confused. Understanding our roles as children first, then sons and daughters, is key to a right relationship with God.

A child is born into this world from a fertilized egg of a woman. This process requires a man and a woman. Only God knows what method science will devise for this in the future. Unfortunately, and with epic stakes, the man and woman can choose whether to be a father and mother to that child. I say unfortunately, because the man and the woman choose whether to embrace the true role of parents. We should require that hen two people produce life, they engage that child as parents to the best of their ability. Regardless of their choice, the child is born. In 2014, over 650,000 women decided to abandon that choice by aborting their unborn child.[1] Besides God, they are that child's life-giver. If they choose to keep their commitment, the child will grow up with a father and mother. As long as those parents provide the basic needs and are civil to the child, the child has little choice until around the legal age of 18 whether those two people are their parents. In a normal scenario, barring any disabilities, the child begins and continues normal child development. This may include learning to feed oneself, potty-training, social development, learning to obey, academic development, and more. The child grows up and learns to be an adult through the parents modeling and teaching life skills for 18 years. Certain children learn this better than others. Most achieve a functional level of adulthood. Child development is so normal that, even in children a few weeks old, failure to express a growth milestone as minute as delayed speech triggers concern. We expect children absent of physical and mental challenges to grow up and learn to be well-functioning adults, established even to the point they can father and mother children of their own.

A father and mother's role is to give the child a loving, safe, and provisioned environment in which that child can grow and learn to be an adult. Even encouraging a child through the development stages and providing opportunities that can challenge growth. It is unusual for a loving and supportive parent to be content with a child that never develops to adulthood, even more, to never learn to crawl.

Likewise, we realize that at an early age in our childhood, whether we have proper fathers and mothers, we must take the responsibility to grow into adults. We learn how the world works, the rules in the home, and our country's laws.

We grow socially and academically, with either positive or negative reinforcement, to overcome challenges and obstacles. It is fortunate for those given a safe home and environment to grow and practice the art of being a responsible human. Most children grow up to be functioning adults. Our innate instinct, coupled with our parents' constant teaching, is a natural part of life and is enough to progress us through the developmental stages to adulthood. Though some continue to wear diapers longer than others, our society, economy, and world does not work well for an adult who has not developed past childhood. Three observations I will make regarding this. One, to function well in this world, we must develop to adulthood. Should we challenge this well-established practice of maturing, it means an even greater challenge: relying on others to care for us in a childlike state as a full-grown adult. Second, as children, we do not choose who raises us, nor at an early age do we have the knowledge to trust them or not. We grow up trusting those who raise us until we can assess their ability to be trusted. That blind trust can be a large contributor to our belief or lack of belief in God as our Father.

These straightforward and rarely contested axioms form a foundation in how we grow up and raise our children. Why, if God is our Father, do we find it challenging to apply the same premise as a starting point for how we might think our relationship with God should be?

Once we decide God is valid and our true Father, we must spiritually mature and grow up the same way as children must grow up physically. The formation of our relationship with God as our Father should not differ from the relationship that exists on earth between children and fathers as long as those fathers are good. In fact, our relationship with a perfect God has the potential to be much better than the relationship with our father on earth. Paul says this about maturing in our spiritual life:

> Brothers, do not be children in your thinking. Be infants in evil, but in your thinking be mature (1 Corinthians 14:20).
>
> When I was a child, I spoke like a child, I thought like a child, I reasoned like a child. When I became a man, I gave up childish ways (1 Corinthians 13:11).
>
> ... until we all attain to the unity of the faith and of the knowledge of the Son of God, to mature manhood, to the measure of the stature of the fullness of Christ, so that we may no longer be children, tossed to and fro by the waves and carried about by every wind of doctrine, by human cunning, by craftiness in deceitful schemes. Rather, speaking the truth in love, we are to grow up in every way into him who is the head, into Christ (Ephesians 4:13-15).

To grow up spiritually is an important part of the transformation to mature into adulthood as learning physical skills to function as adults. To ignore the lack of growth milestones in our spiritual life is as devastating as ignoring physical attributes that are missing.

Without spiritual growth, we will have the challenge of never becoming mature in our spiritual life. That choice leaves us dependent on others mature in their spiritual life who must care for us in a childlike state. Not recognizing the lack of spiritual growth has left hundreds of thousands of believers around the world dependent on institutional church structures and those who are spiritually mature to help them get through the daily spiritual challenges of life. Instead of college like structures that produce mature disciples who then make more disciples, churches become hospitals overrun with widespread epidemics of spiritual immaturity. The institutional church mainly spends its resources on those who already know Jesus instead of caring for those in developing countries with real needs and don't know Jesus. Year after year, the believers who refuse to mature absorb most of the resources instead of using them to make new disciples.

This is especially true for those that cannot decide that God is their true Father. They stay parentless and with no means or help to spiritually mature. It is time that those who believe in Jesus to be discipled, and mature into those who can make disciples themselves.

Jesus shows through His public ministry and the discipleship He provides His twelve that the King and the kingdom of God had come. These words and actions also provide an example of how Jesus expected the disciples and His followers to continue proclaiming the good news of the gospel. The last instructions that Jesus gives His followers are, "Go into all the world and proclaim the gospel to the whole creation" (Mark 16:15). Each of the gospel writers records this command of Jesus in some form known as the Great Commission. As a follower of Jesus, I am to make disciples.

This message and mandate of Jesus to become disciples and then make disciples is largely missing today. Instead, a perpetual cycle of attending church and consuming all the disciple-making resources for ourselves has replaced our discipling commission. It is worth looking at what Jesus showed that our lives should look like compared to what we instead settled for in the life of the believer. George MacDonald says it like this:

> To be a child is not necessarily to be a son or daughter. The childship is the lower condition of the upward process towards the sonship, the soil out of which the true sonship shall grow, the former without which the latter were

impossible. God can no more than an earthly parent be content to have only children: he must have sons and daughters— children of his soul, of his spirit, of his love—not merely in the sense that he loves them, or even that they love him, but in the sense that they love like him, love as he loves. For this he does not adopt them; he dies to give them himself, thereby to raise his own to his heart; he gives them a birth from above; they are born again out of himself and into himself—for he is the one and the all. His children are not his real, true sons and daughters until they think like him, feel with him, judge as he judges, are at home with him, and without fear before him because he and they mean the same thing, love the same things, seek the same ends. For this are we created; it is the one end of our being, and includes all other ends whatever. It can come only of unbelief and not faith, to make men believe that God has cast them off, repudiated them, said they are not, yea never were, his children—and he all the time spending himself to make us the children he designed, foreordained—children who would take him for their Father! He is our father all the time, for he is true; but until we respond with the truth of children, he cannot let all the father out to us; there is no place for the dove of his tenderness to alight. He is our father, but we are not his children. Because we are his children, we must become his sons and daughters. Nothing will satisfy him, or do for us, but that we be one with our father! What else could serve! How else should life ever be a good! Because we are the sons of God, we must become the sons of God. [2]

Journal Pages

This is a great opportunity to journal what you are learning or the action steps you want to take based on this lesson. Doing so will keep all your notes and journaling in this book as future reference. Start by taking a few minutes to pray and ask Jesus to bring to light all you are learning and what transformational changes you can make in your life. If you are reading this in an electronic version, make a digital note and journal.

Journal Pages

TEN

OUR STORY

"I'm looking for someone to share in an adventure, and it's very difficult to find anyone.' 'I should think so, in these parts. We're plain, quiet folk and have no use for adventures. Nasty, disturbing, uncomfortable things, they make you late for dinner."
-J.R.R. Tolkien, The Hobbit

It has been clear while writing this book that its purpose has become to help me figure out my part of the story, our story. To reintroduce the simple message of Jesus as opposed to the very complicated gospel that prevails in the world today. It is easy to understand that we need to get back to the simple message of the Bible. The message of the Bible is simple, not a complicated, church-building, program-creating message. It is one that lives out every day lives in simple ways. Jesus discipling His twelve disciples modeled a simple life. The message was simple for those that accepted Jesus' message of life. It is a message that transforms communities and gives them hope in the coming return of Jesus.

Many, including myself, have lost focus on what our life should express and where our joy originates. Our lives are blended into the status quo of Christianity, living on autopilot with very little differentiation from someone who does not believe in Jesus. Consider where Peter reminds us our hope should lie:

> Blessed be the God and Father of our Lord Jesus Christ! According to his great mercy, he has caused us to be born again to a living hope through the resurrection of Jesus Christ from the dead, to an inheritance that is imperishable, undefiled, and unfading, kept in heaven for you, who by God's power are being guarded through faith for a salvation ready to be revealed in the last time. In this you rejoice, though now for a little while, if necessary, you have been grieved by various trials (1 Peter 1:3-6).

Often our hope depends on the circumstances of the day or hour instead of relying solely on the resurrection of Jesus Christ from the dead. We cling white-knuckled to treasures on earth instead of releasing our grasp on these disposable items and staying focused on the inheritance promised by God that He keeps in heaven that can never perish. That promise is the eternity of our very souls in heaven with Jesus. It is a pity that even when writing this paragraph, I need to remind myself to rejoice in the words I write. God gives us an amazing inheritance and promise. Could we wish for anything grander at the end of our life than a place promised to us in heaven by God? That truth should be more than enough to make us forget whatever this life offers as a substitute. If man could glimpse what eternal life in heaven is like, money would hold no value. We would measure success in helping those who cannot help themselves and how quickly one could give away their own money. This generosity would upend the world's economies because it would end greed and accumulation possessions.

Though well documented, the life and work of Jesus on Earth can look tiny. Measured in today's standards to most churches and mega-churches, Jesus' efforts would be a failure. Yet, the life of Jesus and his small group of followers influenced every part of the world. Twelve ordinary men followed Jesus for three years. At the end of Jesus' ministry, only thousands had seen Jesus or knew His message. Jesus and His disciples shared the message of the kingdom of God around 2800 square miles. During the three years, Jesus taught the disciples to live at a snail's pace. God's speed, two miles per hour, is the speed Jesus walked, discipling along the road, being intentional about relationships, really knowing God, and a few others.

At the end of those three years discipling the twelve, Jesus died, rose again, and ascended to heaven, leaving the rest of the job of telling His message to the disciples and us.

It is a natural assumption that for things in this world to be influential, they need to be big and successful. Yet as we have discovered, the birth, life, and ministry of Jesus was very quiet. The first disciples carried on the work in the same way Jesus modeled for them. Still, the message of Jesus spread like wildfire. Between the first disciples and present-day disciples, discipleship has become less organic, less personal than families meeting daily for teaching and meals together. The rich culture of living daily life together is replaced instead by meeting once a week at a building. It looks a lot like Jewish life before Jesus came on the scene. In Jewish tradition, they met daily at the synagogue as it was the center of Jewish life. On the Sabbath, it was where the community gathered for prayer. Jesus and the disciples spent lots of time around the synagogue.

The synagogue was school, meeting place, courtroom, and place of prayer. In some towns, the synagogue may even have provided lodging for travelers. It was the place where small groups of Jewish students assembled for Scripture reading and discussion of the Torah and oral tradition. This meant that worship and study, friendship and community celebration, and even the governing of the community were all done by the same people in the same place.[1]

It appears that the early church patterned itself after the synagogue and continued the same practice of living and worshiping together as a community, often in private homes (Acts 2:42-47).

The building the Church meets in today looks very different from the synagogue the early church patterned after where they lived and worshiped together as a community.

Hour-long meetings once a week replace everyone working together to meet the community needs. An outsourced church staff replaces individuals taking responsibility for discipleship. Fewer resources are available to take care of the community due to large budgets. We do not sell our possessions and belongings to distribute the proceeds to any with need. Our focus on accumulating possessions is more important than others' needs, even our close friends or family. It is common for people to watch neighbors lose their house or even miss meals and not respond with help. These are people that live right beside them or even go to their church. Not to mention the millions around the world who miss weeks' worth of meals while we make exorbitant mortgage payments on homes with guest rooms big enough for an extra family to live in.

To be influential does not require someone to be rich and successful. Intuitive and caring are not the words that come to mind when most consider the Christians they know or the church they attend. Likewise, what is compelling about these people to drive others to know the Jesus they follow? The message and good news of Jesus, the disciples, and the early Church was life-giving. The message and how they lived out that message was contagious and filled with hope. The way the early Christians interacted with each other was inviting and appealing. Their message, the message of Jesus, changed people for the better. Not only that, the early Christians and disciples showed the same power that Jesus had to bring restoration to all they set their hands to. The Bible says, "And awe came upon every soul, and many wonders and signs were being done through the apostles" (Acts 2:43). Everything about the early disciples' lives showed God's love, power, and the gospel's truth. It was hard to know them and not be compelled to believe in Jesus. The result? "And the Lord added to their number day by day those who were being saved" (Acts 2:42-47).

Why do the lives of the early disciples and believers sound so different from many Christians' lives and churches today? As believers, why do we allow the world to influence us rather than the other way around? Can Christians live just like everyone else in the world and still be effective, modeling the life of Jesus to where others want to know Him?

The answer is no. Jesus warned his disciples in Matthew:

> You are the salt of the earth, but if salt has lost its taste, how shall its saltiness be restored? It is no longer good for anything except to be thrown out and trampled under people's feet.
>
> You are the light of the world. A city set on a hill cannot be hidden. Nor do people light a lamp and put it under a basket, but on a stand, and it gives light to all in the house. In the same way, let your light shine before others, so that they

may see your good works and give glory to your Father who is in heaven (Matthew 5:13-16).

Most believers do not carry the message of Jesus so that they look, sound, or live any different from those who do not know Jesus. It is hard to find Christian leaders who live much different from those they lead. Sure, they might offer the store cashier a more sincere greeting, give a small percentage of their money to the poor, not watch as much filth on TV, or tip the waitress better. But do those actions compare to the compelling lives of the early disciples? Are we content to adjust our expectations so low that going to church on Sundays, being nice to people, and giving 10% of our income to the church is what we think will attract people to the message of Jesus? Are Christians supposed to live like everyone else but appear a bit nicer? Is that the life we think the Bible instructs us to live even though the lives of those discipled by Jesus were so much different? Do we consider those early examples of the Church—the reason you know Jesus– the examples we should follow or just nice stories of the early Church?

A few months ago, while talking with a pastor and asking these questions, he responded by saying, "Thank goodness those early disciples sacrificed in the way they did, meeting daily in each other's houses while having everything in common so we can worship in large, expensive church buildings today."

Through those statements, I understand why the message of Jesus is so hard for many to accept because, other than the stories in the Bible, they see no one else living life any different from the rest of the world. Yet many who know Jesus, though excited that they found Him, never take the first step to tell their co-worker or neighbor about Jesus. They never consider that millions around the world are unaware of the wonderful message of salvation and heaven. These people are stuck in the past, hoping in earnest that "middlemen," an outsourced solution, are busy spreading the message of Jesus. Yet, Jesus was clear that each of us is responsible for making disciples. As far as we can tell, that directive might be the last thing Jesus said to the disciples before He ascended to heaven.

And Jesus came and said to them:

> All authority in heaven and on earth has been given to me. Go therefore and make disciples of all nations, baptizing them in the name of the Father and of the Son and of the Holy Spirit, teaching them to observe all that I have commanded you. And behold, I am with you always, to the end of the age (Matthew 28:18-20).

If the early disciples were alive today, no doubt their lives would be very similar to what they were many years ago after encountering Jesus. They would not shrug away from difficult teachings. Nor would they spend their time building large churches and congregations, content with a comfortable life, waiting for others to lead the charge to spread the gospel. They had met Jesus, and nothing was more important to them than sharing that news with all the world at whatever cost. It is the model the Bible instructs us to follow and the model that the unbelieving world is waiting to see. Although sharing that message today is lost among lesser pursuits, nothing is more important.

Without a doubt, the indifference that most Christians have to our responsibility left to us by Jesus to "make disciples" is disconcerting.

Let us explore what a disciple's life might be like today and how that might differ from the life we are living. In fact, let us explore our story as a disciple.

THEY HAD TO BELIEVE

Our story must start where everything in God's creation starts in the beginning. For Adam and Eve, Noah, Moses, David, and the disciples, there was the first time they met God, Jesus, and the Holy Spirit. There is a first time that each of us first encounter Jesus. You might have met Jesus many years ago, or it is possible you met Him and did not even realize it was Him. Half the world dies without ever knowing about Jesus. Along many people's everyday journey through life, they meet Jesus for the first time. It might be through a good deed, a book, a friend, or even a crisis. When the original twelve disciples met Jesus, they were working their daily jobs as fishermen. Once you meet Jesus, you must accept or reject Him, as there is no middle ground on which to stand. For some, it takes their entire life to follow Him, and for others, only the time it takes to speak His name.

The first disciples were Jews and taught from a young age of the coming Christ, the Messiah. Even expecting Jesus to come, it took many who followed Him time to accept that the Messiah was in person among them. The first disciples met Jesus on an ordinary day. He walked up to them and asked them to follow Him. To be a disciple, you must first accept to follow Jesus as the Messiah.

A good place to learn more about Jesus and the good news He brought the world is to start with the book of John in the Bible. Those who have accepted Jesus may have never committed to learning more of Him than what others have told them. The book of John is a great introduction to Jesus and His life.

Listen to your heart as you read; what is it saying to you? Ask Jesus to show you He is the Son of God and make that real to you. If you want to meet Jesus and settle it in your heart once-and-for-always, He will show you He is the Christ. Remember, He made you, knows you, and has been pursuing you since the day of your birth. He's been pursuing each of us since the day He created Adam and Eve in the garden.

Jesus, the Son of God, died for your sins, rose from death on the third day, and will forgive you of your sins. The Bible says to be saved; a person must, "...repent and be baptized for the forgiveness of your sins" (Acts 2:38). Then you must put your trust in Jesus Christ and believe in Him, and you will be saved (Acts 16:31).

If you are ready to give your life to Jesus, start by repenting for your sins. Tell Him you are sorry for your sins and thank Him for giving His life on the cross for you. Tell Him you believe He rose to life on the third day, and He has saved you from your sins and death and that He has given you eternal life. Begin trusting in Jesus, and you will be saved. Find another Christian who can baptize you, whether in the ocean, pool, or church.

It is that simple to accept Jesus, acknowledge that He is the creator of the universe and you, and start living your life with purpose. It is by faith that we believe in Jesus, and through that faith, we are born again. Now, as we read in 1 Peter, we are "born again to a living hope through the resurrection of Jesus Christ from the dead, to an inheritance that is imperishable, undefiled, and unfading, kept in heaven for you, who by God's power are being guarded through faith for a salvation ready to be revealed in the last time" (1 Peter 1:3-5 ESV). Nothing and no one can take that gift of eternal life away from you. It doesn't mean your life gets easier; many of the disciples found more challenges to life. Jesus will transform your life like the disciples, giving it purpose and use you to tell others of Him.

Once you accept Jesus, there is only one thing left to do, follow Him, and make disciples.

THEY HAD TO FOLLOW HIM

Once we decide that Jesus is the Christ and accept Him as our Savior, as the early disciples did, we need to follow Jesus. For many, that is easier said than done. The disciples had to follow Jesus and commit to a life of learning and a different way of living. In faith, we need to follow Jesus wherever He leads us.

We should expect no less of a life transformation than the disciples experienced. We are accepting the same Jesus and focusing on the same job which they began. It is up to us to finish telling the world about Jesus. We need the same focus, resolve, and dedication as they had. This might be the most difficult challenge, accepting that our lives must focus on making disciples just like in the New Testament. It might look simple to devote one's life to telling others about Jesus and discipling them. Yet that is the directive that Jesus left: go and make disciples. But what are we to do about getting college degrees, building successful careers, raising a family, buying a home, etc.? Are we to accept that Jesus expects us to abandon every hope and dream and successful life for one of making disciples? The Bible is clear; the answer is yes. And let's face it: how many people who are living their lives for themselves, tied to meaningless careers, strapped to exorbitant mortgages, and living life at a break-neck speed are happy? They might act as though they are happy, but they are filling the void with stuff.

> What can this incessant craving, and this impotence of attainment mean, unless there was once a happiness belonging to man, of which only the faintest traces remain, in that void which he attempts to fill with everything within his reach? But it is in vain he seeks from absent objects the relief things present cannot give, and which neither of them can give; because, in a soul that will live forever, there is an

infinite void that nothing can fill, but an infinite unchangeable being.[2]

First off, a disciple who walked with Jesus would live a simple, more meaningful life. Jesus' life was simple; yet no one has nor will ever walk the earth with more meaning and purpose. Many who follow Jesus get confused along with the world of the purpose of life. Our purpose is not for each of us to reconstruct the Garden of Eden, no matter how much we miss it. The only way back to eternity and the "garden" is through Jesus and joining Him in Heaven at the end of our life. Yes, we have a desire for the garden which we were created for. But while the world tries to reconstruct it purchase by purchase, those who follow Jesus can be content that one day we will get the garden back, just not right now. It was no accident that Jesus' life was in stark contrast to the culture, religion, and society that surrounded Him. His behavior, beliefs, and values were different. He opposed the religious leaders and was not concerned that they did not accept Him into their society. Jesus could not even count on the current religious leaders to help Him with His message. They ultimately killed Him because His message was so opposite of theirs.

In the last few years, there has been a movement in the U.S. gaining ground called minimalism. Minimalism is a practice where a person removes the meaningless from their life to make room for the meaningful and purposeful. One practice in removing the meaningless is by owning fewer possessions. By owning fewer possessions, you don't need as much space to live and spend less time cleaning. Organizing and putting away your possessions takes less time and more there is more time for more meaningful pursuits. Often being minimalistic, money goes farther by buying fewer possessions, and you have more time because you work less because you need less income. It is not an oath of poverty, but instead a choice for more freedom in your life by freeing it from consumerism and clutter. Jackie says it well, "There are two ways to be rich: One is by acquiring much, and the other is by desiring little."[3]

I hope to leave a legacy where others say about me, "He chose to be rich by making his wants few, and supplying them himself."[4]

As I mentioned earlier in the book, living in a two-bedroom condo instead of having a larger house was a source of great stress to me. Within just a few chapters of writing this book and after writing about The Lord's Prayer, "Give us this day our daily bread" became a request of contentment for me. I put a note on the wall next to my desk that says, "I have food, clean water, clothes, and a roof over my head today." I found contentment that God does provide us what we need and that it is more than enough. A few weeks later, my wife and I learned of tiny houses and watched a few shows on tiny houses and tiny living. We got excited about tiny living and could envision living in a place even smaller than our condo. I read a short book on minimalism. We decided even though we had been careful with what we fit into our 1,100 square foot condo, we could declutter even more. We emptied closets, dressers, shelves and had a blast. Adopting and then committing to a more minimalist lifestyle has been fun while inspiring others to do the same. I mention this because, as I write this book, Jesus has transformed my life once again from not having much to wanting even less. Earlier in my life, I had reduced what I owned to a backpack of possessions, and it was the most meaningful time of my single life. In just the seven months of a more minimalist lifestyle, we have more meaning and purpose in our life.

It has made us ask ourselves: can we, as Jesus and the early disciples did, live more meaningful and effective lives? Can we live a richer life, desiring less, and being content with what God provides us? We believe we can while using the excess and extra time to make more disciples. Instead of filling the void of happiness with everything within our grasp, we instead find happiness again by clearing away everything meaningless we have surrounded ourselves with. It is amazing how good it feels to get a life pared down to the basics. But no excuses, the lives of the disciples and Jesus while He was on Earth were simple, weren't they? I doubt they had many possessions to start with and certainly a lot less once they sold their belongings and distributed the proceeds to anyone who had need. They had little need for many possessions, and what they had they gave to others. Their lives were simple and very different from the surrounding culture; they were, as Jesus encouraged, "the salt of the earth."

After meeting Jesus, the disciples' lives were minimalistic, purpose-driven, and they cared about others' needs more than they needed possessions in their own lives. It is close to impossible to comprehend this lifestyle. For most of my life, I have known these Bible stories. They are appealing to read, yet I dismissed them as mostly unrealistic. It's as though I categorized these stories as something possible only by the disciples but not by anyone else. The disciples' lives were real. Many of the books in the New Testament are first-person accounts of what they saw. Through their encounter with Jesus, there was a radical change in their lifestyle, and purpose that Christians throughout the ages have had trouble duplicating. Or is it that our encounter with Jesus has been so minuscule: so once-a-week, go-to-meeting; we carry the title, a sure salvation, yet lack the power of the early Church? It is clear the direct infusion of Jesus' power the disciples received through the Holy Spirit has is missing throughout the last 2,000 years. While the modern-day church lacks many of the signs and wonders commonplace in the early Church, the power Jesus gave us, including the faith to live more minimal and purposeful lives, is ours for the asking.

Could it be that many have assumed outsourced discipleship is sufficient through the paid staff they support at the church they attend? That by outsourcing discipleship, it releases them from the responsibility placed on each disciple by Jesus to make disciples? Power or no power, many have deferred their responsibility and feel free to live their lives on an alternative plane than what Jesus asks of His disciples. The Bible is clear that there is no excuse from the responsibilities of making disciples. Outsourcing discipleship to paid staff explains why in two thousand years, a message so amazing is not known by every person on Earth.

If you will remember, for years before Jesus came, God had priests as middlemen between Him and man. It was only the Jews that were God's chosen people. When Jesus came, He changed everything and removed the middlemen. Instead, Jesus became our priest, and through Him, we get direct access to God, for Jesus is a part of the Godhead. Jesus is the one that made it possible for a direct relationship with God again. With the restoration of our relationship came new and exciting changes. Jesus came and died so that everyone, not just Jews, could know God and have Him as their God. There is now a whole world of people who need to hear of Jesus. With no middlemen, we are given the privilege to tell the rest of the world of Jesus. Instead of priests, pastors, or anyone else we might want to put in that role, Jesus gave that role to us. Each of us who is a disciple is to make new disciples. Starting with the first disciples and continuing through the last 2,000 years, those who accept Jesus have the responsibility to spread the message of Jesus. As disciples of Jesus, we do not have the choice of whether to make disciples or not. It is His will and His heart for each of us to make disciples.

We should expect that following Jesus includes experiencing Him in a way that can transform us into disciples with the same power and resolve that the early disciples experienced. Our transformation needs but a sole directive in which Jesus began and left to the disciples: to finish telling the world of Jesus. As with the early disciples, Jesus comes to each of us and asks us to abandon our hopes, dreams, and career paths to follow Him. There is no greater importance in the universe to Him than for each person in the world today to know His name and accept the salvation He afforded by giving His life on a cross. That is how important the discipleship of every living soul is to Jesus; He gave His life. Why, then, should it be less important to us? We must want and learn to follow Jesus wherever He leads, making disciples as we go.

Journal Pages

This is a great opportunity to journal what you are learning or the action steps you want to take based on this lesson. Doing so will keep all your notes and journaling in this book as future reference. Start by taking a few minutes to pray and ask Jesus to bring to light all you are learning and what transformational changes you can make in your life. If you are reading this in an electronic version, make a digital note and journal.

Journal Pages

ELEVEN
WE HAVE TO EMBRACE HIS KINGDOM

It is easy to see the twelve men that Jesus discipled remained confused about Jesus' mission. Jesus came to preach the Gospel of the Kingdom and die a horrible death on the cross to pay for our sins. During their time with Jesus, the disciples thought Jesus was setting up a kingdom on the earth. When the soldiers arrested Jesus, taking Him away to die on a cross, His followers understood that He had not been speaking in metaphors. Jesus had come on a one-way rescue mission to ensure that we will be with Him in Heaven for eternity. Worldly success, power, authority, fame, or any deviation of the plan to redeem us was nowhere on His radar. He came laser-focused on His mission.

As disciples ourselves, we must learn and accept that the mission Jesus was on is the same mission He left for us. Everything Jesus taught, did, and promised concerned His coming kingdom, the kingdom of heaven, not a kingdom here on earth. Jesus came and gave His life for our sins so we could have eternal life. He then commissioned the disciples and us to tell the rest of the world of this gift. Jesus gave us His power and

Holy Spirit to finish the mission. It is a wonderful hope to live knowing that God will give us everything we need. Then at the end of our life here on earth, we will live forever in eternity with Jesus.

For many, the amazing promises of the coming kingdom are not enough. Heaven, at the end of their life, is not enough. Also, they need heaven, or at least a taste of it, here on the earth. Many feel they need to exaggerate the benefits of the Christian life to make it more appealing. It is a travesty that people give more weight to what they get in this short life on earth than the eternal riches they have waiting for them in Heaven. Many teach with acceptance of Jesus; life here on earth will be full of riches and prosperity. Thinking Jesus was setting up an earthly kingdom, the disciples fought over who will be the greatest. Today, church leaders and followers of Jesus jockey for positions of importance and authority instead of taking a servant's role.

Instead, to be disciples of Jesus, we must want His kingdom, not the kingdom of this world. When Jesus taught the disciples to pray, it was to pray, "Your kingdom come, your will be done, on earth as it is in heaven" (Matthew 6:10). It was the will of His Father that Jesus encouraged the disciples to pray for. Jesus spent His entire life focused on God's will.

> So Jesus said to them, "Truly, truly, I say to you, the Son can do nothing of his own accord, but only what he sees the Father doing. For whatever the Father does, that the Son does likewise. For the Father loves the Son and shows him all that he himself is doing. And greater works than these will he show him, so that you may marvel" (John 5:19 & 20).

If Jesus spent His entire life doing only God's will, how can our lives as disciples be less focused on God's will? What exempts us from the need to center one hundred percent of our life on God's will? Do we believe that the mission Jesus was on and the mission we are to be on is different? Why did God the Father have His Son Jesus running all over the countryside spreading the good news of the kingdom, and yet we don't believe it is our responsibility to do the same? Why did Jesus have little in the way of material possessions, yet we believe God has set no limit as to the amount of wealth or possessions we can accumulate? Is there a cryptic message in the words of Jesus when He taught the following?

> Do not lay up for yourselves treasures on earth, where moth and rust destroy and where thieves break in and steal, but lay up for yourselves treasures in heaven, where neither moth nor rust destroys and where thieves do not break in and steal. For where your treasure is, there your heart will be also (Matthew 6:19-20).

The life, mission, and example that Jesus left the disciples are relevant today. Is the reason our lives look so different because we live for ourselves instead of for others? Where we fail, Jesus resisted satan's temptations in the desert by; being content with what God provides, focusing on God's will and not His own, and establishing God's kingdom and rule instead of His own. We are not convinced that the lifestyle and example Jesus left applies to us. We consider our comforts, our pursuit of beauty, our relief of life's stresses, or fill-in-the-blank is more important than God's mission to save the world. Even as we read this, the excuses pop into our heads. As a man, Jesus overcame the same temptations we face today, and we can as well.

Just as us, Jesus overcame the temptation to provide for Himself and live beyond His means; he trusted God and remained content that God was supplying everything He needed. Tempted by satan to turn stones into bread, He instead trusted God's provision rather than His own ability. As Jesus taught us in the Lord's prayer, we too must trust God to give us our daily needs. Trust him, even when we have not eaten for forty days.

In the second temptation, Jesus showed it is God's will we are after, not our own. As disciples, this life is about God and not us. When circumstances do not go our way, we doubt whether we are sons and daughters and if God cares about our life. When tempted by these thoughts from satan, Jesus overcame the temptation. Jesus taught that instead of praying for our will, we should put away our selfishness and pray that God's will is done.

As sons and daughters, we need to bring God's kingdom at all times according to His will, even when tempted to cater to our own. Even when we see an easier, comfortable, or more appealing way to achieve God's will, we must bring glory to God by accomplishing His will in His way. Resisting like Jesus, the temptation to set up our own kingdom here on earth instead of bringing God's kingdom.

The third temptation that satan proposed appeared to be a quick and easier way to finish the mission Jesus was on. But it required Him to worship satan the created, instead of God, the creator. Worshiping the created, whether that is nature, science, or satan himself are the same and break God's commands.

In summary, Jesus overcame the temptation to provide for Himself, create a kingdom for Himself, and worship the created instead of God. Had Jesus failed any one of the temptations, you and I would have no hope. Because Jesus completed His mission we have hope:

born again to a living hope through the resurrection of Jesus Christ from the dead, to an inheritance that is imperishable, undefiled, and unfading, kept in heaven for you, who by God's power are being guarded through faith for a salvation ready to be revealed in the last time. (1 Peter 1:3-5).

God put His trust in Jesus to complete His rescue plan and make disciples who will make disciples and tell the world of His love (Matthew 4:1-11). Jesus put His trust in those He discipled and those who accept Him to tell the world of His love.

But understand this, that in the last days there will come times of difficulty. For people will be lovers of self, lovers of money, proud, arrogant, abusive, disobedient to their parents, ungrateful, unholy, heartless, unappeasable, slanderous, without self-control, brutal, not loving good, treacherous, reckless, swollen with conceit, lovers of pleasure rather than lovers of God, having the appearance of godliness, but denying its power. Avoid such people (2 Timothy 3:1-3).

Most of us trust that someone else is proclaiming the kingdom of God. Someone else is telling the world of Jesus. Someone else is taking care of orphans and widows. We think as long as someone else is doing the work, we are free to live as comfortable and extravagant lifestyle as we can muster until Jesus returns to take us to Heaven. Have you ever stopped to think that maybe God loves the world so much that He is waiting to come back until everyone in the world knows of Him? Estimates are 680 million people do not know of Jesus and do not have access to the gospel. How do we believe that God's will does not need our involvement, while hundreds of millions have no ability to learn of Jesus? How did "Go and make disciples" turn into attend a once-a-week meeting of the saints and live a comfortable and extravagant life? Maybe you go twice a week or are in a small group. Is it enough to go to church each week, give toward missions, and do what we want with the rest of our life and money?

When you look at how important your life and those 680 million people's lives are to God, it is plain to see the price He will pay. "For God so loved the world, that he gave his only Son, that whoever believes in him should not perish but have eternal life" (John 3:16).

Why then, if God will pay His son's life for you and everyone in the world, are we exempt? To begin with, it was our fault that sin entered the world. God paid our debt with His Son's life so that we could live forever in eternity with Him. God is giving us eternity in Heaven, yet we are not willing to live our limited life here on earth, sacrificing our comforts with the same level of love and commitment to save the lost as He affords us? What if the original disciples decided someone else should spread the good news? If we were the ones that had never learned of Jesus, we would want those who knew Him to give their lives to reach us with the message. What if we were the ones that lacked the necessities of life? 748 million people in the world lack access to clean water[1], "About 29,000 children under the age of five dies every day — 21 each minute, mostly from preventable causes.[2] Malnutrition and the lack of safe water and sanitation contribute to half of all these children's deaths." The majority of people who can affect the solution are too distracted by their own lives to help. Life and death regarding eternity might seem distant from the day-to-day, but 29,000 children under the age of five dying every day. Twenty-nine thousand people dying from preventable cause should cut to the heart of everyone.

Granted, it is a hard concept to embrace a lifestyle focused on God's kingdom and not satisfy our wants on earth. I venture to say that few get this right. As followers of Jesus, we embrace His story of what He and the disciples did for us. We rarely see someone willing to live it out for others. No, we are much too focused on our own wants and needs to see past those to others.

Jesus' mission was clear. That mission may not be more misunderstood than in our present day. He was here to find and save the lost while showing us His Father, who sent Him and inviting us to live in the kingdom of God. As Dallas Willard explains:

> Most any New Testament scholar will tell you that Jesus' life and message was all about "the kingdom." What they usually miss, however, is exactly what Jesus did and said about the kingdom. Simply, by his acts and words he invited anyone at all, no matter who or what they were, to live in the kingdom of God now, by trusting—relying on, putting their confidence in—him. The events of his "passion" [dying on the cross] and afterward, as traditionally understood, demonstrated to his followers and other observers that what Jesus said about the kingdom and its availability is true. To live through and beyond torture and the cross in resurrection life shows the presence of a world of God among men.
>
> In the simplest possible terms, the kingdom of God is God in action. It is the range of God's effective will, where what God wants done is done. Jesus is a reformulation and embodiment of the message about God and his kingdom that runs through the history of the Jewish people recorded in the Bible. Jesus said: "Seek above all to live within the kingdom rule of God, and to have the kind of goodness he has, and all else you need will be provided with it." (Matthew 6:33 paraphrase) The Psalmist said simply and

concretely, "The Lord is my Shepherd, I shall not want." (Psalm 23) In one of the historical books of the Old Testament a prophet is quoted as saying: "The eyes of the Lord move to and fro throughout the earth that He may strongly support those whose heart is completely His." (2nd Chronicles 16:9) This is what Jesus knew as he went through his sufferings and death. In that knowledge he simultaneously wrote across the pages of human history the depth of human meanness and brutality and the unlimited reach of God's love and power.[3]

We forget that we can "live right now in the kingdom of God," that is God in action. That action and invitation that Jesus proclaimed is to "seek above all to live within the kingdom rule of God, and to have the kind of goodness he has, and all else you need will be provided with it" (Dallas Willard Matthew 6:33 paraphrase).

4

To be a disciple of Christ is to embrace His kingdom and not be consumed with building our own. To accept His invitation to live within the kingdom rule of God now and to have His kindness holds with it the promise we each want- that God will supply everything we need. No worry, no stress, or striving to carve out a living. But the condition to seek *first* His kingdom is in direct conflict with the world's values. It is the same condition and promise God has offered since the garden. The challenge then and now is trusting God with what He supplies and being content with it. Most of us have been so busy supplying for what we believe we need we couldn't begin to guess how a life of God's provision might look. Many decide we can supply better for our "heaven" on earth ourselves, even if it means living outside the kingdom.

SCOTT MICHAEL RINGO

LIFE IS LIVED OUT IN THE ORDINARY

My family loves summer. While not as cold as much of the United States, winter in Virginia is cold for us. The Chesapeake Bay keeps most of the snow away, but we are in heavier jackets in the winter months. Our family likes things warmer than colder. During the winter months, our family hibernates. Except for the rare occasion it snows, and we can make a snowman, we only go out when necessary. When summer comes, we are outdoor junkies. Most weekends, we go to a festival, the beach, fishing, kayaking, crabbing, hiking, or just hanging out with friends. Every couple of years, we get a yearly pass to the zoo to go unlimited times. As much as we can, we stay outside, soaking up the fun. But during the week, even in the summer, our lives look much the same as any other week of the year. Sure we take the occasional swim or bike ride with the kids in the evening, but not as much as we wish we could. Life happens, and that requires mundane and ordinary activities. Baths, meals, house cleaning, laundry, and lists of everyday activities must happen for our family to have the weekends to have fun. Rarely does anyone in the world has a life where they play seven days a week, three hundred sixty-five days a year play.

While the mountaintop, high-octane thrill rides are fun, life happens in the humdrum, everyday activities such as cooking the meals, eating together as a family, reading to the kids, and even shaving. These are constant, everyday moments that make a lifetime of memories. The biggest challenge to make the right kingdom of God decisions happens in everyday moments. These ordinary and everyday moments are where God writes the story of our lives. It is during those countless hours of the ordinary that our family grows closer that our children learn important life lessons, and we have time to hear Jesus' voice.

The sum of these uneventful, everyday moments, with a few highlights sprinkled in, makes up our life.

Likewise, the Bible shows us the highlights and struggles of many men and women, including Jesus and the disciples. They lived their lives in the ordinary, one step at a time, trusting and following Him. The Bible is full of exciting stories, and makes it hard to remember Jesus and the disciples lived out thousands of hours the ordinary. In reality, most of Jesus and the disciples' lives are not chronicled in the Bible at all.

Not much of Jesus' early life is found in the Bible. There is His birth and a visit from the wise men when he is a child, not a baby. There is nothing of Jesus' life as a child from age twelve[5] until He burst onto the scene at age thirty as a very educated man.[6] It may be hard to imagine Jesus growing up as a youth, teenager, or even a twenty-something. You can be sure as Jesus grew up there was much ordinary in His life. His father Joseph was a τέκτων- the word in Greek is *tekton*, a builder. That could have been a builder who worked with stone, iron, copper, and in wood.[7] Given Jesus' Bible references to farmers, many believe Joseph may have built yokes, plows, and farming tools. Regardless, it was an ordinary job. Ordinary jobs most times make less than ordinary wages, so perhaps Jesus grew up with the necessities and not much more. Interesting because, if desired, God the Father or Jesus Himself could have changed His family's income ability in the blink of an eye. Still, Jesus, who lived a sinless life, was content with His family's financial and social well-being no matter what it was. He had to be; after all it was He, part of the Trinity, who provided for Joseph and Mary. That says much of what we should expect from God. God could supply us with the riches of King Solomon if He wishes. We should pray as He instructs that He supply our daily needs. If He supplies more, then live a modest lifestyle and use the extra to help others. Jesus, as many of us, grew up in ordinary life with most of it lived out in the every day, mundane tasks.

Jesus was without exception, fully man and fully God, and went through the childhood calamities of learning to feed Himself, potty-training, and even learning to talk. As Jesus grew up, there was no extraordinary about His life. We know that because as He starts His ministry, people are amazed at Him. They knew this boy growing up, and now as a man, they can't believe their ears.

> He went away from there and came to his hometown, and his disciples followed him. And on the Sabbath he began to teach in the synagogue, and many who heard him were astonished, saying, "Where did this man get these things? What is the wisdom given to him? How are such mighty works done by his hands? Is not this the carpenter, the son of Mary and brother of James and Joses and Judas and Simon? And are not his sisters here with us?" And they took offense at him (Mark 6:2-3).

They knew Jesus, the neighborhood boy. Now Jesus astonishes them with His wisdom and knowledge of the scriptures. They are wondering, how could the hands of an ordinary carpenter do such mighty works? Jesus, the ordinary boy and teen growing up, is a very different man. People should react to us like this if we spent the ordinary times gaining wisdom, knowledge, and seeking God's will.

Even throughout Jesus' three years of ministry, much of His daily life is not recorded. For example, during His three-year public ministry, Jesus walked 3,125 miles.[8] That is a ton of time spent walking. If He averaged a three-mile per hour pace, it takes twenty minutes to walk a mile. Much of the terrain Jesus walked was challenging, plus the lack of athletic footwear would have slowed the pace. At an average of thirty minutes to walk a mile, Jesus walked over 1,500 hours during his three-year ministry. Fifteen hundred hours of ordinary walking was a great time to teach the disciples. If you want to teach some disciples without distraction, get them out doing fifteen hundred hours of walking. As James Baldwin notes, "Children have never been very good at listening to their elders, but they have never failed to imitate them."[9] Even as much as the miracles Jesus performed, the time walking was rich times for the disciples to learn to imitate Him.

Like the twelve disciples, our life, witness, and ministry happens in the ordinary. Even throughout Jesus' public ministry, it was rare that He was in the social spotlight. He conducted His ministry in the out-of-the-way places. His birth, childhood, and most of His public ministry happened in obscurity. It was His brutal death that made the news headlines. Yet you can be sure that Jesus' entire life stayed focused in prayer and communication with His father, as ours should be.

This is where the real battle rages with the contentment of our life. In the ordinary is where Jesus encountered many of the opportunities to show the world God's love. In the ordinary, like Jesus, we mature as believers so that we can astonish the world with our wisdom and love at the appointed times.

Many of the highlights of Jesus in the Bible read as though He stumbled upon a scene, and the extraordinary happened. Why shouldn't we believe that these events unfolded this way instead of an elaborate theatrical performance? Many times I have assumed He planned these events to carry out His directive. Knowing God's will, He knew where to find these events and how they would unfold. Perhaps He did not plan them but knew where to find them. Think of how many more everyday encounters turned extraordinary that were not written down by the disciples. Instead, the example of Jesus shows that through the ordinary, we face opportunities to show the world God's love, sometimes through simple means and sometimes through the extraordinary. In fact, the opportunities to experience God's glory and show the world His love are all around us every day. We need to embrace the ordinary, for out of those times, we gain the ability for God to do the extraordinary, as Jesus and the disciples experienced.

Theodore Roosevelt said, "Comparison is the Thief of Joy." Our mind makes hundreds of comparisons per hour, and very little steals our joy more than the perceived joy of others: the facade in which people outwardly surround themselves to hide the reality of their true unhappiness. Often people's unhappiness comes from comparing their lives to others' and feeling their own is ordinary and unfulfilling. By making those unsubstantiated comparisons, they have the need or want to surround themselves with more stuff, trips, or seek relief in drugs and alcohol. Alternative lifestyles, a move to a new home, a new job, or even a new state, may feel justified to find the joy we perceive that others have. Moves and change in and of themselves are not harmful if God directs those. But many times when God has us exactly where He wants to use us, or He is teaching us a vital lesson, we try to thwart His plans by looking to stuff or places to fulfill our joy.

A purchase, move, or new relationship rarely fills the joy we seek for more than a short season. Instead of searching for joy outside of Him in things, Jesus wants us to experience real joy through Him. To experience His beauty instead of substituting nature's beauty, to move toward Him and His purposes instead of moving locations, and to build a relationship with Him instead of seeking human companionship.

King David wrote, "You make known to me the path of life; in your presence there is fullness of joy; at your right hand are pleasures forevermore" (Psalms 16:11).

In his life, David understood in a relationship with God is where one finds the greatest joy and true pleasures. Jesus restated the process again with more emphasis:

> As the Father has loved me, so have I loved you. Abide in my love. If you keep my commandments, you will abide in my love, just as I have kept my Father's commandments and abide in his love. These things I have spoken to you, that my joy may be in you, and that your joy may be full (John 15:9-11).

Isn't that what we are all looking for— that our joy may be full? According to Jesus, joy doesn't come from what the world has led us to believe. Instead, it comes from keeping Jesus' commandments, which allows us to abide in His love and as a result Jesus' joy will be in us. When Jesus invited the disciples to follow Him, there was a lot more to His invitation than just giving up their jobs and hanging out. They experienced real joy for maybe the first time through hanging out with Jesus in the ordinary.

As if one or all of the writers for The Hobbit: An Unexpected Journey understood this, they wrote these lines for Gandalf, who represented Jesus:

> Gandalf: I'm looking for someone to share in an adventure.
>
> You will have to do without pocket handkerchiefs, and a great many other things, before we reach our journey's end, Bilbo Baggins. You were born to the rolling hills and little rivers of the Shire, but home is now behind you. The world is ahead.
>
> Saruman believes it is only great power that can hold evil in check, but that is not what I have found. I found it is the small everyday deeds of ordinary folk that keep the

darkness at bay... small acts of kindness and love. (The Hobbit: An Unexpected Journey 2012)[10]

The small, everyday deeds are where people can see the love of Jesus and not just hear the words. This was never more true than in the life of Jesus. Furthermore, I believe many hold great esteem for those that give their lives to meet the needs of those that cannot help themselves: people like Mother Teresa, Amy Carmichael, Jackie Pullinger, and Gladys Aylward gave their lives to show those around them Jesus in a practical way. By seeing a need and meeting it, we show the world the love of Jesus, not just tell them about it. There are two quotes of St. Francis of Assisi that nail this:

> Start by doing what's necessary; then do what's possible; and suddenly you are doing the impossible. (Francis of Assisi)
>
> Preach the Gospel at all times and when necessary use words. (Francis of Assisi)

You may remember that Jesus' message was the Gospel of the Kingdom, the kingdom of God, which is God in action. The example of Jesus fits exactly with His message. He went throughout His ministry meeting others' needs and showing them what the Kingdom of God looks like. There was restoration in everything Jesus did. The kingdom of God had come and restoration with it. Jesus came to restore all, including man's relationship with God.

God in action is restoration. If we look at the entire three-year public ministry of Jesus, it is easy to see that Jesus' actions were a living picture of restoration. The lame could walk, the blind could see, and the outcasts embraced and accepted, and the ordinary people doing the extraordinary. As disciples, we must embrace the ordinary and necessary, and, like the early disciples, we will soon find we are doing the miraculous. A life lived out in the ordinary is full of adventure.

> All that is gold does not glitter,
> > Not all those who wander are lost;
> > The old that is strong does not wither,
> > Deep roots are not reached by the frost. From the ashes a fire shall be woken,
> > A light from the shadows shall spring;
> > Renewed shall be blade that was broken,
> > The crownless again shall be king.
> > (Poem in honor of Aragorn by Bilbo Baggins, The Fellowship of the Ring, Strider)[11]

Journal Pages

This is a great opportunity to journal what you are learning or the action steps you want to take based on this lesson. Doing so will keep all your notes and journaling in this book as future reference. Start by taking a few minutes to pray and ask Jesus to bring to light all you are learning and what transformational changes you can make in your life. If you are reading this in an electronic version, make a digital note and journal.

Journal Pages

TWELVE
LIFE ON PURPOSE

> *And Jesus came and said to them, "All authority in heaven and on earth has been given to me. Go therefore and make disciples of all nations, baptizing them in the name of the Father and of the Son and of the Holy Spirit, teaching them to observe all that I have commanded you. And behold, I am with you always, to the end of the age"*
> (Matthew 28:18-20).

Discipleship, like life, is lived out in the ordinary. Jesus had a purpose for coming to earth, and nothing stood in His way. Jesus made disciples of twelve men while teaching on hillsides. Paul did so by going place to place, starting churches, discipling laypeople, and doing it again and again. Moses conveyed God's message to humanity by teaching a group of people in the desert who had turned away from God. Throughout history, great men kept God's message simple, and the delivery easy. They modeled it.

Today our sophistication makes it tough to get the message out.

It is clear when looking at the life of Jesus, Paul, or any of the twelve disciples the focus and purpose of their life. They made disciples who made disciples. Jesus, Paul, nor the twelve disciples were your every day, Bible-believing Christian. Instead, they were sold-out, life-sacrificing disciples, Acts 29 writing believers. It is what Jesus did; it is what the disciples did, and what He expects from us. To make disciples is the job and purpose He gave to every person who follow in Him, as directed in Matthew 28:18-20.

If we do not stay focused, we can be great at everything but make disciples. In fact, challenge us with the monumental task of building a multi-million dollar building or planting a church we thrive. We will put together a committee, take on exorbitant debt, and spend every last ounce of energy to accomplish it. But ask us to make disciples, and you get blank stares. Does it take any more action to make disciples than what most people pack into their week now? To make a disciple requires engagement with people and possible rejection. Many believe discipleship is a sophisticated process that requires an expertly trained staff. Culture teaches that a life dedicated to good disciple-making requires a complex infrastructure of administration, buildings, and programs. Yet most groups who have these infrastructures make very few disciples. One of our primary roles as a believer is to make disciples. Yet when asked to make a disciple, it confuses us why we are asked to produce such a person. Most assume church staff, pastors, and missionaries are making disciples. After all, the ministry is their career. Jesus is very clear by his example and commission; the work of the ministry is making disciples. We have outsourced the task and hope those hired into full-time ministry is making disciples. Yet, the Bible is clear; we are all full-time disciples and disciple-makers.

Most would be more comfortable if Jesus invited us to build big church buildings and mortgage each church to the hilt. Supply each church with large numbers of staff. Be creative with our marketing message, and people will come to our weekly services where we can share creative stories from the Bible. The fact is we are comfortable with that commission. It gives pastors, church staff, and missionaries job security and gives the believer a reprieve in the disciple-making process. It is straightforward, easy to outsource, and the believer can get back to living and enjoying life without the messy undertaking of making disciples. But those activities do not make disciples, nor can we hire people to take our place making disciples.

Instead, when we look at Jesus' life, we see a life laser-focused on the purpose He came to fulfill. He came to die for our sins and to make twelve diehard disciples who gave their lives to make more disciples. Nothing stopped Him from accomplishing His Father God's will. Not temptations of grandeur, or promised success from satan in the desert, not religious leaders, not even death by crucifixion could derail Jesus from making disciples of each of us. It was not an easy life and the last three years of public ministry were tough. Jesus' life touched those whose lives were messy and complicated. He cast out demons, healed the sick and dead, even brought hope to the prostitute. Most of the people's lives Jesus touched were the ordinary people who had messed up their lives, and He involved Himself in the grimy job of restoring them. Given enough time, that by itself was enough to get Him killed. Yet, Jesus opposed the religious leaders because they had made the temple and the religious leaders' role into a business. They had appointed themselves as CEOs, putting in place rules and mandates to keep the Jewish people under strict control. Then they paid themselves in excess, so they could live decadent and exorbitant lifestyles contrary to God's instruction. Even through these challenges, Jesus mentored twelve men who learned God's way and continued the mission and message even though most died very gruesome deaths because of it. Because of these twelve disciples, billions in the world know the message of the gospel.

No, this life is not what most believers aspire to, but instead, stay at least an arm's length away from. Most stay safely tucked inside a church infrastructure, preferring to outsource their disciple-making involvement to those paid to do it. It has become the accepted lifestyle of the believer.

It is GK Chesterton who said, "The simplification of anything is always sensational." [1]

By Jesus' definition, to disciple someone, is to teach them to be a follower of His, to baptize them in the name of the Father and of the Son and of the Holy Spirit, and teach them to obey everything that Jesus commanded us to do. The commission Jesus gave is simple. There are no substitutes, hiring people or creating structures that fill the individual responsibility Jesus gave us. We either obey Jesus, or we do not. If every one of the 2.17 billion Christians alive today makes a disciple of one other person, then each of those makes one more disciple, the entire world of 7.3 billion people will know Jesus. We will finish the job Jesus left us to make disciples of all nations. Even if one argued that Jesus only spent three years in public ministry, three years is enough given the number of Christians in the world to disciple every last person living.

However, research and trends show that Christians continue to fall short of that commission. Estimates state that there will only be 750 million new Christians by 2050. That is one new follower of Jesus for every three Christians alive today in the next 35 years.[2] In comparison, the same research shows that Islam will increase by over a billion during that same time, edging ever closer to surpassing the number of Christians in the world.

While writing this book, a high school acquaintance of mine wrote: "You said something to me years ago that has stuck with me. Be careful what you subscribe to." So true! I find myself saying that to others now. Be careful not to pick and choose parts of God's Word to believe while discounting the other parts' validity. But rather taking God at His Word and looking at His Word in whole, not in part. I am freaked out by people who pick and choose what parts of the Bible they want to believe and what parts they do not. That is a great reminder that the Bible is a complete book. No part is any more or less important than another, and that includes making disciples.

Jesus lived a life on purpose, and to be a disciple, we must as well. Jesus' life was simple, and so was His message. He had no church building, congregation, budget, or paid staff. Yet He trained twelve men to take God's simple message to the world. Even what the disciples did was simple, and the gospel reached my life. I ask myself, why do we have such a hard time reaching our tiny, individual communities with this message of life? To start, we do not follow the simple pattern of Jesus. Live life alongside a group of those who follow Jesus and teach others to do the same over an extended period of time by living life together.

The message is simple, yet we have made the delivery so complicated. We are the ones who have complicated the message. Imagine the amount of time, energy, and money Christians the world over have spent to make their delivery methods effective and appealing. We can instead spend that time, energy, and money to deliver a message God handcrafted Himself. The message of the gospel does not need a sophisticated delivery method to confirm its worth. We deliver the gospel by living alongside others, demonstrating how we follow and obey Jesus.

Telling the world about Jesus has become complicated in the last 2,000 years. The focus has moved from delivering the message to how and where to deliver the message. Over 3 billion people, half the world's population, have never heard of Jesus. We can never buy or rent enough space to fit half the world's population even once to tell them of Jesus. I am fortunate; I am gifted in finding solutions to difficult problems. However, for God's message to reach humanity, our hearts should be heavily weighted towards the message and not the method. Though I trust I can make any message, secular or spiritual, look great and delivery smooth, God's message does not need my beautification. God's message is beautiful and effective by itself. To the degree, someone needs an infrastructure of buildings, programs, and staff to tell the world of Jesus, is the degree that person lacks the faith in the simple power of the gospel. Buildings, programs, support infrastructures, and paid church staff are man's addition to the gospel message. Jesus did not need them, as He proved the message of the Kingdom works well in the streets delivered by those who are changed by it and where those living in the ordinary can experience it.

I know as a believer, I am the one called to deliver His message as much or as effectively as any professional pastor or paid church staff. My life can have as much impact on the world as any of the twelve disciples' lives did. This is where I am convinced our message gets muddied. Throughout my life as a believer, I have known my "calling" has been to take God's message to the world. Most believers agree they know they are to make disciples. Yet, we get lost in how we are to carry out such a monumental job. But, like the first disciples, we only need to drop our nets and follow Jesus, and do as He did. Yes, it is messy and requires us to stop outsourcing the work we ourselves need to do. Moreover, finding someone to disciple us is not an easy task. A disciple is not made in a church building's four walls, but instead through an apprenticeship. It is hands-on, life training in experiences one might meet during their life. Jesus poured His life, knowledge, eating habits, humility, and everything He was for three years into the disciples. After you live, sleep, eat, and spend every waking hour with a person for three years, you sound, think, and even act like them. The disciples had become much like Jesus by the end of their apprenticeship and were twelve replicas of Him. Their obedience and actions from that time on showed if they were true disciples or just believers. Remember, Judas Iscariot had received the same apprenticeship that the other eleven did. He knew Jesus was the Messiah, yet he failed the final exam of a disciple.

I am convinced the church's message has many Christians and non-Christians confused as there is more administration than a gospel message or ministry coming from our churches these days. Our churches' infrastructure is centered and focused on busyness surrounding delivering a 30-minute message on Sunday mornings. How big a budget, how many staff members, how cool a building, or even what burden of administration does it take to deliver God's timeless truth and disciple others so they can take that truth to the world? Attending a church regularly can be a great start if it stirs you up to love and good works and encourages you while encouraging others. Get your encouragement to obey Jesus from wherever you want. But as a believer, Jesus commissions each of us to make disciples, and that is an individual event. It requires us to be discipled so we can make disciples. That is not the

Sunday morning church meeting most of us are familiar with, but an adventure that will disrupt your life.

There is a quote from J.R.R. Tolkien that describes the reaction of many to the invitation to the adventure of making disciples:

> [Gandalf] "I'm looking for someone to share in an adventure that I am arranging, and it's very difficult to find anyone."
>
> "I should think so—in these parts. We're plain, quiet folk and have no use for adventures. Nasty, disturbing, uncomfortable things, they make you late for dinner. I can't think what anybody sees in them," said our Mr. Baggins, and stuck one thumb behind his braces, and blew out another even bigger smoke-ring.[3]

As we discovered earlier in this book, the desire for adventure is deep inside us. Men need adventure of unequaled magnitude, and women want to share in that adventure. Jesus invites each of us not just into an adventure, but an adventure to live with life-changing purpose for everyone involved. Instead, we have settled for standing on the sidelines, fulfilling but a shadow of our true purpose, so we will not be "late for dinner." If most people could have one true adventure in their life, they would be glad to trade a year of being late for dinner. I remind you of what I wrote in the introduction:

> I love America more than any other country in the world, and, exactly for this reason, I insist on the right to criticize her perpetually.[4]

In that same spirit, I love the Church. Not that I wish to criticize her, but encourage her through love, back to the true mission for which Jesus left for her. To encourage her to consider changing even her finest actions or dismiss them altogether, so she can again find her true direction and commission, fulfilling it and bringing hope to a dying world. I have many responsibilities, but none greater than this: to last, to encourage the Church to finish her work. I want to be the Church's greatest encouragement and defender of the faith.

As I look at the disciple-making task that Jesus left me, I must ask myself if I am single-minded in my focus. When compared to the task of making disciples, baptizing them, and teaching others that Jesus commanded me, have I gotten confused as to my message to those who don't know Jesus? When I look at the financial resources that God has entrusted to me, have I used those as a way to outsource the task Jesus gave me to do? Is my life focused inwardly on my kingdom or externally on God's kingdom?

I have to ask myself, should it take more than 2,000 years for the message and life of Jesus to spread throughout the world? Have we misdirected our focus and resources on a model of making disciples that is not efficient or effective in reaching those who can become disciples? Am I involved with the same model of making disciples that Jesus and His disciples began, or something much different?

For the twelve disciples of Jesus to become true disciples, they had to learn to make disciples, as do we. First, they had to agree to live three years with Jesus, allowing His character to take over theirs. Then they had to agree to reproduce others who carried that same DNA. That mandate was amongst Jesus' final directions to those He had discipled. It is easy to grasp that Jesus lived His life on purpose to do whatever it took to redeem our lives and make disciples. As a true disciple, we must take on the very nature and purpose of Jesus. Our needs must become as simple and focused as His.

Go therefore and make disciples of all nations, baptizing them in the name of the Father and of the Son and of the Holy Spirit, teaching them to observe all that I have commanded you... (Matthew 29:19-20).

Making disciples can be as simple as following the example of Jesus. The early Church knew they did not have to develop a complex or expensive strategy to make disciples. As we read in Acts 2:42-47, living life together with like-minded disciples, taking care of each other's needs, and showing each other love is our part; God will add the disciples. The author of Hebrews offers this simple suggestion:

Let us hold fast the confession of our hope without wavering, for he who promised is faithful. And let us consider how to stir up one another to love and good works, not neglecting to meet together, as is the habit of some, but encouraging one another, and all the more as you see the Day drawing near (Hebrews 10:23-25).

LIVE LIFE WITH LIKEMINDED BELIEVERS

I do not ask for these only, but also for those who will believe in me through their word, that they may all be one, just as you, Father, are in me, and I in you, that they also may be in us, so that the world may believe that you have sent me. The glory that you have given me I have given to them, that they may be one even as we are one, I in them and you in me, that they may become perfectly one, so that the world may know that you sent me and loved them even as you loved me (John 17:20-23).

This prayer that Jesus prays for us comes straight from His heart and gives us incredible insight into how He wants us to not only to act towards each other, but to be in unity with both Him and God and how He wants us to show the world His love. It is clear by Jesus' wording that His wish is:

- For the disciples and every believer to be as one with each other as He and Father God are one.
- For every believer to be one with the Trinity in perfect unity.
- For the world to grasp that God sent Jesus, and understand that God loves them as much as God loves His Son Jesus because of the believers' perfect unity with the Trinity and unity with each other.

This is not a simple prayer hoping for our unity with the Trinity and each other but is instead a directive and invitation from the creator of the universe on how to live in such a way that none doubt the authenticity or love of Jesus. This invitation is the same invitation that Jesus gave the original twelve disciples when He asked them to follow Him. The invitation Jesus extended to those first disciples was far more than a casual offer to be His friends and hang out with Him for three years. It was more than a full-time ministry occupation to preach the gospel and help the needy. As Jesus later pointed out to Nicodemus, it was a complete rebirth of themselves (John 3:3). Jesus' invitation required them to surrender their lives, their very being, hopes and dreams, and instead take on the person of Jesus. They began an apprenticeship in which they agreed to forget everything they were up to at that point and instead embrace and become everything that Jesus was; to become a duplicate copy of Him that continued reproducing itself. Then be in unity with each other in such a way that the world saw the love God had for Jesus, knowing that He sent Jesus, and He loves them equally. Through the believers' perfect unity with the Trinity and each other, the world saw God's love in action. There was no ministry budget or supporters for this new venture, just their faith that He was the Messiah promised by God, regardless of what the rest of the world said.

The twelve Jesus chose believed in the promised Messiah; they only needed to believe He was that Messiah. Raised in Jewish culture, they knew the prophecies: that the Messiah would come to deliver all the Jewish people. Being Jewish, they held to every Jewish religious practice. When they met Jesus, like others who met Jesus throughout His ministry, they faced the decision whether or not He was the Messiah, the Christ. For these twelve men on a very ordinary day, each of them faced a more difficult decision than believing He was the Messiah. Jesus asked them to give up their life and follow Him as an apprentice. Not simply to believe that He was the Christ, but to take action on that belief. This meant to leave everything they had ever known and take on His life, mission, and His very person, and to be one with Him for the rest of their lives. As Jesus' prayer suggests, "... that they may all be one, just as you, Father, are in me, and I in you, that they also may be in us, so that the world may believe that you have sent me" (John 17:21).

Likely that sounds very different from the invitation presented to you when invited to follow Jesus. Nevertheless, the invitation that Jesus offered to the twelve to become disciples and a perfect, duplicate copy of Himself is the only invitation Jesus ever offers. It is to be one with each other and in perfect unity with the Trinity so that the world sees Jesus as the Messiah. The love He has for us requires a person to be willing to be absorbed as a true disciple and transformed into a copy of Jesus.

Discipleship is entering into an apprenticeship, losing yourself to become an exact duplicate of Jesus and taking on His purpose, passion, and mission as though you are Jesus Himself. As a follow-through, we are then to make disciples of our own. The twelve that Jesus discipled agreed to the discipleship program of following Him. Once completed, He expected them to reproduce disciples of their own, mind you, not disciples of themselves, but a duplicate of Jesus, just as they were a duplicate of Him.

The original twelve knew when they accepted the invitation to be disciples it would take them years of non-stop living, eating, traveling, and learning under their teacher.

> The glory that you have given me I have given to them, that they may be one even as we are one, I in them and you in me, that they may become perfectly one, so that the world may know that you sent me and loved them even as you loved me (John 17:22-23).

It is important to note it is not by our own efforts that we become one with each other and Jesus. In the verses above, Jesus says it is because He gave us the glory that God gave Him. The Greek word for glory is *doxa*, which means majesty or belonging to God or Christ. It is because Jesus gave us a relationship and enabled us to belong back to the Father, we can be one with each other, and through that, the world will understand God loves them. We have looked at it over and over in this book, but the picture of unity Jesus prays for His disciples is active in the book of Acts:

> And they devoted themselves to the apostles' teaching and the fellowship, to the breaking of bread and the prayers. And awe came upon every soul, and many wonders and signs

were being done through the apostles. And all who believed were together and had all things in common. And they were selling their possessions and belongings and distributing the proceeds to all as any had need. And day by day, attending the temple together and breaking bread in their homes, they received their food with glad and generous hearts, praising God and having favor with all the people. And the Lord added to their number day by day those who were being saved (Acts 2:42-47).

Verse 44 is the key, "And all who believed were together and had all things in common." The disciples were one with Jesus, the Father, and each other. The glory Jesus says He gives is clearly shown in their oneness and attitude toward each other. The result was that, "... the Lord added to their number day by day those who were being saved" (Acts 2:42-47). I repeat this several times in the book because I believe it is evident that these disciples did not have to do anything else to convince people that God loved them other than allow the people to witness and experience their unity and generosity. These believers had become true disciples who, in turn, were making more disciples.

This form of disciple-making is highly contagious, and what Jesus' twelve disciples experienced in the three years He discipled them. Now they were discipling others the same way. They were a like-minded disciple-making machine.

How influential would Jesus have been to the disciples if He had only met with them for a couple of hours a week? How much would the disciples have learned to be like Jesus if He had spent the majority of His week apart from them? Through the influence of others mentoring, we learn how to do a task, speak a language, and order our lifestyle. Just as parents mentor their children through the life skills of being an adult, we need spiritual mentors to teach us how to be like Jesus. It is hard to picture the disciples learning to do miracles by Jesus giving them instructions, but not showing them it was possible. Instead, Jesus showed and mentored them in everything He wanted them to learn, even death on a cross. By living every day and every hour with Jesus for three years, they knew precisely how He acted in any situation. They could carry on making disciples just as if they were Jesus doing it. They had learned to be an exact copy of Jesus, even when faced with death. When the disciples were killed, it is reported from various sources and the New Testament that of the twelve disciples, five were crucified, two beheaded, two speared, and one clubbed to death for their belief in Jesus.

This is the same mentoring or apprenticeship the early Church continued. They learned to be like-minded by living life with others like Jesus and those they wanted to imitate. Even today, we live life learning to be like-minded with the people we're around; the question we need to ask ourselves is, are we around the right people with which to be like-minded? Are we learning to become true disciples because of the time we spend around true disciples, or to say it another way, those that are very much a copy of Jesus? What disciple have you lived life around that they can say they learned to be like Jesus from you?

Believing is only the first part of discipleship; even satan believes in Jesus. After all, satan is a fallen angel who was in Heaven with the Trinity, who tried to take over Heaven. Once we believe, our call is to take action and live as disciples, among like-minded people, while mentoring other disciples.

> Dear friends, do you think you'll get anywhere in this if you learn all the right words but never do anything? Does merely talking about faith indicate that a person really has it? For

instance, you come upon an old friend dressed in rags and half-starved and say, "Good morning, friend! Be clothed in Christ! Be filled with the Holy Spirit!" and walk off without providing so much as a coat or a cup of soup—where does that get you? Isn't it obvious that God-talk without God-acts is outrageous nonsense?

I can already hear one of you agreeing by saying, "Sounds good. You take care of the faith department; I'll handle the works department."

Not so fast. You can no more show me your works apart from your faith than I can show you my faith apart from my works. Faith and works, works and faith, fit together hand in glove.

Do I hear you professing to believe in the one and only God, but then observe you complacently sitting back as if you had done something wonderful? That's just great. Demons do that, but what good does it do them? Use your heads! Do you suppose for a minute that you can cut faith and works in two and not end up with a corpse on your hands (James 2:14-20 MSG)?

That is why this picture of the early Church is so hard for us to comprehend; this is not a group of people who believed in Jesus while attending a church meeting once or twice a week. They were not getting together once a week, then doing their own thing for the rest of the week. Believers not yet consumed by Jesus cannot live a life of discipleship we see in this early Church. Until we become convinced that our life, stuff, finances, and time are not our own, we cannot look or act as Jesus did. Nor does that mean that our stuff, finances, and time belong to those in the administration of a church building or the pastor who preaches in it. As with the early Church, God trusts us to use what He gives us to help those in need, not only ourselves, and not to outsource it. Many times we try to find happiness through using the resources God gives us to get stuff. It is through a lifestyle of taking care of others we become perfectly one with each other. Through caring and serving others, they experience the unity we have with the Trinity and each other.

Journal Pages

This is a great opportunity to journal what you are learning or the action steps you want to take based on this lesson. Doing so will keep all your notes and journaling in this book as future reference. Start by taking a few minutes to pray and ask Jesus to bring to light all you are learning and what transformational changes you can make in your life. If you are reading this in an electronic version, make a digital note and journal.

Journal Pages

THIRTEEN
JESUS' JOY

Joy is the word that comes to mind when I read about the early disciples in Acts 2. They had glad and generous hearts, and their infectious joy jumps off the page and makes my heart long to be part of them. Their joy is what attracted people to them and learn of the Christian life Jesus offers. Jesus wants us to have joy. But satan will oppose joy; he is out to steal it (John 10:10). Joy is a currency of the kingdom of God that, when we deplete it, we are in trouble. Jesus gives us abundance joy through a simple recipe:

> I am the true vine, and my Father is the vinedresser. Every branch in me that does not bear fruit he takes away, and every branch that does bear fruit he prunes, that it may bear more fruit. Already you are clean because of the word that I have spoken to you. Abide in me, and I in you. As the branch cannot bear fruit by itself, unless it abides in the vine, neither can you, unless you abide in me. I am the vine; you are the branches. Whoever abides in me and I in him, he it is

that bears much fruit, for apart from me you can do nothing. If anyone does not abide in me he is thrown away like a branch and withers; and the branches are gathered, thrown into the fire, and burned. If you abide in me, and my words abide in you, ask whatever you wish, and it will be done for you. By this my Father is glorified, that you bear much fruit and so prove to be my disciples. As the Father has loved me, so have I loved you. Abide in my love. If you keep my commandments, you will abide in my love, just as I have kept my Father's commandments and abide in his love. These things I have spoken to you, that my joy may be in you, and that your joy may be full (John 15:1-11).

Joy is the culmination of everything we ever wish to experience as humans. Imagine for a minute every positive human emotion a person can experience. Can you think of a better emotion you want to experience than joy? As I consider every emotion I wish to have, they all result in me experiencing joy. The pursuit of joy is what I spend my energy trying to get.

Consider the joy that Jesus has. Jesus has perfect joy created by God. John records this promise in Jesus' own words; that not only can we experience His joy in us, but joy abounding or filled to the top so that you will not need more. Though we may forget, man had the fullness of joy that satan stole from us in the Garden of Eden by tricking Eve to eat from the tree of the knowledge of good and evil. God knows joy and is the one who gives joy. God was in the beginning, and so was His joy. For David writes, "You make known to me the path of life; in your presence there is fullness of joy; at your right hand are pleasures forevermore" (Psalm 16:11).

In the Garden of Eden, man and woman were living a perfect life, and because God was present in the garden, they had fullness of joy. When man and woman sinned and God sent them out of the Garden of Eden, they became separated from both the Tree of Life and the presence of God where there is fullness of joy. It was at that moment that satan tried and has been continuing to steal joy from man, not only while here on this earth but for eternity.

When Jesus came to Earth, He came brought complete restoration to fallen man. Restoration is returning something back to its original condition. Besides, our relationship with God, nothing needed restoration more than the fullness of joy we lost in the Garden of Eden. Jesus came to restore our relationship with God and our ability to be again in God's presence, where there is fullness of joy. Through Jesus' sacrifice and our acceptance of Him as our Savior, He restores us to a relationship with God. That gives us the ability to experience overflowing joy, not only for today but for eternity.

I am overcome with awe that my joy is important to Jesus, important enough that He died on a cross to gain it back for me. I know that when I pray, "Your kingdom come, your will be done on earth as it is in heaven," God's will includes that I am full to overflowing with His joy. In John 15, Jesus promises us His overflowing joy that He restored by dying for us, "These things I have spoken to you, that my joy may be in you, and that your joy may be full" (John 15:11).

Right before this promise, Jesus unpacks the condition to gain this overflowing joy. Jesus' overflowing joy is the award of disciple production. If a disciple produces disciples God awards them by *pruning*, encouraging healthy growth and better production. The consequence of not making disciples is God cutting us from the vine, Jesus Himself. Jesus says:

> I am the true vine, and my Father is the vinedresser. Every branch in me that does not bear fruit he takes away, and

every branch that does bear fruit he prunes, that it may bear more fruit. Already you are clean because of the word that I have spoken to you (John 15:1-3).

Jesus lays the foundation by assuring us that He is the true vine and the life-giving source that makes it possible for each believer to make disciples, and His Father severs from Jesus useless believers who do not. The word *prunes* that Jesus uses in the Greek is *kathairō* meaning to cleanse from impurities. Through this promise, Jesus assures the believer who makes disciples that God the Father will enable them to make more disciples. It is clear, Jesus and His Father God expect us to disciple others as a vital part of being a believer.

This should not come as a surprise, as every living thing reproduces itself. Since creation, God put into motion a reproduction cycle for every living thing. He created the universe and then gave the command to be fruitful and multiply. It is no coincidence that Jesus uses a metaphor from creation itself to instruct the disciples in God's action of restoration. Elephants reproduce elephants; humans reproduce humans, and disciples reproduce disciples. If not, there is no need for connection to Jesus and His life-giving ability to make disciples, for they are useless.

GRAPE PRODUCTION

Grape vineyards and grape production is not a process of which many may be familiar. When we want a cluster of grapes or a bottle of wine, most of us buy those items at a fruit stand or store. The creator himself gave grape pruning to man as a tool to get good grape production. Cultivation of grapes is a vital part of getting the best yield from a vineyard. Archeological evidence confirms that using grapes in wine-making dates back to over six thousand years before Jesus. Grains, grapes, and olives were the main crops in Jesus' time. He uses the metaphor they know well of how grapes are grown and vine dressing that ensures good yield. A farmer cultivates soil to get the best yield from his fields. A vinedresser prunes, trains, and cultivates grapevines, so they produce the best yield of grapes.

Grape harvest and wine-making were big social events that the whole community got involved in. It took many workers to pick and crush the grapes. It was a time when the harvest reunited the village with work, wine, and celebration. For those involved in making disciples, this set of teachings reassures them of their success and rewards them for making more disciples.

The vinedresser's role is to create, with the grapevines, the perfect framework to pair just the right number of leaves to the sunlight they receive, so the vine can fully develop the grapes and not waste any resources. Pruning creates this balance, growing a hale and hardy vine void of unneeded vegetation, and ensures a bountiful harvest.

Production of a bountiful harvest is the sole focus of grape production, as Jesus instructs that the sole focus of being a disciple is producing an abundant harvest of other disciples. Jesus' direction to the disciples, including us, is to produce all the disciples possible. Verses 1-3 assures us that God will create the perfect framework to pair us the branches, with Jesus the vine, and ensure a bountiful harvest of disciples.

Producing disciples together with Jesus is the key. Jesus reemphasizes in the next verse that if we do not do it with Him, we cannot make disciples. "Abide in me, and I in you. As the branch cannot bear fruit by itself, unless it abides in the vine, neither can you, unless you abide in me" (John 15:4).

It is plain in these verses that the person who does not live and dwell in Jesus cannot make disciples. Jesus continues in verse 6, saying that His father cuts off and burns in the fire the person who does stay in Jesus because they are useless.

For those who remain in Jesus, there is an unbelievable promise of His joy if we keep His commandments and make disciples. This glorifies Father God and proves they are a true disciple. Jesus promises:

> By this my Father is glorified, that you bear much fruit and so prove to be my disciples. Abide in my love. If you keep my commandments, you will abide in my love, just as I have kept my Father's commandments and abide in his love. These things I have spoken to you, that my joy may be in you, and that your joy may be full (John 15:8-11).

In verse 11 is the promise of Jesus' overflowing joy in our lives. Joy is the very thing each of us wants in life. Joy is the human currency that makes it possible to endure our lives on this earth. Yet we spend every last ounce of our strength and resources to find joy any other way than what Jesus outlines here. Joy comes directly from Jesus by abiding in Him and His love, keeping His commandments, and making disciples.

The Ancient Path to Joy:

- Abide in Jesus, and He will abide in us.
- When we abide in Jesus, we will bear much fruit, which glorifies the Father.
- Keep His commandments, and we will abide in His love.
- Jesus awards us with His love, and our joy will be full.

Jesus authors this blueprint for discipleship while discipling the original twelve disciples. Jesus gives the twelve the commission to make disciples, baptize them, and teach them to do everything He commanded them. They take the blueprint and obey Jesus by becoming one with Him, each other and make disciples, as He showed them. By following Jesus' disciple-making pattern, they thrive at the task as seen in the phrase, "And the Lord added to their number day by day those who were being saved" (Acts 2:47). As a huge bonus to their disciple-making success, their joy is full to overflowing.

As these disciple-making disciples continued outward from Jerusalem, the model remains the same, and the number of disciples grew. For thirty years, Peter and Paul discipled groups throughout Asia and Europe before being martyred in Rome in about AD 66. John led the Christians in Ephesus for more than fifty years until he was exiled to an island to live alone for the rest of his life. Likewise, the other disciples continued outward from Jerusalem, making disciples in the exact manner as Jesus had made disciples of them. They continued making disciples in the model of Acts 2 until many of them were martyred. There is no sign that they changed the method. They had become a duplicate of Jesus, and, like Him, they were wildly successful in making duplicates of Him.

As the number of disciples grew, Jesus continued to give His disciples His overflowing joy as He promised. Their contagious joy and disciple-making began and continues to transform the world. Their joy was not dependent on their circumstances; instead, it came from Jesus because they had learned to abide in Him, His love, and joy. They kept His commandments and continued making disciples, proving they were His true disciples. Just as Jesus did, they focused their entire lives on making disciples. Father God pruned them to enable them to be better at the task, and Jesus gave them His overflowing joy.

Make no mistake, the disciples faced more than their share of trials, hardships, prison time, and horrible ways to die, but they endured those times with Jesus' joy. Nothing could sway them from their task, as referenced by the words Peter writes:

> Blessed be the God and Father of our Lord Jesus Christ! According to his great mercy, he has caused us to be born again to a living hope through the resurrection of Jesus Christ from the dead, to an inheritance that is imperishable, undefiled, and unfading, kept in heaven for you, who by God's power are being guarded through faith for a salvation ready to be revealed in the last time. In this you rejoice, though now for a little while, if necessary, you have been grieved by various trials, so that the tested genuineness of your faith—more precious than gold that perishes though it is tested by fire—may be found to result in praise and glory and honor at the revelation of Jesus Christ. Though you have not seen him, you love him. Though you do not now see him, you believe in him and rejoice with joy that is inexpressible and filled with glory, obtaining the outcome of your faith, the salvation of your souls (1 Peter 1:3-9).

Remember, it is no easy task for the person who mentors disciples, which might give us insight into why Jesus chose only twelve. But twelve was plenty to create over 6 million believers, ten percent of the Roman Empire in just four hundred years.[1] True discipleship creates like-minded, joyful followers who together act as one and change the world.

Joyful, like-minded people who are perfectly one is not a characteristic associated with humans. Joyful unity is unique, and exactly the picture we see in the young Church in Acts. I am astounded that both of these highly successful discipleship programs, Jesus discipling the twelve and the early Church, are largely ignored in making disciples today. Forgotten or even dismissed as an outdated method, they are replaced with large meeting spaces designed to instruct the masses with large sweeping movements. If Jesus could only be effective in discipling twelve, then how can a mere mortal man disciple fifty, one hundred, or even one thousand people in an intimate enough manner that people can be like them? Can a person successfully apprentice an entire room full of people while spending only a few hours a week with them? How did that person become more efficient and effective at discipling people than Jesus, the Son of God? How is an apprentice to become an exact duplicate of a person, taking on their purpose, passion, and mission without being immersed in that person's life?

    The college experience is a great example of this. When entering college, the first couple of years, you take a core curriculum designed to educate students in basic studies to be well-rounded in their educational knowledge. To complete these requirements can take several years of full-time study. You may schedule those classes, so you only attend class a few days a week. The classes are required general classes, and you need not decide on a major course of study until the third year. The third and fourth years of college are where the classes become more specialized depending on the major you choose, such as Engineering or Medicine.

    The professors who teach at a college have at least four years of college, most having a master or doctorate degree. Yet upon graduation, you receive a two or four-year degree, not a degree commensurate of the professors who taught you. Meaning just because professors teach you with doctorate degrees, you do not get a doctorate degree. It is a limited time in class each week with the professor, and the class sizes can be well over one hundred. A professor cannot effectively teach all their knowledge or duplicate themselves with that many people a few hours a week.

If you continue to a Medical Doctorate degree, the class sizes become smaller, more hands-on, and more specialized. Besides the four years of undergraduate school, you will spend another four years in medical school. In medical school, doctors are teaching soon-to-be doctors, and the time spent together increases. Upon completion of medical school is three to seven years of residency before a medical doctor is eligible for a license. Residency is much as it sounds; it is an internship with large amounts of intensive, hands-on training. During residency, students live, eat, and breathe the practice of medicine, elbow-to-elbow with other doctors, many times sleeping at the hospital without enough time to get home between shifts. The student is practicing alongside other doctors who are mentoring them to become a duplicate of them.

It is easy to see the contrast between the four-year degree and the residency in medicine where the soon-to-be doctor is immersed, neck-deep in nothing but the practice of medicine. It is also easy to see the similarity between the medical residency and discipleship. Of course, if you needed surgery, you want the person who has been elbow deep learning it for eighteen years, not someone who had been studying a book on it for a couple of hours a week.

Likewise, it is easy to see the contrast in learning about Jesus a couple of hours a week or being immersed in a community that spends copious amounts of time living life together. The second group of believers live near each other, study together, eat together, share everything, and take care of each other's needs. Which one of these groups will outsiders see

Jesus in easier? Both groups believe and know Jesus, yet the latter can make disciples who then make disciples because the lifestyle is modeled out before them. Because the second group lives life with other like-minded disciples, they abide in Jesus' word and in His love, make disciples, which gains them Jesus' overflowing joy.

You can see it takes a much more involved and immersed lifestyle to make true disciples than attracting an auditorium of people a few times a week. If Jesus Himself had to invest every minute of His life for three years into the twelve disciples, why do we as mere mortals try to make disciples in a few hours a week? In fairness, there has been a lack of those willing to assume responsibility to truly disciple people. When there is no real solution, a substitute will always fill the void.

I want to give equal time to the big-box church. I am curious about the effectiveness of bringing people to church and the church making disciples. We set out looking for the model of generous and joyful disciples like in Acts. We find a meeting place with great worship and good teaching we can attend several times a month. For most, this is an acceptable substitution because we are not looking for something to fill up our lives; we are looking for something that adds meaning. Yet, it is not prone to making diehard, all-in disciples. Is it correct to say we want to attend a church but not become the Church?

A common belief in believers today is that the bigger the church building, the more people we can reach for Jesus. Research shows that to make disciples by building church buildings and employing staff can be a very expensive alternative to disciples making disciples by living life together and inviting people into that community. For example, today's fastest-growing type of church format is the megachurch, characterized by averaging at least two thousand people in attendance every week. The megachurch segment is growing at 8%

per year. Yet only 6% of people who attend a megachurch the first time have never before been to church. If that growth is new believers, that equates to a 6% growth rate or 120 for every 2,000 people that attend those churches. Megachurches are attracting people, but mostly people who already know Jesus. Yet the combined budgets for the top ten megachurches are 611 million dollars. A combined attendance of 1,122,500 of the top 10 megachurches means it took over 611 million dollars to reach 67,350 who did not attend church before.[2] The real question is, how many of the 1,122,500 people that are attending a megachurch are being discipled or making a disciple themselves?

Whether it is a megachurch or traditional church, research shows a common denominator:

> One of the most significant gaps uncovered by the research was the fact that most people cannot recall gaining any new spiritual insights the last time they attended church. Asked to recall their last church visit, three out of five church attenders (61%) said they could not remember a significant or important new insight or understanding related to faith. Even among those who attended church in the last week, half admitted they could not recall a significant insight they had gained.[3]

That is a stark contrast to the early Church living life together, immersed in the apostles' teaching and fellowship, eating and praying together, and taking care of each other's needs. The early Church was the Church, whether eating meals, gathering in their homes or at the synagogue spreading the gospel of the Kingdom

Living in life in relationship with like-minded believers influenced others to join the early Church believers. To live as disciples and make disciples was a daily endeavor and passion for these people. They had true relationships with each other. As Barna Group explains:

> "Again and again, we see people identifying relationships as the most important aspect of their sense of place and belonging," says Roxanne Stone, a vice president at Barna Group and the lead analyst on the study. "As with previous data, adults are clearly prioritizing their relational connections over work, entertainment, church. People move for family, they choose to live within close proximity of friends and family, and it's their friendships they love most about their cities."[4]

We assume we are looking for a church to attend; that is what we are trained to want. With nothing better, we will accept a less engaging substitute. Attending a church in contrast to living as a Church is a safer alternative without the risk of exposing ourselves to a twenty-four-hour a day relationship with others. Limited involvement allows us to control how much we engage with others, yet achieve satisfaction. We are at least doing something. But our heart yearns to find a group of like-minded disciples engaged with each other to live and share life with. As we see in the early Church example, it is worth the risk of being in relationships with others if they are also committed. The challenge is finding people who are more committed to living as true disciples than living life as believers only. The best people to start this disciple- making lifestyle is with is your family. An easy way to understand this idea is by looking at a family with children. Our family is as close as any four people could live and function together twenty-four hours a day. We are mentoring our children to adulthood. We stay engaged with them twenty-four hours a day unless we outsource someone to watch them. If we outsource someone to watch or mentor our children, then they become like that caregiver to the degree they spend time around them. Someone other than my wife and me that spends an hour or two per week around our children has a minor impact on who our children will become. But someone who spends the better part of each day mentoring our children has the potential to equal our influence, good or bad. Like Jesus and His disciples, the early Church spent a large majority of their time around each other. This enabled them to be like-minded, and whole-life focused on becoming and making disciples.

Our family loves and lives in the outdoors as much as we can. The beach and pool are favorites of our family. Most activities with smaller children require preparation and engagement. Neither my wife nor myself enjoy putting sunscreen on the kids. Neither of us wants to be the one who missed a spot that gets sunburned. Each of us tries to ditch the responsibility and disappear until the other has applied the sunscreen. Either my wife or I have to engage the process, or we cannot leave the house. Parents with small children learning to swim do not get the luxury of lying in the sun while the children flail helplessly in the water. Instead, responsible parents get in the water to play with them and even teach them to swim. It would not end well to let them play in water over their head without engagement. To expect a child to learn to swim on their own would end with them drowning.

Raising children well requires engagement and constant involvement. The time we spend with our children is proportionate to how much like us they will become. Sure, they have their own personalities and preferences; but as involved parents, our children will learn moral and life skills from our modeling life before them daily. My wife and I stay engaged with our children because our goal is for our children to be very like-minded to us as adults. When we had children, we were choosing to be their life mentors. We agreed to teach them the skills and moral training they need to live well and duplicate our efforts with their children. We have children to love and enjoy them. Because we love them, we mentor them to be successful adults. What child or disciple can respect and honor a parent or mentor who is not engaged in their lives with transparent and life-giving interaction?

Let me give you an example of this from the business world. Throughout my life, I have started and run businesses. My interest in business differs from many other business people. Business plays a different role for me than making lots of money. First, most of the businesses I started focus on helping others realize their dreams. I enjoy helping businesses achieve the bigger picture, creating real value, and expecting opportunity from that value. Second, my work must never take time away from my family, or my relationship with Jesus. I gravitate to work that affords me more time both of them. I would rather the business suffer from my lack of attention than my family. Our family is not focused on having financial success or having a bunch of possessions. Instead, our focus is on building a quality family and helping others. If possible, we will devote the rest of our lives to helping those who cannot help themselves. Several years ago, I came across a couple of sentences explaining what I have been doing for years both in my companies and encouraging others to do in theirs. Why I do something has always been more important than what I am doing or how successful I am as an individual.

> The master in the art of living makes little distinction between his work and his play, his labor and his leisure, his mind and his body, his education and his recreation, his love and his religion. He hardly knows which is which. He

simply pursues his vision of excellence at whatever he does, leaving others to decide whether he is working or playing. To him he is always doing both. [5]

The goal is not to do business with everybody who needs what you have. The goal is to do business with people who believe what you believe. People do not buy what you do; they buy why you do it. Start with why instead of what when you are rethinking your marketing strategy, which can change how people think about your company and why they should do business with you.

People do business with companies that believe what they believe because of our strong tendency to want to align our actions with our self-perception.[6]

Instead of selling a product or service, communicate why you do what you do. By communicating your passion, you will attract others who agree with what you believe and want to align themselves with your actions. These are loyal and ongoing customers who buy because of why you do, what you do. No one does business with everyone. When you focus on the *why*, you build a loyal base of like-minded customers, you can count on.

Sinek was not the first person to focus on the *why*. The concept of focusing on the *why* instead of the *what* is the message of Jesus and the early Church disciples. The reason that Jesus came to earth was:

For God so loved the world, that He gave His only Son, that whoever believes in Him should not perish but have eternal life. For God did not send His Son into the world to condemn the world, but in order that the world might be saved through Him (John 3:16 & 17).

God loved the world in such a way He sent His Son Jesus to die for our sins so that if we believe in Him, we will have eternal life. God's love for us was the reason *why* Jesus came to earth, healed the sick, made the blind see, discipled the twelve, and died on a cross. His actions then supported and communicated why He came to earth and showed His love in everything He did. He mentored like-minded disciples and gave them the duty of showing the world God's love through their actions of making more disciples. A few examples are:

> You are the light of the world. A city set on a hill cannot be hidden. Nor do people light a lamp and put it under a basket, but on a stand, and it gives light to all in the house. In the same way, let your light shine before others, so that they may see your good works and give glory to your Father who is in heaven (Mathew 5:14-16).
>
> By this [abide in me, and my words abide in you] my Father is glorified, that you bear much fruit and so prove to be my disciples (John 15:8 emphasis mine).
>
> The glory that you have given me I have given to them, that they may be one even as we are one, I in them and you in me, that they may become perfectly one, so that the world may know that you sent me and loved them even as you loved me (John 17:22 & 23).

With that in mind, we see the message of *why* modeled one step further in the early disciples and the early Church. Because God so loved the world, He sent Jesus to mentor them in the life skills they needed to be true disciples. Through their actions of love and generosity for each other and "any who had need," the early Church communicated the message that, "God so loved the world, that He gave His only Son, that whoever believes in Him should not perish but have eternal life" (John 3:16). Their daily actions supported the reason they were disciples. The love they showed, even to the point of selling their possessions to help any who had need, attracted others who they mentored to be like-minded and taught them to show the world that God loves them through their actions. Most people never experience a love that genuine, even from their close family members.

God's love attracted the early disciples and the early Church we read of in Acts. That love motivated them to show that love to others through their actions. They stayed immersed in each other's lives, steeped in the disciples' teachings, and they were full of joy by abiding in Christ. Something else magnificent and unexpected was happening to each of these disciples. They had an adventure worth living. Yes, a dangerous, treacherous, yet romantic adventure! An ancient battle of which none could rival, and their part was significant in its outcome. It is what every man longs for deep within: a battle to fight of epic proportions, and an adventure worth living that takes one's whole life to take in. Through their lifestyle and daily actions, the disciples engaged in rescuing the beauty, the most prized beauty in all of history. The Bible refers to Jesus' disciples as His beloved and His bride. It is the sum of the disciples' lives throughout history that has impacted and changed the world.

Jesus' invitation to those original twelve disciples is the same invitation offered to us: to be a disciple in every sense of the word. We, too, have an invitation into this battle and adventure. This is the story that each of us long for where we live out life with a group of like-minded people and change the world together. Consider the movies *Braveheart, Lord of the Rings,* and *The Lion the Witch and the Wardrobe,* which each depict a group of ordinary people who together embark on an extraordinary adventure to change the world. Again, the first step is to find that group of like-minded people. Like Jesus, it might be easier to disciple that group of people from scratch. If you have a family, start there and let God add to your number when He sees you are ready. if you cannot be in unity with your immediate family, you cannot do it with anyone else. Changing the world is a by-product of a small group of people who takes care of the surrounding need. Jesus was onto something when He chose that ragtag group of twelve. A small group of people are many times more effective than a large group could ever organize. There is a reason when something needs to get done humans do much better in strike teams and specialized, smaller units. Reflect on what the small groups Disney, Skunk Works Labs, Apple Computer, or Black Mountain College accomplished. Each of those groups made their unique mark on the world, empowered by a small group of people who knew they could change the world, and they did. Is it any wonder that God Himself, the creator of man, knew that humans work best in small groups and discipled a group of twelve? It is through those twelve disciples and those in the early Church that I know Jesus. It is through those I disciple, whether that is one or more, that will make the way for others to know Jesus. But I must be willing to let down my guard, be transparent and enter life with others in such a manner that they can see my life modeled out before them, as I do my best to model Jesus' life. Only through that example and mentoring can I empower and make disciples myself.

Allowing ourselves to get trapped behind barriers of fear, insecurity, the convenience of church programs, and even the void of not being discipled ourselves has caused isolation instead of engaging in close, meaningful and life-giving relationships with like-minded people. This has kept us from discovering and experiencing a rich, joyful, and fulfilling life like the early Church.

Instead, the goal is to accept Jesus' command to make disciples and stop relying on others, whether in the church or mission field. It is the battle, adventure, and rescue for which every disciple is made and the ancient path to Jesus' joy we long for.

RESCUE THE BEAUTY

There is beauty all around us. That can be the special person in your life, your children, a sunset, or even the beggar on the street. Though bittersweet, there is beauty in your child's first day at school. There is beauty in laughter, family time, or catching a fish. There is a reason we take pictures— because we want to capture that moment when we saw beauty. Beauty is all around us, and we can look at it all our life. When we experience that beauty, it can truly transform us and bring us delight. But to rescue the beauty, we must engage her foes and fight for her.

We can see a sunset through a window, and it is beautiful. But when you walk outside, it is another experience to see the entire sky lit up and the rays of the sunset kiss your skin with its golden light. You can watch a beautiful woman across the room and marvel at her beauty. But when you talk to her, hear her voice, feel her touch, even live life with her as your wife, there is much deeper joy than simply looking at her. You can watch children play and laugh, and it will make you smile. But enter that child's world by playing and interacting with them and love will captivate you, and for at least the moment, you can escape the grasp of responsibility and become a child again yourself. Yes, there is beauty in that beggar on the street. A human being whose heart beats has feelings like you and me and hopes they can be whole again. They are someone's beauty, mother, child, or friend who lost their way and are begging for someone to help them find their path again. We must engage them to see that they are more than a dirty pile of rags discarded by the world. They are God's beauty He created and sent His Son Jesus to rescue.

While the condo we live in is simple, it overlooks a small cove of water. For eleven years, the beautiful view from our place has given us incredible joy. The sunrise each morning can take your breath away; birds that visit can be awe-inspiring; light dancing on the waves is magic. The view is a moving picture that never grows old. Though I never want to trade it, deep inside is a sorrow that we will need to move one day and the view will no longer be part of our life.

For my birthday a few days ago, I was given a Jon boat, something I have wanted since I was a teenage boy. Launching that boat in the water behind our place goes beyond what words can explain. After eleven years of looking and enjoying that beauty, I entered into and engaged that beauty. I became that beauty and a part of that picture. No longer wonder how it felts to be on that water; I know how amazing it is. Leaving the bank and sheltered cove for the first time was exhilarating. My limited view of observing that beauty from one direction expanded to three hundred and sixty degrees. Trusty fishing pole in hand with the sound of the fishing line whizzing off the reel, and I was fully engaged in the experience. While years of watching the scenery behind our place gave me delight, being immersed and engaged in it was thrilling. When I brought home fish to eat, the experience became life-giving to our family.

This is the rescue, joy, and excitement the early Church experienced living together, engaged with like-minded people.

For as long as any could remember, they had experienced the temple from the outside looking in; but now they had the means to engage the beauty of living with the Trinity and each other in unity. As Jesus promised, those that followed Him as disciples had become fishers of men. By living in unity with each other, their lives and actions became life-giving to others.

Journal Pages

This is a great opportunity to journal what you are learning or the action steps you want to take based on this lesson. Doing so will keep all your notes and journaling in this book as future reference. Start by taking a few minutes to pray and ask Jesus to bring to light all you are learning and what transformational changes you can make in your life. If you are reading this in an electronic version, make a digital note and journal.

Journal Pages

FOURTEEN
ENOUGH IS ENOUGH

In the absence of a real solution, a substitution will always fill the void.
Scott Michael Ringo

When I was in high school at summer camp, I met a guy named Rich Mullins. Little did I know he had just written some of the most influential music that would shape the Christian pop music sound. That week he was a humble music guy at my tiny summer camp. He was an ordinary guy that showed he cared more about each of us at that obscure camp than most ever would. I would later find out that Rich embraced a life of obscurity to care for and love the world's nobodies. Sound like a familiar theme?

Rich never let fortune and fame get to him. Instead, when he made money in the music business, he instructed his accountant to pay him an average man's salary and rest to his church. After becoming famous, he found his true joy moving to a Navajo reservation, teaching music to the children who lived there. Rich never knew the impact he had on the Christian music industry, dying in a car accident in 1997. In 1998, one year after his death, the Gospel Music Association awarded him the Artist of the Year and the next year GMA's Song of the Year and Songwriter of the Year.

That week at camp, Rich took the time to stop and engage me and influence my life with so many others' lives he touched. I do not remember the exact conversations, but they focused on me and what Jesus was doing in my life. Rich touched many people's lives because he believed his life was not his own, but he should spend it on others. In one of his concerts two months to the day before his death, he said:

> So go out and live real good and I promise you'll get beat up real bad. But, in a little while after you're dead, you'll be rotted away anyway. It's not gonna matter if you have a few scars. It will matter if you didn't live. [1]

One of my favorite songs that Rich wrote is *The Color Green*. As he explains the backstory to the song, he captures the essence of what Jesus has been saying to me through this book.

> It started out with this guy who was yelling at this kid for running in the "House of God," because he was running through a church building, and I thought that was funny because I think the Bible was fairly explicit that earth is God's footstool and heaven is His throne - "What kind of house can you build for Me?" I think it's pretty explicit that the Body of Christ is also the House of God - that we are the temple, that it has to do with people, not with buildings. I've often thought, you know, people worry with the Catholic thing of revering Mary, and I've often thought, "Well, maybe it's not that they revere Mary too much. Maybe it's that all of us revere each other too little." And so

I was thinking about this old man going to a meeting and realizing on his way that he'd already been in a meeting. It's just he hadn't been in a corporate meeting. He'd already been surrounded by the presence of God. And he looks out, and of course he's a farmer, and has an appreciation for seasons - has an appreciation for that kind of thing. And all of a sudden he realizes that God invented green. [2]

When God created Earth and us, He did so to have a deep relationship with people. When Jesus came to Earth, it was to restore our relationship to God that we severed in the Garden of Eden. Jesus spent his time here on Earth in deep relationship with His twelve and others while restoring their relationship to His Father. It has taken me my lifetime to figure out that all creation is God's house, not a church building, and I belong out in it, making God known to those who do not know Him. The words to the song "The Color Green" give amazing imagery of this:

> *And the moon is a sliver of silver*
> *Like a shaving that fell on the floor of a*
>   *Carpenter's shop*
> *And every house must have it's builder*
> *And I awoke in the house of God*
> *Where the windows are mornings and evenings*
> *Stretched from the sun*
> *Across the sky north to south*
> *And on my way to early meeting*
> *I heard the rocks crying out*
> *I heard the rocks crying out*
> *Be praised for all Your tenderness by these works*
>   *of Your hands*

*Suns that rise and rains that fall to bless and
  bring to life Your land
Look down upon this winter wheat and be glad
  that You have made
Blue for the sky and the color green that fills
  these fields with praise
And the wrens have returned and they're nesting
In the hollow of that oak where his heart once
  had been
And he lifts up his arms in a blessing for being
  born again
And the streams are all swollen with winter
Winter unfrozen and free to run away now
And I'm amazed when I remember
Who it was that built this house
And with the rocks I cry out* [3]

    Could there have been any better feeling for Jesus than to be in and amongst His creation as He was restoring our relationship to the Trinity? As Jesus walked along the roads of Galilee, He was walking through the creation He made alongside His Father and The Holy Spirit thousands of years prior. As the sun came up, and the rains came down, He celebrated His handiwork as He had done when He rested on the seventh day of creation. As in Rich's song, the time has come for us to awaken and realize we are the temple of God. "... you yourselves like living stones are being built up as a spiritual house, to be a holy priesthood, to offer spiritual sacrifices acceptable to God through Jesus Christ" (1 Peter 2:5). Jesus showed us that by engaging others and making disciples, they could meet and experience Jesus. Discipleship is our charge in God's kingdom. God did not create us to sit comfortably inside church buildings or create perfect little lives for ourselves.

In the words of Rich, "It has to do with people, not with buildings." It is time to say enough is enough with the money we spend on ourselves, on church buildings, on outsourcing ministry and realize as Rich did that:

> Christianity is not about building an absolutely secure little niche in the world where you can live with your perfect little wife and your perfect little children in your beautiful little house where you have no gays or minority groups anywhere near you. Christianity is about learning to love like Jesus loved and Jesus loved the poor and Jesus loved the broken. [4]

BECOME THE SOLUTION

Learning to love as Jesus requires us to become the solution, not just be involved in the solution. Though at first, they might sound the same, they are worlds apart. To be a part of the solution still gives one the ability to stand outside and look in. Becoming the solution is only achieved by placing oneself in the middle of the problem with no way out but discovering the solution. The minimalist movement I mentioned earlier is a start in the right direction. Reducing our possessions, our footprint, and not outsourcing our tasks helps us realize how our lives and resources can impact others. Helping others instead of consuming more and being more comfortable ourselves. It allows us more freedom to become the solution to many of the world's challenges today. It gives us the privilege of becoming part of the greatest mission in the history of the world, to live as Jesus did.

When I look at Jesus, His disciples, the early Church, and the heroes and heroines of the Bible, at the point they are mentioned in the Bible, they are smack dab in the middle of a challenge and willing to be the solution. Each faced challenges, and instead of looking to someone else, they walked right into the middle of it and allowed God to transform them into the solution. At a point in each of their lives, they stopped waiting for someone else to stand up and become the solution. They let go of their lives, let go of what they believed life should offer, and let God define the amazing plans He had for their life. They became a story worth adding to the Bible, not through their own merits but by allowing God to use their lives.

> Pursue the greater things in life. Some of the greatest treasures in this world are hidden from sight: love, humility, empathy, selflessness, generosity. Among these higher pursuits, there is no measurement. Desire them above everything else and remove yourself entirely from society's definition of success.[5]

While those might seem to be high pursuits, they all stem from what Jesus says should be our greatest life pursuit. When the religious leaders asked Jesus which was the greatest commandment, He answered:

> And he said to him, "You shall love the Lord your God with all your heart and with all your soul and with all your mind. This is the great and first commandment. And a second is like it: You shall love your neighbor as yourself. On these two commandments depend all the Law and the Prophets (Matthew 22:37-40).

To love and live like Jesus and His disciples did, we must love God with everything we are. If we do not love God to that degree, it will be tough to let go of our doctrine, stuff, time, fame, fortune, or idea of what life offers and instead love others. It is difficult to find a person, Christian or not, that is desperate enough to engage Jesus or anyone else to the degree that it makes a positive change in their life. Each of us is in desperate shape, but most are not willing to risk our pride, comfort, or privacy to ask for or give help to the degree to which it will impact.

Orphanages are a perfect example. Thousands of organizations and hundreds of thousands of people have devoted time, energy, and finances to improve orphanages and even make them self-sustaining. The real problem is that orphanages exist in the first place. In the absence of a real solution, a substitution will always fill the void. The terminal solution to the problem is two-fold. First, address the reasons parents abandon their children and help reduce the number of children that become orphans. Second, abolish the maddening acceptance that orphanages are a reasonable substitution in which children live. Could we, as a society, afford the parents the resources, support, or help they need to keep their children? We could invite the family into a community of people who take an interest in and care for each other, giving the parents the help they need to raise their child. There are irresponsible people in the world for which no resources will help them make the right choice. The ultimate solution is for each of us to jump into the middle of the problem and become the solution by providing current and potential orphans a place in our own homes, ending the need for orphanages altogether. It would be easier if we lived in community sharing resources with the assurance that no one needs. This is undoubtedly a radical, inconvenient, and obtrusive consideration, but one that shows the love of Jesus. It should be a natural instinct to care for homeless and parentless children. But that requires hands-on engagement and becoming the solution. Instead, we are more comfortable devising solutions that keep us one step away from the real problem and deploy outsourced, artificial stop-gaps. This allows up to sleep at night without getting too messy.

Through the same community focus, we can abolish nursing homes and take care of widows, providing them a proper home and care. Jesus' brother James urges us to have the discipline or strict practice to care and provide for those that cannot help themselves.

> Anyone who sets himself up as "religious" by talking a good game is self-deceived. This kind of religion is hot air and only hot air. Real religion, the kind that passes muster before God the Father, is this: Reach out to the homeless and loveless in their plight, and guard against corruption from the godless world (James 1:26-27 MSG).

The Bible is void of stories that end with the hero having a successful career and retiring well. Instead, many of the stories of wealthy people in the Bible are there as examples of how wealth destroys lives, judgment, and happiness. How is it that so many people settle for a life consumed by their career and piling up retirement for a few easy years at the end of their life? Will they find contentment once retired?

Most of us go through life pretending to have everything together while on the inside, we are scared to death and half the person we pretend to be. Since disobeying God in the garden, most wear the fig leaf with pride. Many never associate themselves with the failure in the garden, yet that sin has traveled with each of us throughout human existence. It is rare to find anyone elated with who they are and who they have become. Most of us are not happy with how our lives are turning out. Not knowing what else to do, we continue to convince ourselves and everyone around us we are bullet-proof. In his book Wild at Heart, John Eldridge refers to it as the poser. Morgan Snyder, a colleague of John's, restates it perfectly:

> We develop this construct, this fig leaf. Every one of us develops this elaborate construction of a person that we use to interact with the world, a person that ultimately at first helps us to avoid pain. That's the first object of a poser, to help us avoid pain. And then it's to answer those deep questions of our heart, these questions of identity and validation.[6]

You may be different, but this describes me. Churches work for most people because, if they are honest, they are not looking for the day-to-day work of discipleship. Attending a church gives us enough participation and social acceptance that we are doing our part. We get to take credit for the product of our belief system— filling our church buildings, without getting our hands dirty or sacrificing our time. Religion is a collection of beliefs and systems but does not require any action. It is not what you believe, but instead, what actions you take based on your beliefs that count. Attendance at a church is not equal to being the Church. Belief in Jesus is not the same as following Jesus. The Hospitaller in the movie Kingdom of Heaven said it well:

> I put no stock in religion. By the word religion I have seen the lunacy of fanatics of every denomination be called the will of God. I've seen too much religion in the eyes of too many murderers. Holiness is in right action, and courage on behalf of those who cannot defend themselves. And goodness - what God desires - is here [points to Balian's head] and here [points to Balian's heart] and by what you decide to do every day you will be a good man... or not.[7]

It is not just a good person God desires, but obedience. Obedience like Jesus, requires us to embed ourselves in the streets, alleys, and gutters of life. It is through our decision to do the right thing every day that brings holiness. Following Jesus requires action, not only belief. Faith without action ends up being nothing but a religious belief system. Throughout the Old and New Testament God calls His followers to holiness through action (Leviticus 19 & 20).

Dallas Willard says this:

> Holiness and devotion must now come forth from the closet and the chapel to possess the street and the factory, the schoolroom and boardroom, the scientific laboratory and the governmental office. Instead of a select few making religion their life, with the power and inspiration realized through the spiritual disciplines, all of us can make our daily lives and vocations be "the house of God and the gate of heaven." It can – and must – happen. And it will happen. The living Christ will make it happen through us as we dwell with him in life appropriately disciplined in the spiritual Kingdom of God.[8]

God quit dwelling in a box, the ark of the covenant, thousands of years ago. With the death and resurrection of Jesus, God moved from a box behind the curtain to giving us a one-on-one relationship with Him again. Yet we continue to build physical and virtual box-like structures and flock to them to find God. As Dallas Willard states:

> So the greatest issue facing the world today, with all its heartbreaking needs, is whether those who, by profession or culture, are identified as "Christians" will become disciples – students, apprentices, practitioners – of Jesus Christ,

steadily learning from him how to live the life of the Kingdom of the Heavens into every corner of human existence. Will they break out of the churches to be his church— to be, without human force or violence, his mighty force for good on earth, drawing the churches after them toward the eternal purposes of God? And, on its own scale, there is no greater issue facing the individual human being, Christian or not.[9]

How many "Christians" know what that means and stay engaged in making disciples? My guess is disciples are not taught to make disciples. Discipleship is outsourced to pastors, church administration, and missionaries. It is difficult for people to be discipled in a large auditorium with a person teaching for twenty or even sixty minutes once a week. Discipleship is not singing on the church worship team, acting on the drama team, serving on the church board, regular tithing, or going on a mission trip once a year. We can do each of these activities and fish every Saturday, but none of them are discipleship. Ask yourself if you are active in making a disciple?

Discipleship is the last and great responsibility Jesus gave each of us who are disciples. To make disciples, we first have to learn to be a disciple. By Jesus' definition, to disciple someone is to teach them to be a follower of His, to baptize them in the name of the Father and of the Son and of the Holy Spirit, and teach them to do all that Jesus commanded us. That happens daily, spending time with those you are discipling. Jesus did it by spending every day with twelve men for three years on 3,125 miles of dirt roads. If it took Jesus that length of time to impart who He was to His disciples in person, it will take us at least that long to teach others to do all that Jesus commanded us. In fact, most of us need someone who will first disciple us to know how to disciple others. If the King of Kings discipled His group on dirt roads using life lessons, it too requires us to get dirty in real-life situations to disciple others or learn to be a disciple. If Jesus, who had all the resources of Heaven at His disposal, did not need a multi-million-dollar budget to make twelve disciples who discipled thousands of others, then neither do we.

It takes each of us to admit that enough is enough, lay down our excessive, narcissistic, and obsessive lives, to become disciples of Jesus. Then we must finish the job of making disciples of the rest of the world. This takes pure grit, obedience, and action. It is not scheduled, it does not take large sound systems, and it does not pay for sports cars. There is no worldly glamour associated with the cost of discipleship. The death of Christ on the cross is the grim reminder of what it costs. No, the glitz and glamour perceived by many in ministry is not a life laid down for discipleship. The beauty of discipleship is seeing the load of despair lifted from a person as they realize for the first time Jesus loves them.

> For those who feel their lives are a grave disappointment to God, it requires enormous trust and reckless, raging confidence to accept that the love of Jesus Christ knows no shadow of alteration or change. When Jesus said, "Come to me, all you who labor and are heavy burdened," He assumed we would grow weary, discouraged, and disheartened along the way. These words are a touching testimony to the genuine humanness of Jesus. He had no romantic notion of the cost of discipleship. He knew that following Him was as unsentimental as duty, as demanding as love.[10]

If glitz, glamour, fame, multi-million-dollar church buildings, big church salaries, and leading worship from a stage is your idea of discipleship, you need to reread the Bible. Likewise, living in a far-off country, discarding your clothes to spend the rest of your life naked with people whose language or culture you do not understand might not be what God has for you either.

It is time to say enough is enough and step away from the excuses we have and instead make the changes necessary to show the world Jesus. Just like the small band of disciples Jesus empowered to make disciples of the world, Jesus also instructs us:

> Go therefore and make disciples of all nations, baptizing them in the name of the Father and of the Son and of the Holy Spirit, teaching them to observe all that I have commanded you. And behold, I am with you always, to the end of the age (Matthew 28:19 & 20).

Jesus did not commission His group of disciples to make Christians or even to start churches. Brands of religion and church department stores are not part of what Jesus taught His disciples. Instead, He sent them out to make more followers and apprentices. Jesus sent them out to make exact duplicates of Him.

It is not expensive, nor is it difficult to disciple people. If engaged in discipleship, most people can be on the same career path, live in the same neighborhoods, even have the same friends as they do now. The difference is to be active in discipling others, which looks very different from what many church leaders have taught us.

The very last thing Jesus tells his group of disciples in person before ascending into heaven is, "But you will receive power when the Holy Spirit has come upon you, and you will be my witnesses in Jerusalem and in all Judea and Samaria, and to the end of the earth" (Acts 1:8).

Jerusalem was the last place that Jesus had led them for Passover, and after His resurrection, where He continued, "appearing to them during forty days and speaking of the kingdom of God" (Acts 1:3). As instructed by Jesus, after His ascension, the disciples made disciples in Jerusalem. Jesus' followers did not build a church building but instead continued to live together and invite others to share life with them. This allowed them to apprentice others just as Jesus had done with them. For many, as the disciples did, we need to get started. Do not be hard on yourself but instead reorient yourself to a disciple-making lifestyle Jesus asked us to live. The key is to move:

> "... forward from the closet and the chapel to possess the street and the factory, the schoolroom and boardroom, the scientific laboratory and the governmental office. Instead of a select few making religion their life, with the power and inspiration realized through the spiritual disciplines, each of us can make our daily lives and vocations to be 'the house of God and the gate of heaven.'"[11]

TRANSFORM YOUR COMMUNITY THEN MOVE OUTWARD

Thank goodness for grace. A few years ago, fourteen to be exact, I read a book titled *What's So Amazing About Grace* by Phillip Yancey that changed my life. A few years ago, a friend gave me a study *The Grace Walk Experience* by Steve McVey. Through that book and study, I understood that none of us will get it right all the time. I learned that the lines blur most of the time between what we should do and what we actually do.

But few books affected me as hard as Brennan Manning's *The Ragamuffin Gospel: Good News for the Bedraggled, Beat-Up, and Burnt Out*. A year ago, when I believe God asked me to write this book to myself, I needed that Good News for the bedraggled me. Though I did not realize how deep I had dug the hole I was in, I knew I felt beaten up and burnt out. I had read *The Ragamuffin Gospel* fifteen years before, but since then, much has happened in my life. Brennan discipled Rich Mullins, who I mentioned earlier. That says a lot about how those who disciple others can make a lasting positive impact, teaching a disciple all that Jesus commanded. As I am drawing to a close and listening to God about what else I should write to myself in this book, He directed me to the Ragamuffin Gospel. I took last week to lay in a hammock on my deck and let my soul soak in the audio version.

Nobody has it all figured out, not even those who will criticize this book and me. Life is messy, understanding is challenging, but thank God for His grace. Brennan's words say it best:

> When I get honest, I admit I am a bundle of paradoxes. I believe and I doubt, I hope and get discouraged, I love and I hate, I feel bad about feeling good, I feel guilty about not feeling guilty. I am trusting and suspicious. I am honest and I still play games. Aristotle said I am a rational animal; I say I am an angel with an incredible capacity for beer.
>
> To live by grace means to acknowledge my whole life story, the light side and the dark. In admitting my shadow side, I learn who I am and what God's grace means. As Thomas Merton put it, "A saint is not someone who is good but who experiences the goodness of God."
>
> The gospel of grace nullifies our adulation of televangelists, charismatic superstars, and local church heroes. It obliterates the two-class citizenship theory operative in many American churches. For grace proclaims the awesome truth that all is gift. All that is good is ours not by right but by the sheer bounty of a gracious God. While there is much we may have earned—our degree and our

salary, our home and garden, a Miller Lite and a good night's sleep—all this is possible only because we have been given so much: life itself, eyes to see and hands to touch, a mind to shape ideas, and a heart to beat with love. We have been given God in our souls and Christ in our flesh. We have the power to believe where others deny, to hope where others despair, to love where others hurt. This and so much more is sheer gift; it is not reward for our faithfulness, our generous disposition, or our heroic life of prayer. Even our fidelity is a gift, "If we but turn to God," said St. Augustine, "that itself is a gift of God."

My deepest awareness of myself is that I am deeply loved by Jesus Christ and I have done nothing to earn it or deserve it.[12]

MEET THE NEEDS OF WHOEVER YOU ARE LED TO

Because of the first disciples' obedience to be witnesses, I too know the love of Christ. I too must be a witness so that others may know. Like the early Church, I need to engage life by being a witness of Jesus with what I have and who I am. That means learning to experience Jesus' joy with others and share in the joy right where I am.

You do that by taking care of the need right in front of you. If you do not see a need, then open your eyes wider. I believe many of us go through life with our eyes wide shut or at least squinting. We believe if we ignore the the surrounding need, it will go away and not mess up our perfect life. I have helped thousands worldwide with information, vision, fundraising strategies, etc., as they set up their nonprofits. There is no lack of places and people where I can be a witness of Jesus and make disciples. It does not take going very far or having any special skills. I need not look any farther than my own street, or in my daughter's case, no farther than a seven-year old's skill set to show people Jesus. Remember, Jesus preached the gospel of the Kingdom of God, and in that kingdom, everyone is restored. Let me give you an example.

This week, it was a chance meeting with a homeless guy named Luke as I headed out on a cold Saturday to check out hunting gear. It took wrestling with myself to stop when I saw a rough cut guy standing next to a building with a large pack next to him. He took me up on my offer to buy him breakfast around the corner. I enjoy helping those on the street that need help, but it is hard to discern those who need from the professional panhandler. Luke came from a rough childhood, dropped out of school, and spent several years following the Grateful Dead when he was fourteen. He never stopped traveling, and at forty-two years old, in his own words it is all he knows how to do. He has no skills, no home, and like most on the streets, turns daily to alcohol to cope with the curveball life has thrown him. Yet his life is worth no less than anyone else's. In many ways, Luke is better off than most: he has no debt, he has no stress, he is on permanent vacation, and he can go wherever he wants to at a moment's notice.

We both enjoyed the hour together, and when I asked if I could help him with some items he might need, he gave me a shortlist. Luke wanted a cheap tent to get out of the cold and a Coleman stove to heat it in the late evenings and early mornings.

Several days ago, as I was getting the stove together for Luke, my daughter asked if she could make a card for him. Her skill set at seven years old is making beautiful handmade cards. For our family, delivering a few homemade meals, a heater, a tent, and a homemade card was the only skill set we needed to meet Luke's needs right here in our *Jerusalem*.

It had been several months since I hung out with someone

living on the street. My path this Saturday led me to someone my family and I could show love to by helping them out. It did not require us to go more than two miles out of our way. Luke asked if I would have breakfast with him on Sunday mornings. Having breakfast with Luke once a week gives us a chance to connect and work our lives together. He wants a friend, not directions to a church he can attend. Luke's life is not perfect, and it does not fit in with how our culture says life works out. That is evident by the constant stares Luke and I receive Sunday mornings while eating breakfast together at a fast-food restaurant. Many of those stares are from people dressed up and headed to church. Our family is grateful for the opportunity to help Luke and apprentice him in life and God's love for as long as he is around. Just as important is the opportunity it presents for me to disciple and apprentice my children in making disciples. Like the twelve disciples with Jesus, my children are learning right beside me as we help Luke.

Remember Hebrews 10:23:

> Let us hold fast the confession of our hope without wavering, for he who promised is faithful. And let us consider how to stir up one another to love and good works, not neglecting to meet together, as is the habit of some, but encouraging one another, and all the more as you see the Day drawing near (Hebrews 10:23-25).

The Bible requires me to live out its truths in a manner that encourages others to be more loving and helpful people. Our family encouraged each other to be loving and helpful to Luke. I do not have to worry about the outcome. I need only to keep looking for opportunities to love and be helpful to others. Through my actions, I can show Luke his worth of who he is not based on his circumstances.

For most of us, the simple focus of loving and helping others will jumpstart a life of making disciples. For many, the quest to make disciples is very different from what they have experienced attending church. Like my example with Luke, making disciples for most will not be running around naked in a foreign country, but simply loving and helping others you meet each day.

The challenge is getting past the reasoning this book makes that discipleship does not occur in most churches. There is nothing wrong with churches as long as we do not use them to outsource our individual responsibility to make disciples. Once past that offense, as Dallas urges, we can:

> "... break out of the churches to be his church— to be, without human force or violence, his mighty force for good on earth, drawing the churches after them toward the eternal purposes of God"[13]

Discipleship can happen in a church building, but it is very tough. Yet, they are great places for evangelism. Remember, Jesus and early disciples were meeting at the temple and synagogue to share the gospel of the Kingdom. For those that face the larger challenge of it being illegal to make disciples, it might help to think about the words of Paul in Acts as he was heading into Jerusalem and to face the hardest part of his missionary life:

> And now I am going to Jerusalem, drawn there irresistibly by the Holy Spirit, not knowing what awaits me, except that the Holy Spirit has told me in city after city that jail and suffering is ahead. But my life is worth nothing unless I use it for doing the task assigned me by the Lord Jesus-the work

of telling others the Good News about God's wonderful kindness and love (Acts 20:22-24).

I am irresistibly drawn to the work of telling others about Jesus' wonderful kindness and love; there is nothing else I would rather do. No matter what lies ahead on my quest, His peace and love are strong in my life, as I hope they are in yours.

David, the shepherd boy waiting to take his role as king while King Saul is hunting him, penned this encouragement:

> Point me down your highway, God; direct me along a well-lighted street; show my enemies whose side you're on. Don't throw me to the dogs, those liars who are out to get me, filling the air with their threats. I'm sure now I'll see God's goodness in the exuberant earth. Stay with God! Take heart. Don't quit. I'll say it again: Stay with God (Psalm 27:11-14 MSG).

My three-year-old son makes an "Om nom nom" sound as he eats food he loves. As I write, he is finishing up lunch to which I added a few strawberries for dessert. My children love fruit. As my son bites into each strawberry, "Om nom nom" accompanies each chew as his senses are overtaken with enjoyment. Just hearing him makes you long for the experience.

Likewise, when I read the words, "Stay with God!" they resound in my spirit and beckon me with courage. Maybe that is why David repeats them a second time. David's resolve is unwavering, and He stands with confidence that God will deliver him.

I knew nothing of discipleship as I grew up going to church. I struggled through life as a Christian to the point of despair. I knew there had to be more to living a Christian life than just living life on my terms and attending church on Sunday and

Wednesday. Not even a stint doing missions work satisfied my thirst for real meaning nor gave me a lifelong answer for disciple-making. I was fortunate to meet a group who were making disciples by working with refugees in Europe through Life Transformation Groups. A Life Transformation Group is a grass-roots tool developed by Neil Cole that in his words: "... empowers the common Christian to do the uncommon work of reproductive discipling." Within days of arriving in Europe, I was making a disciple myself. Not only was I making a disciple named Jakim, but I was doing so in an easy way he could duplicate. It took no specialized training, no multi-million-dollar church budget, or even an ordained pastor. I did not spend hours telling Jakim about Jesus or giving him advice on how to get his life together. In contrast, I cultivated a friendship by hanging out each week playing volleyball, eating lunch together or seeing the sights in Rome where we both lived. Then each week on our own we read twenty-five chapters of the Bible. Each week when we got together we would ask each other questions we had agreed upon concerning our character. Our conversations would often turn to what we were both reading that week in the Bible. Through simply reading the Bible and modeling what I knew about Jesus a few hours a day with Jakim for six weeks, he accepted Jesus as his Savior. That day is still a major highlight of my life. Life Transformation Groups are a great starting place to follow Jesus' command and learn to disciple others. The groups work and it only takes a desire to follow Jesus and spend time with those who do not know Him. Jesus never gave us a more important role in history than to make disciples. As Jesus showed us, making disciples takes nothing more than loving people and showing them His love.

SCOTT MICHAEL RINGO

WE NEVER GET TO PERFECT UNTIL HEAVEN

Other than a few times in high school, I have spent my life fishing off the shore. There is not any size boat or amount of gear that ensures a fisherman a guaranteed catch. Sure, many spend tens of thousands on boats, comfortable seats, expensive rods and reels, even the bait they use. Until this last summer, I have never had a boat. Like I mentioned before, my family bought me a Jon boat for a birthday present. A friend gave me a trolling motor to power it. I have always wanted a small boat to fish in; nothing expensive, just enough. The first time I took it out with my Dad was a blast, but we caught no more fish than I catch off the shore. A boat did not make me a better fisherman or put me onto more fish.

It is the same in many situations in life. I know a guy who owned a Lamborghini and, except for the few times he opened it up for a few miles on the interstate, his car did not get him to the grocery store any faster than my twenty-year-old car. His car did not make him a more important person, and it was too loud inside to hear each other speak. Bigger houses, bigger salaries, more expensive diamonds, better vacations, or larger church size does not mean your life is any more valuable than anyone else's. It does not mean you are a better provider for your family, better at business, more loved, or more needed than anyone else. Bigger churches do not, necessarily, make more disciples than smaller ones or individuals. We can keep adding gadgets and buying bigger and better boats, but you do not catch fish until you go fishing and practice. Fishermen are made on the water. It is only when you go fishing you learn what catches fish. That is how fishing works, you might get lucky a few times, but fishermen know there is no substitute for time on the water, which equals experience.

Discipleship works the same way with the added benefit

that Jesus has a vested interest. I am not saying that Jesus does not care about fishing, but I believe He has more interest in us making disciples. Even the original disciples Jesus found struggling to catch fish did well at making disciples.

You might get the idea by reading this book that I have spent a lot of time fishing. Until the last couple of years, there were 20 years I did not fish once. You might also think I have spent much of my life discipling others; I have not. I grew up attending church, but that did not equal making disciples. Except for my time in Europe and Youth With A Mission, I have not spent as much time making disciples as I could have. After writing this book to myself, I plan on doing both a lot more in the coming months and years.

If that sounds like you the good news is in reading this book; we have spent time learning truths from the Bible. Together we can get busy on the life project Jesus left us. If you are new to both Jesus and discipleship, then you are fortunate on both accounts. It should be simple to dive in and share with others what helped you meet Jesus.

THERE IS NEVER A BETTER TIME TO START TO BE A DISCIPLE

Unfortunately, unlike the small group that Jesus discipled, we do not get to hang out with Him for three years in person. However, Jesus and the Holy Spirit are as close to us as our own skin. Besides, we have the recorded accounts of the disciples as Jesus discipled them. It is important never to let the Bible become optional, for through it, the disciples left us their witnesses of Jesus (Acts 1:8).

We are learning how to become sons and daughters. Jesus and the Holy Spirit are growing us up just as they did the disciples. Whether we like it or not, we are Jesus' witnesses to the world; He is waiting for us to show them how to be like Him.

> His [God's] children are not his real, true sons and daughters until they think like him, feel with him, judge as he judges, are at home with him, and without fear before him because he and they mean the same thing, love the same things, seek the same ends. For this are we created; it is the one end of our being, and includes all other ends whatever.[14]

FORGIVING ENEMIES

Forgiveness is difficult when someone wrongs us. We do not want that person to escape justice for their crime against us. Whatever the offense or violent crime, we want to hold the offender responsible.

While writing the latter part of this book, my family and I were the target of an ongoing, daily offense. It was one of the tougher challenges of my life and could have turned dangerous. The law did not protect us; we were an island. The offense cost us our freedom, our comfort, our legal rights, and threatened our enjoyment of life. My prayer life increased, and I prayed every verse and phrase I knew against my enemy. I clung to Jesus' intervention and His rescue. Yet days turned into months while this person continued their wrong against us. We knew that satan was trying to use this person to steal our joy. Set against my enemy, I knew that the battle is won through fervent prayer.

What I did not know in the beginning was Jesus needed the fervent prayer to change me more than He needed it to change my oppressor. Jesus had my ear, and through this, He wanted to teach me a kingdom truth I could learn no other way than being right in the middle of it, as He taught His disciples.

While praying one day, Jesus led me to this verse:

You have heard that it was said, 'You shall love your neighbor and hate your enemy.' But I say to you, Love your enemies and pray for those who persecute you, so that you may be sons of your Father who is in heaven. For he makes his sun rise on the evil and on the good, and sends rain on the just and on the unjust (Matthew 5:43-45).

Then several others:

But I say to you who hear, Love your enemies, do good to those who hate you, bless those who curse you, pray for those who abuse you. To one who strikes you on the cheek, offer the other also, and from one who takes away your cloak do not withhold your tunic either. Give to everyone who begs from you, and from one who takes away your goods do not demand them back. And as you wish that others would do to you, do so to them (Luke 6:27-31).

A new commandment I give to you, that you love one another: just as I have loved you, you also are to love one another. By this all people will know that you are my disciples, if you have love for one another (John 13:34-35).

Beloved, never avenge yourselves, but leave it to the wrath of God, for it is written, "Vengeance is mine, I will repay, says the Lord." To the contrary, "if your enemy is hungry, feed him; if he is thirsty, give him something to drink; for by so doing you will heap burning coals on his head." Do not be overcome by evil, but overcome evil with good (Romans 12:19-21).

Even Jesus forgave those that crucified Him on a cross. "And Jesus said, 'Father, forgive them, for they know not what they do.' And they cast lots to divide his garments" (Luke 23:34).

Jesus has more interest in my heart than serving justice. Jesus overcame satan and in an instant He can change everything about my circumstance. Heaven can open and the armies of the living God can wipe out every wrong coming against me. On the day Jesus returns for His bride, He will wipe out every injustice, every tear, and every sorrow. In the meantime, Jesus wants my heart. Jesus wants all of me: my spirit, soul, body, heart, mind and will.

I have never understood what it means to love my enemies and reading those verses is hard when a battle rages around you. Nothing happens in Heaven or earth that God does not allow. You might remember the story of Job where God allowed satan to test him. Terrible injustices happened to Job: his children were killed, his wife and friends abandoned him, his health deteriorated ending with Job sitting naked and alone. God never abandoned Job and restored to Job twice as much as he lost. Dallas Willard says:

> With this magnificent God positioned among us, Jesus brings the assurance that our universe is a perfectly safe place for us to be. The very heart of His message, as well as of His personality and actions, is found in such well-known words as these from Matthew 6:25 "Therefore I tell you, do not be anxious about your life, what you will eat or what you will drink, nor about your body, what you put on. Is not life more than food, and the body more than clothing?"[15]

Through these verses Jesus urged me to forgive and pray for the person and his wife that continued to wrong us. It was hard to forgive and pray for them. It was unthinkable that I would love them. I obeyed Jesus and forgave them. As I saw these people daily, I prayed peace and blessings on them. I assumed by their actions they did not believe in Jesus. Jesus impressed on me I might be the only person who had ever prayed for this couple. This might be the only time they had interaction with a son of God. The offenses continued, but by daily forgiving and praying for them, my heart changed. I cared for their future and prosperity. By forgiving and praying, I began to love them, not their actions. I am a son of the King of Heaven and my actions must show that, no matter my circumstances. Even in the midst of satan's attacks, I can be like Jesus. Jesus will use whatever means necessary to mature me and mold me into being Him.

Jesus allowed this person to get my attention in such a way I could not ignore to learn to forgive, pray for and love my enemies. This person, not aware they were desperate for my prayers, found the only way to get me to pray for them. There is no other way to learn to love an enemy other than to have an enemy to love. At the final editing of this book, 5 months later, the attacks continue. I continue to forgive and pray. Others have come alongside to help. Regardless of the outcome, I have grown and learned a priceless lesson in the kingdom of God. By obeying Jesus, He has taken another person's behavior and used it to make me a better disciple. We live in a world at war. Everyone faces challenges, some are better at posing than others and making it look like life is easier than it is.

> James, the Lord's brother, began his message to the church by instructing us to be "supremely happy" when troubles come upon us: "When all kinds of trials and temptations crowd into your lives, my brothers, don't resent them as intruders, but welcome them as friends! Realize that they come to test your faith and to produce in you the quality of endurance." (James 1:2-3 Phillips). When endurance or

patience has been given full play in the details of day-to-day existence, it will make us "perfect and complete, lacking in nothing" (v. 4)[16]

It hits me like a ton of bricks as I realize how much I need to grow to become a true son, a true disciple. Even so, I am the son of the High King, the Creator of the cosmos. I realize the time has come for me to say enough is enough.

Journal Pages

This is a great opportunity to journal what you are learning or the action steps you want to take based on this lesson. Doing so will keep all your notes and journaling in this book as future reference. Start by taking a few minutes to pray and ask Jesus to bring to light all you are learning and what transformational changes you can make in your life. If you are reading this in an electronic version, make a digital note and journal.

Journal Pages

FIFTEEN
INTERACTIVE RELATIONSHIP

> *"Twenty years from now you will be more disappointed by the things you didn't do than by the ones you did do. So throw off the bowlines. Sail away from the safe harbor. Catch the trade winds in your sails. Explore. Dream. Discover"* — H. Jackson Brown, Jr.[1]

It is sad that the closer and more mature we get in our relationships, the less we say to one another. Guys might struggle with this more than women. The six months after I met my wife until we married, we stayed up late each night, barely getting enough sleep. We spent our time asking each other deep questions about our life dreams. Too tired to continue, we traveled to our respective homes. We get into those conversations less, and when we do, the kids interrupt our conversation before it goes deep. Now that we have children, I find no time to get into a conversation with any weight. Interruptions by children thousands of times has resigned me to saying and sharing less of my thoughts and feelings with my wife. It is easy to see how two people living in the same house might become strangers in the short eighteen years it takes to raise them. Once the kids leave for college and the constant interaction through them is gone, the two people might find themselves living with a stranger. In seven years of raising children, keeping the family close and your spouse closer is vital.

The more my children grow up, the less I need to cater to them every minute. I have the extreme privilege of working from home, so I have been with my two children 24-7 for the last seven years. At a young age, they must be on your radar every minute they are awake. As babies, I talked to them nonstop unless they were sleeping, or I was on the phone. When they were babies, talking to them as they were taking their bottles were special times. I felt such a connection to them as they looked into my eyes with yearning as if those eyes might speak. It is not probable they understood what I said, and my voice resembled the adult voice on Charlie Brown movies. I was so thankful when both kids could feed themselves. A year later, I miss those forced intentional times of connection when I fed them.

Now my kids are more self-sufficient, and even my three-year-old plays well on his own. Glad for the relief; I get busy. Yes, life must happen, and my attention can focus elsewhere. It is easy to let the children get swept off into a day when I interact with them only when they need something. Even the kids playing on their own, there are still only twenty-four hours in a day. I can sense the space between us widening. Even now, as I write the final words in this book, my son has deposited three matchbox cars on my desk. It is his subtle way of saying, "Daddy, play with me." He is my constant reminder of the danger of getting caught outside the magical world of play. As each day draws to an end, guilt washes over me for not taking a few extra minutes to interact with my children. Our family life is simple compared to most we know. We cook and eat every meal at home together with a well-thought-out menu. We shun extra-curricular activities to focus instead on each other. Our work rarely falls outside nine-to-five or into the weekends. We do not have a yard to keep. Still, spending every weeknight and our weekends together, our relationships can slip. It takes a focused and conscious effort to make sure we are looking at one another in the eyes often and engaging in daily quality time with each other. It is much too easy to live in our own worlds, even with two small children. I am thankful I recognize the error, and I am quick to make the adjustments to keep our family close.

The emptiness I described above visits me many nights when heading to bed, and my thoughts turn to God. I can get through most days without incident, without engaging God. There are other days I only speak to God on the minimum levels needed for Him to guide me through varied activities and decisions. Too many days, I have spent the day talking *at* God instead of with Him. I am embarrassed that days go by I have not talked with God so that I know Him any better. There are days I have not talked with God as a son who focuses on His will or is growing to be more like Him. I complete those days with His guidance, but not with an engaged, meaningful, and relationship-building purpose. Heading to bed, I feel like an orphan, not because my Father abandoned me. Instead, He was waiting patiently for me to acknowledge Him.

You will remember I started this book to hear what God wanted to say to me through it. I've learned there are no short-cuts. Each day of writing required many more days of listening and living what God wanted me to write. Some may write a book in a matter of weeks or months. God wanted to interact with me and illustrate what He was saying. There are a hundred or more stories that God put in place while writing this book to show me and tell me what to write. God wanted to write and create this book with me, and through this process, for us to be closer as a Father and son. This is God's book for me and a journey we have taken together for the last year and five months.

The worst mistake mankind can make is to have at our immediate and constant availability, the High King and creator of the cosmos, and not engage Him. A perfect example happened to a scientist named Loren, while on the beach one morning:

> I did not realize at first what it was I looked upon. As my wandering attention centered, I saw nothing but two small projecting ears lit by the morning sun. Beneath them, a small neat face looked shyly up at me. The ears moved at every sound, drank in the gull's cry and the far horn of a ship. They crinkled, I began to realize, only with curiosity; they had not learned to fear. The creature was very young. He was alone in a dread universe. I crept on my knees around the prow and crouched beside him. It was a small fox pup from a den under the timbers who looked up at me. God knows what had become of his brothers and sisters. His parent must not have been home from hunting.
>
> He innocently selected what I think was a chicken bone from an untidy pile of splintered rubbish and shook it at me invitingly. There was a vast playful humor in his face. "If there was only one fox in the world and I could kill him, I would do." The words of a British poacher in a pub rasped in my ears. I dropped even further and painfully away from human stature. It has been said repeatedly that one can never, try as he will, get around to the front of the universe. Man is destined to see only its far side, to realize nature only in retreat.

Yet here was the thing in the midst of the bones, the wide-eyed, innocent fox inviting me to play, with the innate courtesy of its two forepaws placed appealingly together, along with a mock shake of the head. The universe was swinging in some fantastic fashion to present its face, and the face was so small that the universe itself was laughing.

It was not a time for human dignity. It was a time only for careful observance of amenities written behind the stars. Gravely I arranged my forepaws while the puppy whimpered with ill-concealed excitement. I drew the breath of a fox's den into my nostrils. On impulse, I picked up clumsily a whiter bone and shook it in teeth that had not entirely forgotten their original purpose. Round and round we tumbled for one ecstatic moment. We were the innocent thing in the midst of bones, born in the egg, born in the den, born in the dark cave with the stone and ax close to hand, born at last in human guise to grow coldly remote in the room with the rifle rack upon the wall.

But I had seen my miracle. I had see[n] the universe as it begins for all things. It was, in reality, a child's universe, a tiny and laughing universe. I rolled the pup on his back and ran, literally ran for the nearest ridge. The sun was half out of the sea, and the world was swinging back to normal. The adult foxes would already be trotting home.

I think I can safely put it down that I had been allowed my miracle. It was very small, as is the way of great things.

Loren continues:

For the moment, I had held the universe at bay by the simple expedient of sitting on my haunches before a fox den and tumbling about with a chicken bone. It was the gravest, most meaningful act I shall ever accomplish...[2]

My eyes tear up as I read this story. Because Loren, an evolutionist, missed the universe's very creator, God, sitting right in front of Him. His statement was true that for the moment, he had held the universe at bay sitting in front of a fox den. God used that fox as if to say: "Loren, Loren, I am God your creator; I am real."

As I read Loren and the fox's story, I cringe to think of the many times God has tried to engage me in a tumble that I ignored. Yet as holy and divine as God is, He is a Father to me as I am a father to my children. He loves to tumble and play with me as much as I do with my children and not for just five minutes as with the fox but every second I will give Him. It is important to remember back to the start of creation. He made me to have a relationship with Him; there is no other reason. He created us and loves us. God made us to play, frolic, adventure, rest, and even write a book together. My eyes well with tears as I remember the amazing time I have had writing with the God of the Bible, with my Father. It has been as grand an adventure as Bilbo Baggins had when he accepted the invitation to join Gandalf and the dwarfs on a journey seeking the treasure of Erebor in The Hobbit. God's ultimate goal in making us is to be in unity with us just as Jesus and God are in unity (John 17:20-23).

In the third chapter of Genesis, man sinned, and that separated us from God. The rest of the Bible is God's love story of everything He did to rescue us so we can be with Him again. God wrote that love story by *tumbling* with hundreds of thousands of people's lives for thousands of years and compiling those encounters into the Bible. Yet, He still has the time and patience to write the pages in this book with me. The crazy part is He is my creator and the creator of the cosmos. He enjoyed writing this with me as much as I did. This time with Him is part of my design as much as Mary's was to give birth and raise Jesus, the Son of Man.

It is in a one-on-one relationship where Jesus, as He did with His disciples, wants to spend His time with me. It is the same relationship He wants with everyone. Through Him spending time with me, I learn to be His witness. This is how I learn who He is and how to be more like Him.

Like it or not, through this book, you might see Jesus differently than you did before. The gospel of the kingdom may sound different from how you heard it before. For the first time, you may have seen your life in a different role than you knew it before. Many times reading God's word on the subject looks different than what we are told. Like I have discovered by writing this book, you may see how simple the gospel is and how key our role is. Granted, the Bible is a big book compiled of hundreds of stories made from thousands of people's lives. Yet, the stories and people have one thing in common. The stories in the Bible are people learning to become and make disciples. Some follow their own desires, reject God and His plan for their salvation, and their role in making disciples. Some encounter God in the Old Testament. Others meet Jesus in the New Testament. But some people hear the gospel and accept God's plan for salvation, and embrace their role of disciple-making.

> But you will receive power when the Holy Spirit has come upon you, and you will be my witnesses in Jerusalem and in all Judea and Samaria, and to the end of the earth (Acts 1:8).

Only at the end of our lives here on earth can we look back and see the total for what our life counted. For the first time, we can see clearly what we did with the life God gave us. Often, we get too self-absorbed or lured into the skeptic role too long that we lose the ability to see past our own hand. If we are fortunate along the way, the inconvenience of an event, book, or friend helps us see our self-preoccupation and invites us back to the adventure.

There is an invitation for us to join with the creator of the cosmos and live the grandest, wild, incredible, and satisfying adventure we could ever imagine. An adventure to disciple and save all mankind from destruction. You might have seen that storyline played out in a movie or two? That faint tug each of us has as though something or someone is beckoning us to play a part in saving the world is not déjà vu or coincidence. Remember, Neo, the main character in the movie The Matrix? At the beginning of his adventure he has a choice between the blue pill and the red pill.

> This is your last chance. After this, there is no turning back. You take the blue pill—the story ends, you wake up in your bed and believe whatever you want to believe. You take the red pill—you stay in Wonderland, and I show you how deep the rabbit hole goes. Remember: all I'm offering is the truth. Nothing more.[3]

That is an invitation straight out the pages of the Bible and an invitation Jesus made to His small, intimate group of disciples when He said, "Follow Me." Had they said, "No," they might have never known Jesus at all, but rejected Him as the Messiah as did many Jews. They would have never had the amazing journey they did as walking with the Messiah and creator of the universe for three years as disciples. Each of the disciples would have had a much smaller story since it was their time with Jesus that made them into great men. Jesus offers us the same invitation. Say no, and you can have a safe, ordinary life void of making disciples. The story ends, you wake up in your bed and believe whatever you want to believe.

In J.R.R. Tolkien's The Hobbit, the parallel of Jesus' invitation to the disciples sounds like this. One morning Bilbo Baggins, who has lived his entire life sheltered in the safety of his shire, meets a visitor named Gandalf the Grey. Gandalf has assembled a group of dwarves for an adventure for which he needs one more member. Though intrigued at first, Bilbo is resolute. He wants no part of an adventure. Bilbo says:

> We are plain quiet folk and have no use for adventures. Nasty disturbing uncomfortable things! Make you late for dinner! I can't think what anybody sees in them.[4]

The next day through a fun and spirited dinner party, which is a complete surprise to Bilbo in his own house, he is again invited on the expedition of epic proportions. The dwarves who have now eaten everything in his house invite him on an adventure outside the squire's boundary to reclaim the treasure stolen by the dragon Smaug. Though Gandalf and the dwarves piqued Bilbo's interest again, and despite Gandalf's pep talk, he refuses the invitation and does not sign the contract to be a part of the excursion. The next morning when Bilbo wakes up, Gandalf and the dwarves have left him behind in the quiet of his home. He knows his fear has caused him to miss out on the biggest adventure of his life.

You might know the feeling to be invited to something too big to say yes, yet, too big to say no. The minute you say yes, you might faint, and the second you say no, you might regret it for the rest of your life.

This is the place I again have to quote the most inspirational words I've heard in the last ten years. You will remember they came from John Moorhead, who passed away from cancer two months after I heard them. "We never know what life really has to offer until we manage to let go of what we believe it should offer [and] lay down the false self."[5]

Gandalf, inviting Bilbo into what will become the largest adventure of his life, very much resembles Jesus inviting each of us on the epic quest to join the creator of the cosmos in discipling the nations. In the least, His invitation includes a one-on-one, intimate relationship with our creator. Who loves us so much that He sent His only son to die on a cross to restore the relationship we foolishly threw away for a piece of fruit, and a lie that God did not have our best interests at heart.

Oh, it's a dangerous mission, one that will cost each of us our lives [not that life doesn't cost everyone their life]. I've lived long enough to know there is more to this life, and I want all it offers. There is a choice to sit comfortable and bored to death at what many consider life, or give my life to Jesus and join Him in the grandest of adventures. I do not know about you, but it's time for me to lay down this book and run headlong at top speed into what Jesus created me to be, a disciple who makes disciples. I will not stop until I squeeze every ounce out of the adventure God made me for alongside my Father, the High King, and the creator of everything. I will leave you with this scene as Bilbo realizes he must leave his comfortable squire for the adventure he must live.

It is morning. Bilbo wakes up on his bed and suddenly realizes that his house is very quiet. He walks all around his house, expecting to run into the dwarves; however, there is no one there. The house has been cleaned up completely from the mess of the party last night, almost as if it had never happened.)

[Bilbo:] "Hello?"

(Bilbo looks a bit lonesome. He sees the Contract sitting on a table; he looks at it, then looks up with a determined face.)

(Bilbo runs out the door of Bag End and down the path,

wearing a traveling pack and holding the contract. He runs through Hobbiton, jumping over fences and pumpkins in his haste. His neighbors shake their heads at him.)

[Neighbor:] "Hey! Mr. Bilbo! Where are you off to?"
[Bilbo:] "Can't stop, I'm already late!"
[Neighbor:] "Late for what?"
[Bilbo:] "I'm going on an adventure!"[6]

I do not know about you, but I'm right behind him!

Journal Pages

This is a great opportunity to journal what you are learning or the action steps you want to take based on this lesson. Doing so will keep all your notes and journaling in this book as future reference. Start by taking a few minutes to pray and ask Jesus to bring to light all you are learning and what transformational changes you can make in your life. If you are reading this in an electronic version, make a digital note and journal.

Journal Pages

EPILOGUE

EPILOGUE

As I write this morning, I am sitting in our condo that my family has rented for 12 years. The thing we love is the sliding door that goes out to our deck that overlooks a saltwater inlet. It is that view from our deck that gives me an incredible picture of this amazing world and life that God has given us. We are His sons and daughters He created in the beginning. We and the world are broken and have been since the garden. But through Jesus' death on the cross, He has restored us to our rightful place and gives us His power to live our lives with joy and purpose.

My three-year-old son plays with a truck, running it over a bump he has made in the rug. He is off on an amazing adventure in that imaginary place I call God's world. My daughter is at school, where a few days ago, she tested out in the top 99 percentile of the gifted program. My wife is at work, a sacrifice she makes, so I can write this book. As I look out the sliding door, the morning is misty and overcast, the kind that makes me want to grab a cup of coffee and settle in with a good book. Instead, this morning I write to you because I can because I have this opportunity to affect your life. For the last year and five months, our family's simple lifestyle granted me the ability to share with you through this book, the reason for life, and the reason for Jesus' life.

Our family's life is simple, uncluttered, and meaningful. We are ordinary, and others might look at us and think we have a pitiful existence because we have little to accumulated for the years we have lived. Yet we have everything we need today; food, clean water, clothes and a roof over our heads. I have not always thought that way, and many years I struggled with how to get the things I felt I needed for my life to count. Over the years and culminating with writing this book, I have realized that God has provided us what we need for today. Tomorrow is tomorrow.

That is not the case for 795 million people in the world who do not have enough food to lead a healthy, active life. That's about one in nine people on earth.[1] Nor do many take action, Christian or not, that 42% of the world's population has never heard of Jesus.

I can change that one person at a time.

Dear Lord, grant me the grace of wonder. Surprise me, amaze me, awe me in every crevice of Your universe. Delight me to see how Your Christ plays in ten thousand places, lovely in limbs, and lovely in eyes not His, to the Father through the features of men's faces. Each day enrapture me with Your marvelous things without number. I do not ask to see the reason for it all; I only ask to share in the wonder of it all.[2]

Shortly after praying this the first time fishing this summer, I caught twelve Sea Trout in one hour...duly noted!

APPENDIX

HELP ALONG THE JOURNEY

"A dead thing can go with the stream, but only a living thing can go against it." – GK Chesterton, The Everlasting Man, 1925 [1]

CHAPTER QUESTIONS

CHAPTER ONE QUESTIONS

These questions are great for journaling and applying God's truth to our life.

Chapter One

- Do most people regularly pray to God?
- Do most people trust God, the one who sustains all life? Or do they trust money, the tool that God gives me to barter for goods to supply their needs?
- If there was a perfect plan for your life or day, and you wanted to know it, would God show it to you?
- Do you think praying the "Lord's Prayer" is a good way to pray?
- We want God to provide for us, but we are many times too busy providing for ourselves. How can you let go of providing the stuff you want and let Him supply your needs?

Chapter Two

- What does the creation account in Genesis tell us about God that He would create the animals, earth, and man?
- Have most people seen God's invisible attributes, namely, his eternal power and divine nature, have been clearly perceived, ever since the creation of

the world, in the things that have been made (Romans 1:20)?
- What does the account of creation and sin in the Garden of Eden tell you about yourself?
- Do you find yourself making the same mistake the first woman and man made in the garden by disobeying God's commands and sinning against Him?
- How can you apply the Lord's Prayer and the formula for living out our lives in a broken world in your own life?

Chapter Three

- "So God created man in his own image, in the image of God he created him; male and female he created them" (Genesis 1:27). What does that tell us about God?
- How much like Him does God make man and woman?
- Do you think it is fair that God gave man three chances?
- Do you find it easy or hard to love others like 1 John 4 instructs? What does that tell you about yourself?
- How can you love others as God loves you? Can you think of someone you can show love to this week?

Chapter Four

- What can we learn about God that He sent Jesus to rescue us from sin?
- What are some differences that God made into the man and woman?
- Why do you think God kept the birth of Jesus so quiet?
- What was it like when God rescued you? How was His rescue unique to you?
- 1 John 4:8 says, "Anyone who does not love does not know God, because God is love." What does this tell you about yourself and whether you know God?

Chapter Five

- If people open their eyes and look, can they see God's love for them in creation around them? What does that say about God?
- What does it say about God and the Trinity that they would sacrifice one of their own for us?
- Why do you think Jesus chose ordinary men to follow Him and be His disciples? Can He powerfully use your life?
- How might God be asking you to trust Him and respond to His love and role to change the world?
- How can you spend time the next few days asking how He is asking you to change history forever?

Chapter Six

- Why did God build us to count, as water is made to run downhill?
- Do most people believe their life is significant with a divine purpose?
- Do you think most people have a preconceived idea of what their life has to offer?
- How have you been striving for significance through other means rather than what God has planned?
- Instead of meaningless stuff perceived to make life meaningful and significant, how can you place your emphasis on gaining wisdom and knowledge from God?

Chapter Seven

- What does it say about God that He gave the Bible to answer the questions to creation, life, and our purpose?
- Do most people spend a concerted effort to research the meaning of life and include an in depth look at the Bible?
- What does it tell us about humans that we often follow beliefs, instructions, and even religious rules without researching it out ourselves?
- Has your life been unfounded and complicated by beliefs, traditions, or rules from family, friends, or colleagues?
- How can you accept Jesus' love for you without

believing you have to earn it?

Chapter Eight

- What does it tell us about God that He calls Himself our Father?
- Do most people have a hard time with the role of God being a father?
- Do you think in most churches, the message of Jesus is complicated?
- Is it attractive to think about being part of a group that learns, cares, and takes care of each other like in Acts 2?
- Is there a smaller group of Christians to be a part of or start to be more like the early Church in Acts?

Chapter Nine

- Do most Christians have a son or daughter relationship with God? What does it say that God desires for us to be sons and daughters?
- Do most children struggle with proper son and daughter roles?
- Do you think most Christians have a challenge in maturing in their spiritual life?
- What can you learn about your role as a son or daughter from Mark 15:16?
- How can you take steps to make disciples and fulfill Jesus' commission?

Chapter Ten

- Do most people live for themselves, tied to meaningless careers, strapped to exorbitant mortgages, and living life at break-neck speed?
- Do many Christians you know believe and follow Jesus with the devotion we see of the first disciples?
- Do you think most peoples' hope depends on the circumstances of the day or hour instead of relying solely on the resurrection of Jesus Christ from the dead?
- Do you find your life blended into the status quo of Christianity, living on autopilot with very little differentiation from someone who does not believe in Jesus?
- How can you, as Jesus and the early disciples did, live a more meaningful and effective life?

Chapter Eleven

- Are most people confused that the mission Jesus was on is the same mission He left for us?
- Do most people give more weight to what they get in this short life on earth than the eternal riches they have waiting for them in Heaven?
- What does it tell us about ourselves that the life, mission, and example that Jesus left the disciples is relevant today?
- If Jesus spent His entire life doing only God's will, how can we as disciples, be more focused on God's will?

- Granted, it is a hard concept to embrace a lifestyle focused on God's kingdom and not satisfy our wants on earth. How can you focus on the small, everyday deeds are where people can see the love of Jesus and not just hear the words?

Chapter Twelve

- What does it tell us about God that He invites each of us not just into an adventure, but an adventure to live with life-changing purpose for everyone involved?
- What can we learn about Jesus that He lived a simple life on purpose and trained twelve men to take God's simple message to the world?
- When compared to the task of making disciples, baptizing them, and teaching others that Jesus commanded us, do you think many have gotten confused at the message to those who don't know Jesus?
- How does it change your life that invitation that Jesus offered to the twelve to become disciples and a perfect, duplicate copy of Himself is the only invitation Jesus ever offers?
- As you look at the disciple-making task that Jesus left us, how can you be more single-minded in your focus?

Chapter Thirteen

- Consider the joy that Jesus has. Jesus, a member of

the Trinity, has perfect joy. Joy is important to Jesus, important enough that He died on a cross to gain it back for us. What does that tell us about God?
- John 15:4 says, "Abide in me, and I in you. As the branch cannot bear fruit by itself, unless it abides in the vine, neither can you, unless you abide in me." What does it mean to abide in Jesus?
- Do you think like in grape production, there is the perfect blend of disciple-making ingredients to fully develop disciples and not waste any resources?
- Imagine for a minute every positive human emotion a person can experience. Can you think of a better emotion you want to experience than joy?
- How can you become a better fisher of men by finding others to live in unity with?

Chapter Fourteen

- What can we learn about God by understanding creation is God's house, not a church building?
- Do most people view themselves as the temple of God rather than a building?
- What do you think it means that "... you yourselves like living stones are being built up as a spiritual house, to be a holy priesthood, to offer spiritual sacrifices acceptable to God through Jesus Christ" (1 Peter 2:5)?
- How do the words of Acts 20:22-24 make you feel? What can you learn about yourself from these verses?

- How can you take steps to be true sons and daughters by learning to "think like him, feel with him, judge as he judges, are at home with him, and without fear before him because he and they mean the same thing, love the same things, seek the same ends." [1]

Chapter Fifteen

- Do most people, even Christians, go through each day talking *at* God instead of with Him?
- What does the interaction between Loren and the fox say about God? Like Loren playing with the fox, do you think most people miss the times God interacts with them?
- Do you think most people want a relationship where Jesus wants to spend His time with them as He did with His disciples?
- Do you see Jesus differently than you did before? Does the gospel of the kingdom sound different from how you heard it before? For the first time, have you seen your life in a different role than you knew it before?
- There is an invitation for us to join with the creator of the cosmos and live the grandest, wild, incredible, and satisfying adventure we could ever imagine. An adventure to disciple and save all mankind from destruction. What can you do to join in the adventure?

ACCEPTING JESUS

There is a first time that each of us first encounter Jesus. You might have met Jesus many years ago, or it is possible you met Him and did not even realize it was Him. Half the world dies without ever knowing about Jesus. Along many people's everyday journey through life, they meet Jesus for the first time. It might be through a good deed, a book, a friend, or even a crisis. When the original twelve disciples met Jesus, they were working their daily jobs as fishermen. Once you meet Jesus, you must either accept or reject Him, as there is no middle ground on which to stand. For some, it takes their entire life to follow Him and for others only the time it takes to speak His name.

The first disciples were Jews and taught from a young age of the coming Christ, the Messiah. Even waiting years for Jesus to come it took many, time to accept that Jesus was in person amongst them. The first disciples met Jesus on an ordinary day. He walked up to them and asked them to follow Him. To be a disciple, you must first accept to follow Jesus as the Messiah.

A good place to learn more about Jesus and the good news He brought into the world is to start with the book of John in the Bible. Those who have accepted Jesus may have never committed to learning more of Him than what others have told them. The book of John is a great introduction to Jesus and His life.

Listen to your heart as you read; what is it saying to you? Ask Jesus to show you He is the Son of God and make that real to you. If you want to meet Jesus and settle it in your heart once-and-for-always, He will show you He is the Christ. Remember, He made you, knows you, and has been pursuing you since the day of your birth. He's been pursuing each of us since the day He created Adam and Eve in the garden.

Jesus, the Son of God died for your sins, rose from death on the third day, and will forgive you of your sins. The Bible says to be saved, a person must, "...repent and be baptized for the forgiveness of your sins" (Acts 2:38). Then you must put your trust in Jesus Christ and believe in Him, and you will be saved (Acts 16:31).

If you're ready to give your life to Jesus, start by repenting for your sins. Tell Him you are sorry for your sins and thank Him for giving His life on the cross for you. Tell Him you believe He rose to life on the third day, and He has saved you from your sins and death and that He has given you eternal life. Repent of your sins and begin trusting in Jesus and your salvation from eternity in Hell is secure. Find another Christian who can baptize you whether it be in the ocean, pool, or church.

It is that simple to accept Jesus, acknowledge that He is the creator of the universe and you, and start living your life with purpose. It is by faith that we believe in Jesus, and through that faith we are born again. Now, as we read in 1 Peter:

> Blessed be the God and Father of our Lord Jesus Christ! According to his great mercy, he has caused us to be born

again to a living hope through the resurrection of Jesus Christ from the dead, 4 to an inheritance that is imperishable, undefiled, and unfading, kept in heaven for you, 5 who by God's power are being guarded through faith for a salvation ready to be revealed in the last time. (1 Peter 1:3-5).

Nothing and no one can take that gift of eternal life away from you. It doesn't mean your life gets easier; many of the disciples found there were more challenges to life. Jesus will transform your life like the disciples, giving it purpose, and use you to tell others of Him.

Once you accept Jesus, there is only one thing left to do, follow Him, and make disciples.

Taken from *Ancient Paths, Untangling the Complexity of Discipleship*, Scott Michael Ringo

WHAT WILL YOU DO?

> *"An adventure is only an inconvenience rightly considered. An inconvenience is only an adventure wrongly considered."*
> – G. K. Chesterton[1]

What will you do with what you have read?

As with everything in life, you will find yourself in one or more of three groups. Those in one group will toss it aside as a nice read and go on about their lives as before. Those in the second group will find words of fault and criticism. They will feel the need to write or speak negatively regarding its content and me as the author. There is a long list of books this group has an issue with. Every book ever written worth its value has met criticism by those in this group. To that group, I offer this:

> Know this, my beloved brothers: let every person be quick to hear, slow to speak, slow to anger; for the anger of man does not produce the righteousness of God. Therefore put away

all filthiness and rampant wickedness and receive with meekness the implanted word, which can save your souls.

But be doers of the word, and not hearers only, deceiving yourselves. For if anyone is a hearer of the word and not a doer, he is like a man who looks intently at his natural face in a mirror. For he looks at himself and goes away and at once forgets what he was like. But the one who looks into the perfect law, the law of liberty, and perseveres, being no hearer who forgets but a doer who acts, he will be blessed in his doing (James 1:19-25).

I do not take issue with those that oppose this book as I have carefully written exactly what I should write. It is not me but Jesus that they criticize by doing so to this book and most likely have an issue with the Bible itself. It is only to Jesus that I must answer for what I have written here. "Let the words of my mouth and the meditation of my heart be acceptable in your sight, O Lord, my rock and my redeemer" (Psalms 19:14).

There will be a third group. I call this group the Simple Few. The Simple Few includes me, and it is this group Jesus wants to inspire through the pages of this book. This group, if only my family and myself— but hopefully millions more— believe living a life for Jesus and making disciples is their call to action. Something in the pages of this book stirs your spirit deep inside to say, "Yes! I will take the leap." It is this group that has been looking for more meaning from life and more from God. There is more in the kingdom of God. All it takes is the faith to let go of what we believe life should offer; ask our Father, "Where are we going today, Father?"

Like the disciples who accepted Jesus' invitation to follow Him, this group will have the winning story from this life.

NEXT STEPS IN DISCIPLESHIP

I often need a reminder of what success in the Kingdom of God looks like. Thankfully, I only need to look at the simple example of Jesus' discipling His twelve disciples. Jesus defined success by making disciples who made disciples. They lived, ate, hung out, had all things in common, and proclaimed the gospel message.

Success in the kingdom of God is being defined by Jesus Himself as making disciples that make disciples. From this point forward, there is no more guessing how Jesus is building His Church. True disciples are those that abide [follow] His word and glorify God by making many disciples (John 8:31, John 15:8).

We know that this is what Jesus taught the twelve disciples because this is what they do after Jesus ascends to heaven.

> And they devoted themselves to the apostles' teaching and the fellowship, to the breaking of bread and the prayers. And awe came upon every soul, and many wonders and signs were being done through the apostles. And all who believed

were together and had all things in common. And they were selling their possessions and belongings and distributing the proceeds to all, as any had need. And day by day, attending the temple together and breaking bread in their homes, they received their food with glad and generous hearts, praising God and having favor with all the people. And the Lord added to their number day by day those who were being saved (Acts 2:42-47).

We know that God approved because He multiplied their efforts, "...the Lord added to their number day by day those who were being saved" (Acts 2:47).

Disciple-making is hard work. Proclaiming the gospel message and making disciples of the kingdom of God is a life-long pursuit. Doing this work by yourself will leave you wore out. Doing the work within a community of believers who are together all the time and have everything in common, while challenging, is fun and exciting. Jesus knew exactly what to model with His disciples to train them to carry on the work in a sustainable model. The challenge is to find believers that want to be true disciples and commit their time, energy, resources, and daily life to make disciples. Being a disciple of Jesus is not going to a church building once a week to listen to a sermon, sing some songs, then waiting a year to mention Jesus to your neighbor through fellowship evangelism. Making disciples is living life together, eating together, studying the Bible, and modeling the life of a disciple.

"Immediately they left their nets and followed Him" (Matthew 4:20). The disciples who followed Jesus immediately left everything the minute they met Jesus. Then they followed Him as a community of vagabonds learning to make disciples. This ragtag group of disciples of Jesus changed the world.

Simply Scatter Seeds

This is what the kingdom of God is like.

> And he said, "The kingdom of God is as if a man should scatter seed on the ground. He sleeps and rises night and day, and the seed sprouts and grows; he knows not how. The earth produces by itself, first the blade, then the ear, then the full grain in the ear. But when the grain is ripe, at once he puts in the sickle, because the harvest has come" (Mark 4:26-29).

According to Tim Chester and Steve Timmis, "...approximately eighty-five million people in the United States have no intention of attending a church service. In the United Kingdom its forty-million— 70 percent of the population."[1] Many have walked away from the attractional church event and are looking for a more biblical model of discipleship. Yet, many have become frustrated trying to do house church or community because their training was in the attractional church and try to do what the institutional church does in a house. However, Jesus came proclaiming the Kingdom of God has come. In these verses, Jesus shows us a simple picture of how the Kingdom of God comes and grows. There are millions of people in every country looking for a gospel community of true disciples of which to be a part. Your job is to become a community of true disciples in which God can add others.

Many times farmers sow by himself. This sowing mostly happens in obscurity. The man's task is to scatter seed on the ground. After that, it grows, but that is not the man's task. His next task is to put the sickle to the harvest when the full-grain is in the ear. That harvest comes from the seed that falls on good soil. Mark 4:8 says, "And other seeds fell into good soil and produced grain, growing up and increasing and yielding thirty-fold and sixtyfold and a hundredfold" (Mark 4:8). The man harvests and brings that harvest into the barn, community.

A community of believers is not a community of unbelievers. The community in Acts was believers and God added to the community others who are being saved (Acts 2:47). The believers' position was to be in unity (John 15,) and show the world a picture of the Kingdom of God. In Mark 4:29, the farmer scatters seed. God does the growing and then the farmer reaps.

Looking further, when Jesus talks about the good soil, even when the seed is scattered on the ground, only some fall of good soil and sprout and grow (Mark 4:8).

Every person's community looks different. Sometimes our community is going to be only our family, as there is no good soil around producing a harvest. Other times we will scatter seed and much of the ground will be good soil. The key is to be consistent to scatter seed and look for the harvest. The second is to be consistent to mentor, apprentice the community God gives us.

Someone must first want to be a disciple and the seed fall on good ground. The seed must then sprout, God grows and then you gather into the community of believers. God adds to the community. If you form the community out of nonbelievers, you will have a very mixed bag as Mark 4:1-8 shows and the most likely tear the community apart.

The process to get started may seem overwhelming, especially if you are looking for others to do this with. It is hard to find people who believe in Jesus, who want to follow Him in making disciples. Even if you are part of a small group from your church, you know how hard it is to get everyone to show up weekly. It is near impossible to have participation in ongoing activities to transform the surrounding community. As easy as it sounds, getting twelve or fewer people together once a week to eat, study, and care for each other is daunting.

Married couples should start with your spouse. If you have children, it is important to include them. If you are single, start with yourself and find someone of the same gender. If you have extended family who lives within a few minutes of you in town, include them. It is hard to have a community or ongoing activity if your group is fifteen minutes away from each other. It will be easier to start small and let God add to it than to start with several who are not committed. Begin studying the Bible and eating together once a week. If you are a family, commit to studying the Bible, eating most of your meals together, and helping those with need. Commit to an outreach activity like outlined in this book. If you are a family or close group of friends, it is easier to get a rock-solid commitment. If those in the group cannot commit from now on to getting together to study the Bible, eat together, and do outreach activities you need to find those that will. It will never work perfectly, but discipleship is about teaching others to be like Jesus as you become like Jesus. The twelve disciples wanted to follow Jesus and learn His ways. Jesus kept them engaged, learning, and in community with each other.

Stay Simple

The encouragement here is to start with whom you have, but make sure you build community with believers who have repented of their sins, trust Jesus, and want to do the work of making disciples, not just carry a title. Stay small until you find or make committed disciples. Stay small even after you find committed disciples. There is nothing, if not less, to gain with a large group. Read and follow the Bible and the examples of Jesus, it needs no professional education. Success as a disciple of Jesus is in making other disciples who make disciples. Jesus says, "By this my Father is glorified, that you bear much fruit and so prove to be my disciples" (John 15:8). That verse is the definition of success in the Kingdom of God.

The group you are a part of may never be large, but there are few stories of size in the Bible. The Bible is one large story of God made up of all the smaller stories of obedient sons and daughters. To make a disciple proves you are a disciple of Jesus, and that is all that matters.

NOTES

Introduction

1. James Baldwin Notes of a Native Son (Boston: Beacon Press, 1955), 9.

Preface

1. "News Release Number: STScI-2012-37," Hubble Goes to the eXtreme to Assemble Farthest Ever View of the Universe, last modified September 25, 2012 01:00 PM, http://hubblesite.org/newscenter/archive/releases/2012/37/image/a/.
2. Hubble pointed at a tiny patch of southern sky in repeat visits (made over the past decade) for a total of 50 days, with a total exposure time of 2 million seconds. More than 2,000 images of the same field were taken with Hubble's two premier cameras — the Advanced Camera for Surveys and the Wide Field Camera 3, which extends Hubble's vision into near-infrared light — and combined to make the XDF.

    "The XDF is the deepest image of the sky ever obtained and reveals the faintest and most distant galaxies ever seen. XDF allows us to explore further back in time than ever before," said Garth Illingworth of the University of California at Santa Cruz, principal investigator of the Hubble Ultra Deep Field 2009 (HUDF09) program.
3. Unless otherwise noted, all biblical passages referenced are in the English Standard Version.
4. "Path." Merriam-Webster.com. Accessed May 20, 2016. http://www.merriam-webster.com/dictionary/path.
5. C.S. Lewis, The Lion, the Witch and the Wardrobe (New York: Macmillan, 1950).

1. God's Economy

1. CdeBaca, Luis (11 July 2013). The State Department 2013 Trafficking in Persons Report. state.gov. United States Department of State. Retrieved 27 July 2014. http://www.state.gov/j/tip/rls/tiprpt/2013/index.htm
2.
3. Oxfam. (2014). Working For The Few. (Accessed on September 19, 2014) Data File

NOTES

4. Department of Health & Human Services. (2013) 2014 Poverty Guidelines. U.S. Retrieved from http://aspe.hhs.gov/poverty/14poverty.cfm
5. Oxfam. (2014). Working For The Few. (Accessed on September 19, 2014) Retrieved from http://www.oxfam.org/sites/www.oxfam.org/files/bp-working-for-few-political-capture-economic-inequality-200114-summen.pdf
6. Mary-Lou Weisman. (1999). The History of Retirement, From Early Man to A.A.R.P. The New York Times. (Accessed on April 28, 2015) Retrieved from http://www.nytimes.com/1999/03/21/jobs/the-history-of-retirement-from-early-man-to-aarp.html

2. God's Creation

1. (2003) Animal. In World Book Encyclopedia. 16 vols. Chicago, IL: World Book.
2. McVeigh, T., & Finch, I. (June 14, 2014. Fathers spend seven times more with their children than in the 1970s. The Guardian. Retrieved from http://www.theguardian.com/lifeandstyle/2014/jun/15/fathers-spend-more-time-with-children-than-in-1970s
3. Technostress. (2005). The New Oxford American Dictionary (2nd ed). Oxford, UK: Oxford University Press. Retrieved October 1, 2014, from Oxford Reference Online database.
4.
5. Centers for Disease Control and Prevention. (2010). Prescription Drug Use Continues to Increase: U.S. Prescription Drug Data for 2007–2008 [Data file.]. Retrieved from http://www.huduser.org/Datasets/IL/IL08/in_fy2008.pdf
6.
7. Deuteronomy 31:6, Deuteronomy 31:8, Joshua 1:5, 1 Kings 8:57, 1 Chronicles 28:20, Psalms 37:28, Psalms 94:14, Isaiah 41:17, Isaiah 42:16, Hebrews 13:5
8. Crosby, Stills, Nash & Young. "Woodstock." iTunes audio, 3:54. 1970. https://music.apple.com/us/album/woodstock/321974224?i=321974260.

3. God's Love

1. Crosby, Stills, Nash & Young. "Woodstock." iTunes audio, 3:54. 1970. https://music.apple.com/us/album/woodstock/321974224?i=321974260.

NOTES

4. Jesus' Love

1. Brennan Manning, The Furious Longing of God (Colorado Springs: David C. Cook, 2009), 43.
2. John Eldredge, Wild at Heart: Discovering The Secret of a Man's Soul (Nashville: Thomas Nelson, 2010), 17.
3. Ibid., 16-17.
4. John Eldredge, Wild at Heart: Discovering The Secret of a Man's Soul (Nashville: Thomas Nelson, 2010), 9.
5. Ibid., 70.
6. Ibid.
7. Ibid., 16-17.

6. Significant Life

1. Shall We Dance, DVD, produced by Simon Fields, directed by Peter Chelsom, Miramax, 2004.
2. Dallas Willard, The Divine Conspiracy: Rediscovering Our Hidden Life In God (New York, 1998), 14-15.
3. Ibid.
4. Ibid., 15.
5. "#009: Nearing the End of My Beginning, 2015," Podcast, posted by Morgan Snyder, January 26, 2015, http://www.becomegoodsoil.com/009-nearing-the-end-of-my-beginning-podcast/.
6. Charles Spurgeon, "The Fourfold Treasure," sermon 991, Accessed on July 24, 2015, http://www.spurgeon.org/sermons/0991.php
7. Robert M. Groves, "Census Bureau Releases National-Level Data on Education Levels, Bachelor's Degree Attainment Tops 30 Percent for the First Time," Commerce.gov, February 24, 2012, http://www.commerce.gov/blog/2012/02/24/census-bureau-releases-national-level-data-education-levels-bachelors-degree-attainm.
8. Washington's Blog, "How Many People Have Lost Their Homes? US Home Foreclosures are Comparable to the Great Depression," Global Research.org, May 17, 2013, http://www.globalresearch.ca/how-many-people-have-lost their-homes-us-home-foreclosures-are-comparable-to-the-great-depression/5335430.

7. Complicated Life

1. Taken from The Jesus Storybook Bible: Every Story Whispers His Name by Sally Lloyd Jones Copyright © 2007 by Sally Lloyd Jones Used by permission of Zondervan. www.zondervan.com.

NOTES

8. The Simple Message

1. MacDonald, George, Unspoken Sermons: Series I., II., III. (London: THE PROJECT GUTENBERG EBOOK UNSPOKEN SERMONS, 2005), (Kindle Locations 8-9).
2. MacDonald, George, Unspoken Sermons: Series I., II., III. (London: THE PROJECT GUTENBERG EBOOK UNSPOKEN SERMONS, 2005), (Kindle Locations 8-9).
3. Greg Demme and Jonathan Sarfati, "Big bang critic dies" (Fred Hoyle), http://creation.com/big-bang-critic-dies-fred-hoyle.
4. Hoyle on Evolution," Nature, Vol. 294, 12 November 1981, 105.

9. Becoming Sons and Daughters

1. Center for Disease and Control. 2018. "Abortion Surveillance — United States, 2014." November 22, 2018. https://www.cdc.gov/mmwr/volumes/66/ss/ss6625a1.htm?s_cid=ss6625a1_w.
2. MacDonald, George, Unspoken Sermons: Series I., II., III. (London: THE PROJECT GUTENBERG EBOOK UNSPOKEN SERMONS, 2005), (Kindle Locations 2812-2826).

10. Our Story

1. Ray Vander Laan. 2020. "He Went To Synagogue." That the World May Know. https://www.thattheworldmayknow.com/he-went-to-synagogue .
2. Blaise Pascal (Pensées)
3. Jackie French Koller, 1948.
4. Part of Ralph Waldo Emerson's 1862 Eulogy and Tribute to Henry David Thoreau May 9th, 1862

11. We Have To Embrace His Kingdom

1. World Health Organization and UNICEF. Progress on Drinking Water and Sanitation, 2014 Update. (New York, NY: Division of Communication, 2014), 8.
2. UNICEF, "Millennium Development Goals," Goal: Reduce child mortality, Accessed on July 22, 2015, http://www.unicef.org/mdg/childmortality.html
3. Ed. Jorge Gracia, Mel Gibson's 'Passion' and Philosophy: The Cross, the Questions, the Controversy, (Peru, Illinois: Open Court Publishers, 2004)
4. Ed. Jorge Gracia, Mel Gibson's 'Passion' and Philosophy: The Cross, the Questions, the Controversy, (Peru, Illinois: Open Court Publishers, 2004)

NOTES

5. Luke 2:41-47, Luke 2:51-52
6. Mark 6:2-3
7. M.G. Easton, "Easton's Bible Dictionary," Carpenter, 1893, Accessed on July 24, 2015, http://eastonsbibledictionary.org/727-Carpenter.php
8. Arthur Blessitt, "Miles Jesus and Mary walked," How far did Jesus and Mary Walk?, Accessed on July 27, 2015,http://www.blessitt.com/Inspiration_Witness/MilesJesusandMaryWalked/MilesJesusandMaryWalked_Page2.html
9. James Baldwin, Nobody Knows My Name: More Notes of a Native Son 3 (New York: The Dial Press, 1961), 17.
10. The Hobbit: An Unexpected Journey, directed by Peter Jackson (2012; USA: New Line Cinema, 2012), DVD.
11. The Fellowship of the Ring, directed by Peter Jackson (2001; USA: New Line Cinema, 2001), DVD.

12. Life on Purpose

1. G.K. Chesterton, Varied Types (New York: Dodd, Mead and Company, 1905), 118.
2. Daniel Burke, "The World's Fastest Growing Religion Is...," Accessed on August 5, 2015, http://www.cnn.com/2015/04/02/living/pew-study-religion/
3. J.R.R. Tolkien, The Hobbit or There and Back Again (New York: Estate of J.R.R. Tolkien, 1989, 1990, 2006), 9.
4. James Baldwin Notes of a Native Son (Boston: Beacon Press, 1955), 9.

13. Jesus' Joy

1. Robert Louis Wilken, The First Thousand Years: A Global History of Christianity (New Haven/London: Yale University Press, 2012), 65-66.
2. Online Christian Colleges, "Megachurch Megabusiness," Accessed on August 5, 2015, "http://www.onlinechristiancolleges.com/megachurches/
3. Barna Group, "2015 Sees Sharp Rise in Post-Christian Population," Accessed on August 17, 2015, https://www.barna.org/barna-update/culture/725-friendships-are-the-top-thing-people-love-most-about-their-cities#.VdIuOHi8uyM
4. Barna Group, "Friendships Are the Top Thing People Love Most About Their Cities," Accessed on August 17, 2015, https://www.barna.org/barna-update/culture/725-friendships-are-the-top-thing-people-love-most-about-their-cities#.VdIuOHi8uyM
5. Unknown
6. Simon Sinek, "Start With Why" (New York: Penguin Group, 2009), 70.

NOTES

14. Enough is Enough

1. Rich Mullins, Lufkin, Texas July 19, 1997
2. Pursuit of a Legacy, Accessed on September 16, 2015 http://www.20thecountdownmagazine.com/rich-mullins-bonus-videos/
3. Rich Mullins, A Liturgy a Legacy and a Ragamuffin Band, Provident Label Group, LLC, 1993, compact disc.
4. Pursuit of a Legacy, Accessed on September 16, 2015 http://www.20thecountdownmagazine.com/rich-mullins-bonus-videos/
5. Joshua Becker, A Helpful Guide to Stop Comparing Yourself to Others, Accessed on September 1, 2015, http://www.becomingminimalist.com/compare-less/
6. Morgan Snyder, Good Soil Intensive: Session 2 From False Self to True Self, Ransomed Heart, 2014, MP3.
7. Kingdom of Heaven, directed by Ridley Scott (2005; Los Angeles, CA: Twentieth Century Fox Film Corporation, 2005), DVD
8. Dallas Willard, The Sprit of the Disciplines: Understanding How God Changes Lives (New York: HarperCollins, 1988), xii
9. Dallas Willard, The Great Omission: Reclaiming Jesus's Essential Teachings on Discipleship (New York: HarperCollins, 2006), xv
10. Brennan Manning, The Ragamuffin Gospel: Good News for the Bedraggled, Beat-Up, and Burnt Out (Colorado Springs: Multnomah Books, 2005), 101
11. Willard, The Sprit of the Disciplines, xii
12. Brennan Manning, The Ragamuffin Gospel: Good News for the Bedraggled, Beat-Up, and Burnt Out (Colorado Springs: Multnomah Books, 2005), 25
13. Willard, The Great Omission, xv
14. George MacDonald, Abba Father!, Accessed on February 11, 2016, http://www.online-literature.com/george-macdonald/3669/
15. Dallas Willard, The Divine Conspiracy: Rediscovering Our Hidden Life In God (New York, 1998), 65.
16. Dallas Willard, "Looking Like Jesus:
    Divine resources for a changed life are always available," Published in Christianity Today, August 20, 1990. ©1985 Ron Harris Music. Available in The Great Omission, San Francisco: HarperCollins, 2006., last accessed March 23, 2015, http://www.dwillard.org/articles/artview.asp?artID=105

15. Interactive Relationship

1. H. Jackson Brown, P.S I Love You: When Mom Wrote She Always Saved The Best For Last (Nashville: Rutledge Hill Press, 1990), 13

NOTES

2. Loren Eisley, The Unexpected Universe (Orlando: Hardcourt Brace & Company, 1969), 209-212.
3. The Matrix, directed by Andy Wachowski and Larry Wachowski (1999; Burbank, CA: Warner Bros. Pictures, 1999), DVD.
4. The Hobbit: An Unexpected Journey, directed by Peter Jackson (Burbank, CA: New Line Cinema, Metro-Goldwyn-Mayer (MGM), 2012), DVD.
5. "#009: Nearing the End of My Beginning, 2015," Podcast, posted by Morgan Snyder, January 26, 2015, http://www.becomegoodsoil.com/009-nearing-the-end-of-my-beginning-podcast/.
6. The Hobbit: An Unexpected Journey, directed by Peter Jackson (Burbank, CA: New Line Cinema, Metro-Goldwyn-Mayer (MGM), 2012), DVD.

Epilogue

1. World Food Programme, Hunger Statistics, Accessed 0 February 5 2016, https://www.wfp.org/hunger/stats
2. Prayer of Jewish Rabbi, Joshua Abraham Heschel

Appendix

1. G. K. Chesterton The Everlasting Man (St. Athanasius, 2018).

Chapter One Questions

1. George MacDonald, Abba Father!,

What Will You Do?

1. G. K. Chesterton, On Running After Ones Hat, and Other Whimsies (New York: Robert M. McBride & Company, 1935), 6

Next Steps in Discipleship

1. Tim Chester and Steve Timmis, Everyday Church, Gospel Communities On Mission (Wheaton, IL: Crossway, 2012), 25.

ABOUT THE AUTHOR

I have food, clean water, clothes and a roof over my head today. Tomorrow can worry about itself.

Scott Michael Ringo lover of Jesus, Husband, Father, and adventurer, is a seasoned author who writes from his experience around the world. Scott has had the fortune in life to be as the ancient explorers, living life at its fullest and always curiously looking down the unexplored, overgrown trails that lead to new beauty. Jumping aboard a schooner bound for the open sea or charting an island that needs finding, full of riches in every turn. Join with Scott and explore and discover this amazing world that God created for us to live our life glorifying Him by making disciples, while being in an intimate relationship with our passionate lover, Jesus. Scott enjoys a simple life and the simple purpose each of us has to disciple others.

Become a world-changer

What if Jesus called us to be a disciple like he did the fishermen? Would we drop everything and follow Him?

Take a journey walking along the road with Jesus that once again transforms a group of disciples into His likeness, and change the face of your church, your city, or even the world.

Available at amazon.com/author/scottringo in print or ebook.

TITLES BY SCOTT MICHAEL RINGO

Transform, Transformed by Our Encounter with Jesus

James, Lesson from a Fisher of Men

Coffee for One, Devotionals that Inspire

Simple Fundraising, Easy Non-Profit Fundraising

Explosive Marketing

Simple Non-Profit Fundraising